The Ethnic Dilemma
in
Social Services

The Ethnic Dilemma
in
Social Services

Shirley Jenkins

 THE FREE PRESS
A Division of Macmillan Publishing Co., Inc.
NEW YORK

Collier Macmillan Publishers
LONDON

THE FREE PRESS
A Division of Macmillan Publishing Co., Inc.
866 Third Avenue, New York, N.Y. 10022

Collier Macmillan Canada, Ltd.

Library of Congress Catalog Card Number: 80-2155

Printed in the United States of America

printing number
1 2 3 4 5 6 7 8 9 10

Library of Congress Cataloging in Publication Data

Jenkins, Shirley.
  The ethnic dilemma in social services.

  Bibliography: p.
  Includes index.
  1. Social work with minorities—United States.
2. Ethnic attitudes—Case studies.   I. Title.
[DNLM: 1. Ethnic groups.   2. Health services.
3. Social work.   WA 300 J52e]
HV3176.J45   361.3'089   80-2155
ISBN 0-02-916400-1

To my sons,
Ian and Peter

Contents

Preface

The ethnic dilemma posed in this book is the question of how, where, and when ethnic factors should be incorporated in service delivery. A range of possibilities has been suggested, all the way from the use of bilingual workers to separate ethnic agencies. Between these two extremes, varying degrees of importance have been placed on the matching of clients and workers, workers and supervisors, adoptors and adoptees, and therapists and patients.

This dilemma is not unique. It is part of the larger search for a balance between integration and separation, and between group identity and intergroup empathy. It is related to the question of how to decide when our commonalities outweigh our differences, or when our differences must be respected before our commonalities can be recognized.

Issues of human relations, in particular interracial and interethnic questions, have been of long-standing personal, professional, and political concern. From my late husband, Dr. David Ross Jenkins, who taught Maori children in his native New Zealand, I learned about the Treaty of Waitangi (February 6, 1840), in which a native people, buttressed by a supply of arms, were able to negotiate for territorial rights, arrangements that later led to separate political, educational, and social institutions. Work in the 1940s as associate editor of the *Far Eastern Survey,* Institute of Pacific Relations; as political officer for the Security Council, United Nations Secretariat; and as a research associate for the

Institute of International Education laid the base for cross-cultural research. The study, *American Economic Policy toward the Philippines* (1954), was relevant to later work on Puerto Rico; both countries had legacies from and were victims of the Spanish-American War.

On the personal side, I participated in the struggles in the 1950s for interracial housing and against school segregation, and my professional work then turned to domestic issues. My doctoral thesis, *Reciprocal Empathy between Negroes and Puerto Ricans in New York City* (1956), helped me to understand that much could be learned from the way in which minority groups relate to each other. Eighteen years of work in child welfare research at the Community Council of Greater New York and the Columbia University School of Social Work produced data that consistently implied there were services needed but not received by ethnic families, in particular Blacks and Puerto Ricans. These findings are reported in three books: *Paths to Child Placement* (1966), *Filial Deprivation and Foster Care* (1972), and *Beyond Placement: Mothers View Foster Care* (1975).

The present study is an outgrowth of work begun while on sabbatical leave from Columbia and serving as visiting research professor at the Graduate Center, City University of New York. During that time I collaborated with the late Dr. Leonard S. Kogan, director of the Center for Social Research, on a social indicators project that produced the book *Indicators of Child Health and Welfare* (1974). That research continued after my return to Columbia. Because of my interest in pursuing work on indicators related to ethnicity, Dr. Kogan generously facilitated a subcontract with City University to provide the initial funding for the Columbia ethnic studies project. The sustained support over the years of the Children's Bureau, then part of the Office of Child Development, U.S. Department of Health, Education and Welfare, is gratefully acknowledged.

The ethnic studies on which this book is based involved five years of field work and research in many parts of the United States and overseas, followed by two years of writing and analysis. During that time I was fortunate to have as my research associate on the project Dr. Barbara Morrison, then an able doctoral student, a solid researcher, and an important contributor to the present study. She undertook the literature review, participated in all phases of the research including field interviews in the United States, and did essential work in statistical analysis. Her contributions are highly valued.

Just as one sabbatical provided the impetus for the research, another sabbatical provided the finis. A semester as visiting professor at the Paul Baerwald School of Social Work, Hebrew University, Jerusalem, Israel, afforded the opportunity to visit over twenty-five programs for Sephardic Jewish children and for Arab children. The kindness of Professor Jona Rosenfeld, then director of the Baerwald School, in making this appointment possible is much appreciated. Dr. Eliezer D. Jaffe, also of Hebrew University, who has written on ethnicity in Israel, reviewed the material prepared there. In England the opportunity to visit over fifteen programs for West African, West Indian, and Asian children and families was facilitated by Mr. David Jones, who provided study space at the National Institute for Social Work Training in London, of which he is principal. I am also very grateful to Juliet Cheetham of Oxford University, Department of Social and Administrative Studies, and a member of the British Commission on Racial Equality, for reviewing the British material.

There are many people to thank for assistance along the way to completion of this project. First and foremost are the people of the ethnic groups with whom the study was concerned and the fifty-four agencies that cooperated in the study process. I am grateful to the Asian American, Black, Chicano, Indian, and Puerto Rican consultants, social workers, parents, clients, and colleagues who not only shared knowledge of their own cultures and people and helped in the research but, most important, trusted me enough to wait and see what I would do with the material. I hope the findings warrant their confidence.

Finally, any far-ranging exploration needs a home base. For me that has been the Columbia University School of Social Work, whose dean, Mitchell I. Ginsberg, has provided a climate that supports and values independent research, and whose faculty and students are always ready for both discussion and argument.

My former professor, Dan Dodson, who directed the Center for Human Relations at New York University and who sponsored my own doctoral thesis, had an incisive question for the dogmatic and the too sure. He would ask, in his Texan style, "Who anointed you?" The burden of this work is that I am not among the anointed—hence the choice of "dilemma" for the title. My hypothesis is that the dilemma posed by this study can be resolved only by a serious search, and not by an easy answer.

Shirley Jenkins

The Ethnic Dilemma
in
Social Services

Part I
The Dilemma

I

The Ethnic Issue

In a renowned mental hospital in a major city, there was a psychiatric conference about a serious symptom of a newly admitted elderly patient—refusal to eat. Various theories of oral functioning were offered, but no solution was found until an intern on his rounds noticed the patient wearing a yarmulke, a head covering worn by many religious Jews. The young doctor asked the patient three questions: Are you Orthodox? Are you kosher (observant of Jewish dietary laws)? Would you eat if I ordered a kosher diet? The answer was yes to all three. At the next psychiatric conference the intern reported that his patient was still crazy, but at least he wasn't hungry.

A group of institutionalized Puerto Rican men in the same city were found to have an extremely high rate of schizophrenia, which led to extensive speculations on their cultural inheritance. It was then learned that all psychiatric diagnoses for these men had been made through interpreters; not a single Spanish-speaking psychiatrist had been involved.

About the same time in a general hospital elderly chronically ill Chinese patients were subjected to special study because they had severe weight loss in long-stay hospital care. The medical tests were ineffective in explaining why this occurred. It was an observant hospital worker who reported the widespread dumping of uneaten Western food—meat and potatoes—unacceptable to the

Chinese palate. It was only then that a Chinese dish with a rice staple was added to the daily hospital menu.

These anecdotes are not atypical. They simply illustrate our predilection for accepting differences but ignoring their consequences. In other areas, such as civil rights, education, employment, and housing, ethnic needs and issues have been the subject of major national debates over the past few decades. But the social welfare field, although deeply involved in serving ethnic clients and training ethnic workers, has only recently and in peripheral ways acknowledged the need for ethnic content in therapeutic and service approaches.

The relevance of such content cuts across all fields of practice but has special meaning for family and child welfare. The state acts *in loco parentis* to a disproportionately high number of children from ethnic groups. An important issue is the extent to which the state can function as the appropriate ethnic parent. For Indian children, for example, the tribal council is involved in decisions on adoption and surrender of parental rights.

Background study suggests that the need to direct attention to ethnic factors in the delivery of services has become increasingly important because of the growth of the public sector of the delivery system. In an earlier time in U. S. history, when self-help groups, immigrant associations, and language and religious societies took it upon themselves to aid new arrivals, understanding of the cultural background and ethnic differences of clients was taken for granted in the very nature of voluntary and self-help organizations. When services moved into the public sector, an egalitarian approach was the goal, presumably unrelated to culture. It was an approach, however, that reflected dominant cultural patterns, and was devoid of empathy and comprehension of differences. This created barriers for minorities in obtaining access to their appropriate entitlements.

In recent years there has been increasing pressure from minority groups for recognition of ethnic differences, but as each new group makes its stand still another emerges on the scene, in an unending procession of fragmentation and fission. The present book attempts to systematize an approach to ethnicity by means of a comparative analysis. It is our hypothesis that a typology can be developed that is broadly applicable to different groups and different settings, and that can serve as a standard-setting guideline to facilitate differential service patterns.

Before describing the design of the study on which the book is based, it may be useful to define the key term *ethnic group* as used in this research. Ethnicity is not a precise concept but nonetheless it is a viable one. There is a substantial literature on ethnicity, and although there may be disagreement on some of the components of the definition, there is general agreement on the core meaning of the concept. Two definitions are cited as relevant. Weber defines ethnic group as "a collectivity based on an assumption of common origin, real or imaginary."[1] Schermerhorn defines it as "a collectivity within a larger society having real or putative common ancestry, memories of a shared historical past, and a cultural focus on one or more symbolic elements. . . . A necessary accompaniment is some consciousness of kind among members of the group."[2] Among these symbolic elements, Schermerhorn includes physical contiguity, language or dialect, religion, phenotypical features, kinship patterns, and nationality, or any combination of these.

In describing ethnic patterns, it is apparent that different configurations exist depending on the situation. Religion may be critical in defining certain groups, national origin for others, language for others. Typically a combination of factors is important, and often the identity of the group may be more apparent to "insiders" than to "outsiders," a distinction described by Merton.[3] Differences often become explicit at points of conflict.

The comingling of the two phenomena of conflict and ethnicity in our history and our social awareness may be one reason why ethnic characteristics are so rarely presented in a positive or constructive light. This is a country settled and built by immigrants, and each new wave carried with it a legacy of cultural differences. But each new group inevitably faced instituionalized prejudice and discrimination as they made their place in the new society. In the religious area, it was necessary to create an organization for "antidefamation." In the racial area, a major study posed the issues of differences as creating "an American dilemma,"[4] not an American opportunity. In other countries as well the association of conflict and ethnicity has been pervasive. Parkin, the British sociologist, goes so far as to define ethnicity as "the articulation of cultural distinctiveness in situations of political conflict or competition."[5] Does this definition, however, stand the test of reversal? In other words, if political conflicts were not present, would ethnic differences disappear?

There is active debate on whether ethnicity is currently thriving, reviving, or declining among immigrant groups in the United States. Gans suggests that acculturation and assimilation are continuing to occur, but that there may be a new kind of ethnic involvement concerned with identity. This is expressed in use of ethnic symbols rather than cultures or organizations.[6] He documents his hypothesis, however, with references only to white ethnic groups, such as Jews, Italians, and Poles, and does not discuss the issue of race. For nonwhite groups assimilation has not been a major goal. Where racial characteristics and cultural differences are the core of identity, as with the nonwhite population, another path is being pursued. The issues are different for the groups which in the past have been referred to as the "minorities" on the ethnic scene: Asian Americans, Blacks, Puerto Ricans, Chicanos, and Indians.

The application of the term *minorities,* which originally referred to Black and other nonwhite victims of racial discrimination, has been widened to provide a catchall category for other groups with problems, regardless of their actual numbers or situations. Women, for example, gays, veterans, and other entities who have been disadvantaged in one way or another all receive the minority designation, to the consternation of some ethnic groups who feel the hard-won gains achieved under civil rights legislation are being eroded and diffused. The proposed substitution of "Third World people,"[7] however, leads us right back to an entirely political characterization of ethnicity and has questionable validity on the international scene.

A more careful analysis of the "minorities" appellation is given by Schermerhorn in his *Comparative Ethnic Relations.* He states that there are three concepts that need to be understood before an appropriate characterization can be made. The first is *ethnic* group, already defined, and the second is *dominant* group, which Schermerhorn defines as "that collectivity within a society which has authority to function both as guardians and sustainers of the controlling value system, and as prime allocators of reward in the society."[8] A dominant group may be either a numerical majority of the population or a fraction of it with most of the power, called an *elite.* Schermerhorn next circumscribes the meaning of *minority* group as one of two possible subordinate categories, based on size and power. If the group makes up most of the population, they are called *mass subjects,* as in a colonial country. If they are a fraction of the population, they are designated a *minority* group.

Thus presumably in the United States an Irish Catholic millionaire in high elective office would belong to a dominant elite, leaving the minority group designation to those who meet the criteria of being both powerless and relatively few in number in the larger society. This definition appears appropriate to the United States at this time, and it is the context in which the present book refers to ethnic minorities.

The five groups considered here—Asian Americans, Blacks, Chicanos, Puerto Ricans, and Indians—have all been designated as appropriate for affirmative action in order to redress earlier discrimination. They are of particular significance for the social welfare field since many of their number are poor, and they are disproportionately high among clients of social agencies. It is for these groups that consideration of ethnicity in the delivery of social services is particularly appropriate, although it is also relevant for members of other groups who seek such help.

Ethnic factors in service delivery can be incorporated at an individual case level, or they can be conceptualized in broader terms. A theoretical interpretation of why ethnicity may have particular importance for child welfare arises from the hypothesis of two sociologists, Litwak and Dono.[9] They suggest that ethnicity may serve as an intervening variable between the family, or primary group, and the large bureaucratic organization. If the ethnic group has characteristics of an in-between structure, then it may meet the demand for noninstrumentality for large numbers of people. Translated into practical terms, if there ever was a need for a noninstrumental, nonbureaucratic approach in service delivery, it is in the care of children. This is a service that undertakes primary group functions, and it does so most effectively when it individualizes care and preserves family values. To practice family and child welfare without regard for ethnic variables is to truncate the potential for service.

Perhaps because ethnic issues have been related to both conflict and discrimination, as in racism, or to self-interest, as in affirmative action, they have been neglected by social work practitioners. Ballard, a social scientist who studied the Sikh community in Leeds, expresses concern that the training of practitioners does not prepare them for working with racial and ethnic minorities. He states:

> Although discussion of the practicalities of the provision of effective services for the ethnic minorities is almost inevitably shot through by political and ideological dilemmas, it nevertheless needs to be

stressed that the issues raised can also be approached on a straightforward professional level. For the practitioner the question as to whether the minorities ought, or ought not, to remain ethnically distinct is irrelevant. The fact is that they *are*. In so far as his specialism, whatever it is, demands that he should take into account the social and cultural worlds in which his clients live, he needs to make some responses to ethnic diversity. If he does not his practice is inadequate in purely professional terms.[10]

It is in this professional context that the research reported here was undertaken. The search for a general theory of ethnicity continues, but it is impeded by two main contaminating variables, the issues related to class and poverty, and the fact that cultures are themselves in a state of flux, so that even descriptive data on ethnic group behavior is often out of date by the time it has been analyzed.

For the field of social work and social welfare, however, the task of meeting the needs of the ethnic minorities has not been successfully fulfilled. This book seeks to identify those special problems associated with delivery of services to ethnic groups, to recognize impediments to this task, and to develop a typology for such service delivery which will be relevant for a variety of groups and situations. Each chapter raises different but related questions.

- What are the issues that concern ethnic minority professionals as they cope with service delivery?
- What are the attitudes toward these issues of child welfare workers in both traditional and innovative settings? Can an instrument be validated to measure these attitudes?
- Can we operationalize the definition of an *ethnic agency* to see what works and what doesn't work in delivery of services to clients?
- How do parents of children served in agencies see the issues? Do the perceptions of ethnic parents and ethnic workers differ in relation to service delivery?
- Is the conceptualization of the ethnic issues developed in the United States relevant to ethnicity in other countries? In particular, what are the ethnic issues in delivery of services to Sephardic Jewish children and to Arab children in Israel, and to West African, West Indian, and Pakistani children in Great Britain?
- Can a typology for incorporation of ethnic factors in service delivery be developed that could be applicable for different

groups in varied places and provide a basis for teaching and training for social workers in ethnic settings?

Notes

1. Max Weber, "The Ethnic Group," Talcott Parsons et al., in *Theories of Society*, vol. 1 (New York: The Free Press, 1961), p. 305.
2. R. A. Schermerhorn, *Comparative Ethnic Relations: A Framework for Theory and Research* (New York: Random House, 1970), p. 12.
3. For a discussion of this concept see Robert K. Merton, "Insiders and Outsiders: A Chapter in the Sociology of Knowledge," *American Journal of Sociology* 78: 1 (July 1972): 9–47.
4. Gunnar Myrdal, *An American Dilemma* (New York: Harper & Row, 1944).
5. David Parkin in A. Cohen (ed.), *Urban Ethnicity, U.S.A.*, Monograph 12 (London: Tavistock, 1974).
6. Herbert J. Gans, "Symbolic Ethnicity: The Future of Ethnic Groups and Cultures in America," *Ethnic and Racial Studies* 2: 1 (January 1979).
7. *New York Times*, April 22, 1979.
8. Schermerhorn, *Comparative Ethnic Relations*, pp. 12–14.
9. Eugene Litwak and John Dono, "Forms of Ethnic Relations, Organizational Theory and Social Policy in Modern Industrial Society" (Unpublished paper, Columbia University, December 21, 1976).
10. Roger Ballard, "Ethnic Minorities and the Social Services: What Type of Service?" in Verity Saifullah-Khan (ed.), *Minority Families in Britain: Stress and Support* (London: Macmillan 1979), p. 164.

2

The Common Needs

In a field study conducted in 1954 on reciprocal empathy between Blacks and Puerto Ricans, a Black woman in a New York City housing project was asked what problems she had in common with her Puerto Rican neighbors. Her answer was, "None." The interviewer persisted; "How about jobs, housing, discrimination?" "Yes we have the same problems," was the answer, "but you asked what we had in common. To have a problem in common, you have to feel it together. And we don't feel our problems together." By that definition commonalities of problems among ethnic groups have still not been identified. Yet such a typology is needed if service delivery is to respond to ethnic needs.

Sociologists continue to seek a general theory of ethnicity that would explain the processes of interracial and intergroup relations for all groups under a range of circumstances. In a far more limited field, it should be possible to develop the needed typology for service delivery to ethnic groups. But the response to the 1954 empathy study must be kept in mind—the same problem is not necessarily a common problem. Explorations are needed in the context of each of the ethnic groups to see if underlying dimensions can be identified reflecting similar needs for different groups, even though group demands assume disparate forms. That might be a first step to establishing the commonality of service delivery.

To this end a review of ten years of literature was undertaken, primarily of works by minority writers on ethnic needs. From this review, which gave special attention to ethnicity and social work in child care settings, four major areas of concern were identified. The issues that were relevant across ethnic groups are the lack of recognition on the part of planners and practitioners of the diversity of ethnic patterns and cultures of the client population; the lack of appreciation of language differences and of the importance of bilingualism as a necessary component in service delivery for non-English-speaking clients; the persistence of stereotypes which have hampered the understanding of the ethnic communities, their problems, and their special needs; and the threat to the survival of the group as a cultural entity, exacerbated by many aspects of the service system.

Ethnic Cultural Patterns

A major theme throughout the literature is the concern of minority group members for recognition of their distinctive cultural patterns in the planning and delivery of services. This is not to imply that there is a homogeneous ethnic position on all cultural questions. Factors such as age, birthplace, education, recency of migration, extent of acculturation, and social class affect the degree to which members of the group will hold to tradition or seek ways to change. The direction is not always predictable, since return to tradition may be the expression of the ethnic identity ideology. Social services, in particular family and child welfare, are intimately concerned with individual and family life-styles, but these are often ignored in planning traditional service delivery.

Changing family forms pose problems for child welfare, and the shifts are particularly dramatic for ethnic groups. The traditional Confucian family system, for example, is still part of the basic values of many Chinese American families, and this includes prescribed status, which gives every man and woman a definite place in society. Whenever feasible, the extended family system encourages relatives to live together. Filial devotion is a major component, and young people are expected to obey their elders and exert self-restraint. It is apparent that this tradition will clash with the current modes, especially for second-, third-, and fourth-generation Chinese Americans. Fong discusses the nature of this cultural conflict for the Asian American child:

It is common in the American culture to teach the individual to make his own decisions and to assert his own independence, which is contrary to the Chinese approach. The bicultural child may then develop some conflict-laden identifications, with two social worlds, the one of the parents and the other of the teacher and peers.[1]

A cultural pattern to which the helping person working with the Chinese community and its children should be sensitive is the special relationship that exists between father and eldest son. Fong characterizes this relationship as follows:

The Chinese admonish the male, as soon as he is able to understand, to obey his parents, especially the father, to the fullest extent; that it is bad behavior to question his wisdom or decisions; that it is good to do whatever he wants done without the slightest regard for one's own feelings; that it is not desirable to commit oneself to any independent line of action; that it is sinful to do anything which disturbs his father in any way.[2]

The special stresses this places on the eldest son in particular mean that he will probably have the greatest difficulty in resolving the cultural conflicts between the Chinese traditional values and the values of the dominant society in which he must function. This was discussed by Nicol in a study of Chinese American children in New York who had social and emotional problems. She reports:

The preponderance of first males in the study might indicate that they are the focus of much stress, both intrafamilial and intercultural. Families "moor" the eldest son most securely to tradition, while currents of cultural change would tend to sweep him along. Eldest sons are expected to be most passive in absorbing cultural values. Passive individuals, however, may experience the greatest difficulties in acculturation. The eldest son would seem to be the most vulnerable to withdrawal and isolation or its alternative (found not infrequently in Chinese culture) pronounced aggression.[3]

The issue of parental authority is not confined to the Chinese. Many parents in ethnic groups which value obedience to parental authority, particularly that of the father, find themselves at odds with their children who are being socialized to different values in the dominant culture. As Fong noted in a paper on the changing social roles in the Chinese community:

The tensions arising from reduced authority of parents in modern American families are not unique to the Chinese. In a study of American Indians, for example, Erikson ... indicates that the "weakest relationship" ... seems to be that between the children and their fathers, who cannot teach them anything and who in fact have become models to be avoided.

... The consequences of social change on patriarchal families in several ethnic groups seem to be familiar. In their study of Japanese and Mexican patriarchal families in America, Clark and Kiefer ... reached the following general conclusions about the younger generation: "While they have been taught like their parents that proper family relationships are always respectful and based on appropriate role behavior, they do not share their parents' belief that, despite the personal conflicts involved, formalized interaction may be the best way of arranging things in an imperfect world. ... The common complaint of young ... Mexican Americans, like their Japanese American counterparts, is that there is no communication between them and their elders—that everything is a game, a ritual that they cannot escape and that serves no positive purpose."[4]

Similar observations of the interaction between Samoan American youth and their parents were made by Chen:

Young Samoans have problems similar to those of other American young people. They are not sure of themselves in a society in which their roles are not clearly defined. They have identity problems in relation to their families, their island ties, and the strange city life that surrounds them.

The problems of young Samoans are intensified by cultural conflicts. Some who are overwhelmed by new demands on them develop a deep sense of shame and defeat. ...

At home the youth is told to obey the father or Maitai, but in school he is told to obey American laws—and there may be a conflict between the two. The old cultural values contradict the American values; in this country equality, democracy, and individuality are esteemed above the family. The young Samoan is told that he should compete to get ahead, but the average Samoan youth is not geared toward intense competition and attainment of material possessions.

Young Samoans who are adjusting to the American way of life begin to question Samoan values. They cease to believe that the Maitai's word is law, that the father is always right or that they need to obey their older siblings.[5]

In relating to the Mexican American child, the social worker needs to be aware that the Mexican American family has traditionally experienced strong paternal authority.

The family is under the firm authority of the father, while the mother assumes the traditional subservient and severely prescribed role of the homemaker, the model of purity, bearer and trainer of children. This is a reflection of "hombria" or "machismo," i.e., the supreme male dominance, the male individualism, assertiveness, and extreme pride—attributes which strongly influence nearly all phases of Spanish-American life.[6]

It is important to understand this characterization of relationships to avoid inadvertently increasing conflicts between the Chicano child and his family. Ballesteros, for example, warns that conflicts can be created for the Chicano child when such relevant cultural factors as machismo are not understood:

What makes the Spanish-speaking child appear "uneducable" is his failure in an educational system that is insensitive to his cognitive styles and cultural and linguistic background. An example of this would be the suppression of the male-dominant image that Mexican American boys bring to school. In school he is confronted by Anglo female teachers (unlike in Mexico where the majority are male). If he is to succeed in school he becomes a feminized male, if he retains his *macho* characteristics he more than likely becomes a failure and a discipline problem. He is rewarded only for behavior accepted by the teacher.[7]

If the child becomes conflicted or has to make a forced choice between his parents' values and those of the outside society, extreme tension may be experienced, and high dropout rates and absenteeism may result. Chicano parents who see their children being caught between conflicting value systems are beginning to express their concern and to take what they believe to be protective measures. In Tucson, Arizona, for example, Mexican American parents have apparently been removing their children from an experimental educational program because of differences in child-rearing patterns. An article entitled, "Innovative School Losing Pupils: 'Cultural Clash' Gets the Blame," which appeared in the *Tucson Daily Citizen,* reported:

Parents of some children trapped in a "cultural clash" at the former Miles Elementary School apparently have become disturbed at the results of an experimental program there and have begun removing their youngsters.

... Ronald DeWitt, principal of the Exploratory Learning Center, said that the innovative program is aimed at giving each child as much freedom of choice as possible. "This form of education is in conflict with those from more impoverished backgrounds, those with limited experiences," DeWitt said, specifying that he referred to Mexican-American and black families in the program.

The article went on to relate some of the responses of parents to the innovative program:

> "That school isn't teaching my children anything but how to be rude," said one mother. "They have no discipline and can talk back to anyone they want. . . . You teach your children how to behave at home and they go to that school and lose it all."

Summing up the major issue, which is the challenge to parental authority, the principal stated:

> It is true that we have a different set of values. . . . Mexican-American families have an authoritarian system and what father says goes. But we teach the children to question and they end up questioning father.[8]

A different conflict is seen in the experience of the Native Americans which causes problems for the child welfare worker who is concerned with child development. This is the conflict between patterns of competition, a deeply ingrained value of the dominant culture, and noninterference, a traditional value of the Native American. Braswell states:

> It is my opinion that there is more conflict between the traditional Indian values and the values of the dominant non-Indian society than with any other ethnic minority.
>
> One example of value conflict . . . is between the Indian value of generosity and sharing and the non-Indian value of material achievement. The Indian value is to get in order to give, while the non-Indian value is to get to keep.[9]

Other authors have expressed similar views. Locklear, of the American Indian Study Center in Baltimore, has said: "Generosity is still the paramount virtue among Indians. An Indian cares more about being able to work at a satisfying occupation and earn enough to share with relatives and friends than about putting money in the bank and purchasing a home in the city."[10] Jerdone states:

> Some of the characteristics he [the Indian] has developed through living on the reservation do not enable him to cope well with his new environment (urban). For example, on the reservation he is likely to have learned to be cooperative and to share with others, whereas, in the urban center, a competitive spirit and a responsibility limited to one's immediate family alone are necessary.[11]

Furthermore, reports Levy, "The competitive person who competes with and exploits his peers is definitely a problem in the Navajo culture and may be suspected of being a witch."[12]

The Indian value is not only to disown competitiveness but to support the philosophy of noninterference. As Farris states:

> The Indian has always had a special concern and respect for each person's right to live his own life without interference as long as he does not hurt his fellow man. For example, an Indian prayer to the Great Spirit says: "Before being critical of one's neighbor, one should walk a mile in the neighbor's moccasins." This philosophy is further reflected in the Indian natural reluctance to be competitive or aggressive in personal relationships. He has always stood ready to give assistance to and share with his needy fellow men. Ironically, the settler's early survival depended on the help freely offered by the American Indians.[13]

The importance American Indians place on self-determination without competition and without interference from others was emphasized by Camp, chairman of the American Indian Movement (AIM), in an interview in *Akwesasne Notes:*

> Our problems are only as far as they are related to the white economic system. Once we are divorced from that, we won't have to worry about "upgrading our standard of living." We can live by what would be considered a poor standard of life by white standards and still have a good life and be happy.
>
> That is one of the differences between us and the struggles of other minority groups. We are not concerned with having a $10,000 median income for our people. We are concerned with our people being free and living the way they want to live.
>
> ... We're not looking for a 9–5 job, a white collar job for all our Indian people. We're not looking for upward mobility in the social structure of the United States. We don't need that, we don't want that, we don't want anything to do with that. We're looking for our sovereignty, our ability to govern ourselves, and for every person to live as a free person. To live the way they want to live.[14]

This is a strong ideological statement, not necessarily subscribed to by all members of the group. But it has a unique quality in that few leaders of minority groups would disavow "upward mobility" as a political goal.

It is important for planners of programs for Indian children to be aware of cultural differences. Even something that may seem as trivial as rewarding a child in the day-care center for some small achievement can be dysfunctional in these terms. In a paper prepared by the Shiprock Indian Agency in New Mexico for use by its staff, "Culture and Its Relationship to Values in Conflict for Indian People," it was suggested that workers in a school should "reward progress or advances made by a student in such a manner that he will not gain the enmity of his peers; gold stars opposite his name can be very embarrassing to some tribal groups."[15]

The Indian philosophy of noninterference also has many implications for deciding which helping methods will be most effective in working with Indian biological, foster, or potential adoptive parents. As noted by Good Tracks:

> All methods usually associated with the term *social work intervention* diminish in effectiveness just to the extent that the subject has retained his native Indian culture. The reason is that any kind of intervention is contrary to the Indian's strict adherence to the principal of self-determination. . . . The Indian child is taught that complete noninterference in interaction with all people is the norm, and that he should react with amazement, irritation, mistrust, and anxiety to even the slightest indication of manipulation or correction.[16]

In addition to being aware of the culture patterns, the social workers need to understand the way the Indian client perceives the social work process, and to adjust helping methods accordingly. Good Tracks states:

> From an Indian client's point of view, the worker is expected to perform only the superficial and routine administrative functions of his office. . . . These tasks involve no real social involvement, as involvement is understood by both Indians and non-Indians. The Indian client does not allow or desire the worker to have any insight into his inner thoughts. That would not be a proper part of work.
>
> This expectation does not, of course, correspond to the professional social workers' own concept of his function. . . . Nevertheless, the workers must not intervene unless the people request an intervention and he is likely to wait a long time for such a request. The credentials of his profession, his position, status, knowledge, skills, achievements, and authority, though respected by the agency, are in most cases completely without merit among Indians. Such things belong to the Anglo culture and are not readily translatable into Indian culture.[17]

In an article on "Ways of Working with Navajos Who Have Not Learned the White Man's Ways," Polacca advised program planners to be aware of the Indian value of noninterference:

One important thing for the person working with the Navajos to remember is that they do not like being pushed. No matter how eager one may be to hurry things along, too much pushing may slow down the progress.

Polacca cited a statement by Paul Jones, Navajo tribal chairman, to reinforce her point: "We Navajos will look you over for a couple of years, and then decide whether we are for you or against you."[18]

Bilingualism: Handicap or Advantage?

For those ethnic minorities whose mother tongue is other than English, the recognition of their linguistic background is of cultural importance. The literature of Chicanos, Puerto Ricans, Asian Americans, and American Indians has all expressed concern that services for group members be planned and implemented by persons familiar with their language, as well as other aspects of their cultural background.

Hayden, for example, said in 1966:

In many Southwest schools the use of Spanish is forbidden in class and on the playground; often there have been attempts to devalue it by ridicule and other means. It would be unnatural if such negation of Spanish did not create resentment and defensive reinforcement of loyalty to *la raza*. The aim of Anglo school authorities is to make Spanish-American students proficient in English. However, instead of this the unintended consequences are likely to be alienation of the student from the Anglo world and its language, early school leaving, reduced respect for the process of education, rebelliousness and delinquency, and a low level of aspiration.[19]

In a paper on "Understanding the Bicultural Child," Ballesteros added, "We so often err in equating bilingualism with a handicap, or at least with some sort of special problem. A Spanish-speaking child's state of socioeconomic disadvantage, which is usually accompanied by a lack of knowledge or a limited knowledge of the English language, is nearly always interpreted as a 'language handicap.'"[20]

In their recently published set of guidelines for bilingual-bicultural programs for the Chicano child, Interstate Research Associates suggested ways in which educators can help the

Spanish-speaking child not only to appreciate his native language but to develop proficiency in both languages. They stated that educators should attempt to foster the following:

- the enhancement of the child's self-concept by building on his cultural strengths and differences . . .
- to link the home with the school by utilizing and/or recognizing the language, tools, decoration, food and customs of the home . . .
- enhance language development through the use of both languages . . .
- prevent educational gaps by allowing the child to learn skills and concepts in whichever language he best understands . . .
- preserve the child's sense of history, culture, identity, and language.[21]

For the American Indian child and his family, whose language may be one of 550 distinct Indian tongues, the importance of recognition and appreciation of linguistic diversity is just as great. In working with Navajo children in boarding schools, Bergman put himself in the position of the Indian child forced to learn English. He empathized with the dilemma of the Indian child who must function in a world that refuses to recognize the validity of his mother tongue.

> I have been trying to learn Navajo and find it a very difficult language; it seems reasonable to assume that for the Navajo-speaking child, English is equally difficult, yet these children are expected to come to a large, strange, crowded institution and manage in an almost totally English-speaking environment. Elsewhere when children are expected to learn a second language, reading, writing, and arithmetic are taught in their native language and concurrently they are instructed in another language. It would seem logical to do this with Indian children, and start teaching English only when the children have reasonable mastery of the language. Submerging the student in English from the first is now so long established a custom, however, that it seems rarely to be even questioned.[22]

Asian American children are also subject to conflicts both within the family and in their relationships outside the home because of language difficulties. Fong notes:

> Most Chinese parents want their children to learn the language, customs, and manners of their ancestors. In a manner, they have

given the Chinese school the task of socializing their children. Many of the youths react negatively to this experience. . . .

When the child goes to American public schools he learns a new language, and he acquires greater facility as he goes through school. The time will come when he speaks mainly English with his peers. He speaks English increasingly at home with his brothers and sisters. The parents may soon find that they are losing contact with their children and some communication problems develop. At school the child also learns new skills and social values which may be foreign to those of his parents. It is common in the American culture to teach the child to fend for himself, to make his own decisions, to stand on his own feet. Instead of being led by an authoritarian figure the pupil is encouraged to be self-reliant and independent. In fact the child may be encouraged to assert himself.

The seeds of cultural conflict are sowed, then, at an early age, and the mind of the sprouting child may be bent, at some point, by the winds of perplexities.[23]

Official encouragement for bilingual competency was given by the Office of Child Development for children who speak English as a second language in its *Day Care Handbook*, which states:

Children should be encouraged to verbalize in more than one language. . . . Teachers should be bilingual to serve as good listeners and speaking models. Teaching of standard English should not be approached as a "phasing out" of another language or dialect and a child should be given recognition, praise, respect, and encouragement in his use of both languages. When appropriate, prereading and prewriting activities should be conducted in both languages.[24]

Other references in the literature suggest that a bilingual approach should be taken in the delivery of services at all levels for those who speak English as a second language. The New York Committee for the Care of Puerto Rican Children, for example, stressed the need for a bilingual approach in the foster care process, stating:

Information given to Puerto Rican families about child welfare programs must be written in Spanish as well as English. . . .

There should be most extensive use of Spanish-speaking personnel during the intake and home study procedure and during the initial contacts with Spanish-speaking natural and foster parents. . . .

Foster parents should be provided information in Spanish on all legal matters such as the Foster Parents Preference Law and the 24 Month Family Court Review, and the Subsidized Adoption Law. . . .

Bilingual–bicultural personnel should be used to administer psychological tests and provide treatment to children after they are placed. Personnel with this background also should analyze the test results. We are all aware that Puerto Rican children have often been labeled "retarded" or dull simply because of their inadequate knowledge of English. . . .

The agency should no longer use the excuse that the Puerto Rican family speaks little or no English to rationalize lack of services. It is the agencies' responsibility to hire Puerto Rican personnel who can ensure effective communication with the child and his family and with whom they can identify.[25]

Language has always been a problem for new non-English-speaking immigrants, and there has always been a strong movement among such groups to learn English as a way to achieve in the new society. The ethnic perspective, however, rejects the "melting-pot" ideology and holds that success is more likely if ethnic groups maintain their identity and political base. What is new is the combined emphasis on both bicultural and bilingual programming with retention of the native tongue through life. There is also pressure to learn languages long forgotten, or never known. If such moves gained strength, there would be a possibility of a multilingual society in which substantial numbers speak both English and another language associated with their ethnic origins, whether Swahili, Yiddish, Spanish, or Cantonese. This is an unlikely prospect, however, since there are few rewards in our society for bilingual competence.

Stereotypes and Prejudgments

To some extent, all ethnic groups suffer from stereotypes and prejudgments. When these are institutionalized in the social welfare field, they affect the type of service delivered to minority clients. Although this surfaces in different ways for different groups, stereotypes have been found to have cross-ethnic relevance.

In the case of Asian Americans, there is some evidence that they may have been denied needed services because of overly positive stereotypes. They have been seen as the "model minority"—self-sufficient, successful, and capable of meeting their needs from their own resources. As Kuramoto said:

The myth of the American Dream as illustrated by the Asian experience not only involves the problems of identity and recognition imposed by the majority, but includes the myth that all Asians are affluent. Most Asians are believed to have too much money to be considered a "poverty" category, yet many live in extreme poverty.[26]

Chen maintains that there are cultural values within the Chinese community that foster reinforcement of the model-minority myth among the Chinese:

> The myth that Chinese people have no problems is a fallacy. The Chinese people in America have problems now, have had them in the past, and will continue to have them in the future. Two significant factors contribute to the misconceptions about the Chinese population in America: (1) the general public's tendency to stereotype ethnic groups and (2) the Chinese people's tendency to hide the darker side of their culture. It has been assumed that traditional strong family ties among the Chinese have reduced their problems to a minimum and that the Chinese people can take care of their own problems. The Chinese people themselves tend to reinforce and exaggerate these distortions and thereby add to the general misconceptions about them. Honor and pride have prevented them from making their problems known to the public.[27]

The consequences of this myth for the provision of social welfare services have been that many much needed services have not been sought after by Asian Americans and therefore not provided. In writing of New York's Chinatown, Nicol states:

> At least one manifestation of the conflict between Chinese and American cultures has a direct bearing on the provision of services to Chinatown residents. Stereotypes on the surface favorable to the Chinese have apparently limited awareness by the general public and the Chinatown residents themselves of the unmet psychosocial problems in Chinatown. According to Cattell, many social and health needs of the Chinatown residents go unmet because of the idealized conception that problems of its residents can be met without extra-community help. Chinatown leaders have actively perpetuated this stereotype, supporting the notion that relationship groups and other protective associations within the community could meet the needs of their members.[28]

The consequences of the model-minority myth for Asian Americans were strongly stated by Kim:

The maintenance of the convenient myth of Asian Americans as a model minority excludes them from nationwide concerns and education, health, housing, employment, and social welfare programs. However, behind the busy, prosperous shops and restaurants of Chinatown's little Tokyos are thousands of unattached old people wasting away their remaining years in poverty and ill health and children of new and not-so-new immigrants left at home without adequate adult supervision while their parents work long hours to support them. Unnoticed and ignored by the social welfare community are uncounted numbers of deserted and abused wives and children of American service men.[29]

The literature reviewed implied that a major belief that has governed policy formation in social services for the American Indian is that the Indian cannot live in a bicultural fashion—taking the best from the tribal world and the dominant culture and synthesizing these into a viable life-style. The belief has been that the Indian must be forced to assimilate into the white culture if he is to survive, and he must completely abandon tribal ways. As McNickle states:

> In discussing the Indian situation it is customary, almost compulsory, to refer to the individual tribesman as a man caught between two worlds, as a man who must break free from the past in order to find his place in the future—everyone recognizing that his hold on the present is precarious. The Indian world is dead, the inference runs, and the tribesman must get on with the business of making over his life.[30]

This policy of forced assimilation has been especially directed toward Indian children, and no better example of it can be given than that of the boarding schools. Some years ago an article in the *New York Times* stated:

> Under so-called remedial and welfare programs ... one Indian child in four is presently taken from his reservation home and sent off to boarding schools or to some form of foster care.
>
> Boarding schools are operated by the Government for disturbed children with behavior problems or for children with disrupted families, but they really are homes of detention with no rehabilitative services at all.
>
> About 40,000 Indian reservation children, half of them Navajos in the Southwest, are taken from their families and sent to boarding schools, sometimes hundreds of miles away.[31]

Wauneka, in a paper presented at a workshop on "Emotional Problems of the Indian Students in Boarding Schools and Related Schools," stated that the Navajo people do not wish to send their children away from home and that the policy of the Navajo tribe is to seek the means of educating their children as close to home as possible.[32]

The problem of the education of Navajo and other Indian children goes far deeper than just the unwillingness to provide facilities at the local level. The boarding school where the Indian child is Anglicized has been the instrument of forced assimilation. Although there have been efforts to change this institution in recent years, the schools still arouse concern among proponents of Indian culture. Bergman states:

> In the world of the boarding school, not only the Navajo language but almost all things Navajo are rated very low. The children are frequently told not to be like their parents and they are often admonished against following the traditions of their people.[33]

Many Indians believe that they can be truly bicultural and they see enormous value in this. Braswell has proposed a policy of "selective acculturation":

> This aspect of self-hood is closely related to the self-ideal. The values which have been internalized are the building blocks from which this dimension of self is constructed. This is another area in which many of our Indian people are caught in a bind, especially our young people. They are not certain what they want to be, an assimilated white Indian or a traditional Indian completely, one who has reverted to the old tribal way as totally as possible. I believe that there is a third alternative, one which many of our people seek to follow today. It has been termed "selective acculturation without assimilation." This means cultural interaction without loss of cultural identity, to be culturally eclectic, to take from both cultures those elements we want and to mold them into a way of life that alienates us from neither.[34]

Like the American Indian, the Chicano is believe by some to be a man or woman who must make a choice between the ways of the forefathers and the dominant American culture. Social scientists have been quick to point out cultural traits that hamper Mexican American children in their "necessary" acculturation to the values of the Anglo society. In a review of research, Montiel states:

The following child-rearing practices are viewed in the literature as factors that hamper acculturation and assimilation: parents indulge male children, which limits their desire to achieve; do not encourage independence; teach their children lax habits; do not stress education; are oriented to the past; speak only Spanish, and think too much about their own misfortunes.[35]

Montiel quotes Burma to represent the attitude of many social scientists who believe that the Chicano cannot survive as a bicultural man: "It appears necessary for the Mexican American to make up his mind which culture he wishes for his own, rather than to drag willy-nilly with unrelated parts of each."[36]

In most of the literature about Mexican American and Puerto Rican cultures there are numerous references to the extended-family network, with its informal system of mutual obligation, including the care of dependent children. If planners assume that this traditional informal network obviates the need for child welfare services, however, they are misreading the social needs.

There are important cultural factors in the Latin tradition of which workers should be aware. Mizio characterizes the traditional Puerto Rican family as follows:

> The Puerto Rican family is, in contrast to the American, an extended family; intimate relationships within the kinship systems are of high value and a source of pride and security.... The Puerto Rican family encompasses not only those related by blood and marriage, but also those tied to it through custom. The *compadrazgo* and *hijos de crianza* are important parts of the Puerto Rican family system.
>
> The *compadrazgo* is the institution of *compadres* ("companion parents"), a network of ritual kinship whose members have a deep sense of obligation to each other for economic assistance, encouragement, support, and even personal correction. Sponsors of the child at baptism and confirmation assume the role of *padrinos* ("godparents") to the child and compadres to the parents. Witnesses at a marriage or close friends also assume this role. *Hijos de crianza* ("children of upbringing") is the cultural practice of assuming responsibility for a child, without the necessity of blood or even friendship ties, and raising the child as if he were one's own. There is no stigma attached to the parent for surrendering his child or to the child who is given up. This may be a permanent or temporary arrangement.[37]

Similar institutions are reported as important for the Mexican American family. Aquilar, for example, states:

To Mexican Americans the extended family is of great significance in their pattern of living; they take it for granted that in time of trouble they can always count on the family to help out.[38]

This analysis is supported by Sotomayor, who characterized the Mexican family, including the phenomenon of *compadrazgo,* as follows:

In the extended family pattern, the members often rescue the head of a household by sharing their goods to meet the daily needs of his family.... Various members of the family assume the physical and affective care of the child when stress from the external system causes self-preoccupation of an individual parent. This process is also present at times of internal crisis, such as the birth of a new child, when the extended family gives care to the mother during her convalescence and to the older youngsters.[39]

The perception of the extended family as a viable resource also has implications for the way in which a worker will handle a crisis. Garcia, for example, suggests:

Aware of the extended family pattern of the Chicano, the worker should not suggest out-of-home placement of the elderly or disabled relative. The Chicano has close family ties, and he assumes responsibility for those relatives who can no longer care for themselves. His training from early childhood has conditioned him to the tradition of the young and able person assuming the responsibility for the elderly and disabled.[40]

The degree to which the extended family exists in the present Mexican American and Puerto Rican cultures is an appropriate subject for systematic research, since many cultural patterns have been diluted and modified. If service delivery strategies are to be limited because of the presumed existence of informal child-caring resources, it is important to know whether these "resources" in fact exist. As Mizio says:

To write about the Puerto Rican family living in the United States as if there were a universal model would be deceiving. Families are affected by strains in different ways, and the Puerto Rican family system must be viewed as being on a continuum. At one end is the extended family system with traditional Puerto Rican values, and at the other end is the nuclear family system with an American value system.[41]

This qualification must be made for the Mexican Americans as well. Montiel states that the recent studies and surveys done of the Chicano community indicate that the extended family is almost nonexistent. He cites a finding by Ulibarri, who surveyed migrant families in the Southwest and found that the concept of the extended family had been lost. He notes further that Brebler and associates found that only 4 percent of the Chicano families in Los Angeles and only 3 percent in San Antonio were extended households. Montiel concludes, "If these studies accurately represent the urban Chicano family, then the extended stable family has never been as extensive as many social scientists have claimed."[42]

There are in fact several issues to be investigated. One is whether the extended family persists, with several generations living in the same household. A second issue is the quality of relationships, and the persistence of family loyalties and feelings even when the household comprises only the nuclear family. Finally, and most relevant for service delivery, is the capacity of the family unit to extend help. Since poor people tend to be related to poor people, the large extended family may mean shared needs rather than shared resources.

Myths, stereotypes, and unsupported theories about Blacks permeate the social science literature, with important consequences for service delivery. Perhaps the most pervasive stereotype with relevance for child welfare is the concept of the so-called pathology of the Black family, widely publicized in the Department of Labor publication of 1965 popularly known as the "Moynihan Report":

> At the heart of the deterioration of the fabric of Negro society is the deterioration of the Negro family. . . .
> There is no one Negro community. There is no one solution. Nevertheless, at the center of the tangle of pathology is the weakness of the family structure. Once or twice removed it will be found to be the principal source of most of the aberrant, inadequate or antisocial behavior that did not establish, but now serves to perpetuate, the cycle of poverty and deprivation.[43]

Moynihan did not originate the thesis that the disorganized Black family resulted from the constraints of slave society and the social crisis that accompanied emancipation. The Black sociologist E. Franklin Frazier, who was widely influential in combatting racist scholarship, nonetheless, according to Gutman, "underestimated the adaptive capacities of slaves and ex-slaves and therefore wrote that their families, 'at best an accommodation to the slave order, went to pieces in the general breakup of the plantation system.'"[44] Frazier continued:

> What authority was there to take the place of the master's in regulating sex relations and maintaining the permanency of marital ties? Where could the Negro father look for sanctions of his authority in family relations which had scarcely existed in the past? Were the affectional bonds between mother and child and the solidarity of feeling and sentiment between man and wife strong enough to withstand the disorganizing effects of freedom?[45]

It is Gutman's thesis that "retrogressionist" beliefs that emancipation caused Black retrogression to "African barbarism" distorted perceptions of Afro-American family life and sexual behavior. This gave rise to a major stereotype that still affects understanding of Black families.

In Gutman's own work[46] he traces the records of Afro-American families from 1750 to 1925, using plantation records, census reports, genealogies, letters, names retained, and other available documents. His findings show substantial evidence of adaptive social and cultural arrangements within the slave experience, of the development of the slave family and slave kin networks, and of the persistence of strong marital and familial ties through emancipation. The data go to 1925, when a survey of 13,924 Black households and subfamilies, nearly all in central Harlem, showed 85 percent of kin-related Black households to be headed by two parents, and five of six children under the age of six living with both parents.

Gutman's finding is that family disorganization did not follow southern Black migrants north, and he suggests that the vast structural unemployment and underemployment affecting Black men had more to do with family breakups than did either slavery or Reconstruction. This work has important implications for the social service field, since it shifts perceptions of Black family history and offers new insights into family strengths. One relevant application is the possibility of rethinking the prevalent "acceptance of illegitimacy" stereotype, which implies that special services are not needed for the unmarried Black woman who is pregnant since this situation is nothing unusual. Saunders says this is a misconception:

The black family, first of all, is an extended family. Relatives readily share responsibility for child-rearing. The family usually comes to the aid of a troubled member; for example, it is unusual for a young black unwed mother to give up her child for adoption. More likely the baby will be accepted into the larger family and be reared by the maternal grandmother, behavior that although frequently the target of criticism by whites, reflects a human quality. . . . Contrary to popular statistics, the young black female is not more promiscuous than her white counterpart. Nor do black families condone illegitimate pregnancy; they simply have more compassion for the child once it has been conceived.[47]

The stereotype is also discussed by Fischer, who says that in rationalizing why so few Black children are placed, the following attitudes are frequently expressed:

"After all, the black culture does not permit the giving away of children."

"Everyone knows the unwed mother and her illegitimate child are easily assimilated into the family in the black community."

"The statistics on unrelated adoptions do not take into account the high number of related adoptions among black people. Those figures show that large numbers of black children are being adopted."[48]

A final stereotype applied to Blacks and to other minorities as well is generalizing a single model of family structure to all members of the group. Willie makes an important contribution in reporting on Blacks of three income groups: the middle class, who he designates as "affluent conformists"; the working class, "innovative marginals"; and the lower class, the "struggling poor."[49] Not only do life-styles vary, so do family size, marital relationships, and goals and aspirations. He concludes that whereas all Blacks must of necessity adapt to white society because of discrimination, the unique adaptation by Blacks is further differentiated by the key variable of social class.

Threats to Group Survival

Underlying most of the concerns of ethnic minorities about child welfare is the conviction that children must have ethnic supports if the group as a whole is to survive. Two major themes in the literature emphasize this: the priority given to the natural family as the service base, and the opposition of most groups to transracial or out-of-group adoption.

Since the family serves as the primary socializing agent and purveyor of culture, it is also critical for the passing on of ethnic patterns. Billingsley and Giovannoni emphasize the role of biological families:

> Adoption agencies should have more to offer natural parents than adoption. A fundamental issue arises here. If the primary function of adoption is to provide babies for couples wishing to adopt, then the natural parents and their children will remain of secondary concern. If, on the other hand, the primary function is to provide homes and services to children, then the natural parents are a valuable resource, and a multifunctional approach becomes vital. The commitment to such a function is one of the most fundamental changes that agencies must make if they are to adapt to the needs of black children.[50]

The New York Committee for the Care of Puerto Rican Children also recommends that priority be given to the maintenance of the natural family, and link this with ethnic concerns:

> Every effort must be made to avoid placement of Puerto Rican children in foster homes or institutions. Before these are considered as alternatives, attempts must be made to help the child remain in his own family.
>   Very often because of a lack of understanding on the part of agencies of the family's importance in Puerto Rican culture, and their inability to communicate adequately because of the language barrier, the decision is made to place a child in a foster home. How can a practitioner assess the needs of a family if he cannot communicate with them?
>   Agencies should emphasize services to families that help maintain, support and strengthen them so as to avoid the separation of children from their homes. . . .
>   If a child must be placed, the natural family must remain a priority. Effective services must be established to expedite the child's return home.[51]

Most child welfare agencies have a philosophic commitment against unnecessary placement of children when the natural family can be helped to cope with the children's needs. Because of racism, misunderstanding, and lack of recognition of the cultural patterns and values that shape the life of the ethnic minority family, misjudgments may be made about its adequacy to care for its own children. Jenkins and Norman report on an extensive study of natural families with children in foster care:

> Parental rights also emerge as a matter of increasing concern. For any poverty group, there is a built-in problem of equity in access to available resources. Children can be moved from and returned to parental care for a range of reasons—some appropriate, some not—and these reasons may reflect arbitrary, discriminatory, or capricious decisions. One part of the problem in New York City, for example, is that for the large Spanish-speaking population decisions on child care may be based on inadequate comprehension of language or life-style.[52]

Because the minority group family is so easily misunderstood, it is often blamed for the shortcomings of children. As Montiel notes:

> Casework services and early education programs for the culturally deprived are essentially designed to improve the functioning of individuals. The Chicano family, as described by social scientists, possesses certain characteristics that explain the "failures" of its young. Thus it logically follows that if these forces impinge on the "proper" socialization of Chicanos they must be replaced by traits that foster "successful" socialization.[53]

Foster care is an area in which the recognition of ethnicity can be crucial. Many of the recommendations of spokesmen for ethnic minorities are concerned with the maintenance of cultural continuity for the child in substitute care. The Puerto Rican Committee cited above, for example, states:

> It frequently happens that, as a result of faulty placement, Puerto Rican children find themselves in foster homes where no Spanish is spoken. The result is that when they do finally return home, they can no longer communicate with their families in Spanish.... Part of the training in foster homes should be the teaching of Spanish and Puerto Rican culture and history.[54]

The committee recommends that foster parents be of the same ethnic and linguistic background as the child, and that everything possible be done to recruit Puerto Rican foster parents when placement outside the home becomes absolutely necessary.[55]

The service area in which ethnic groups feel most threatened is adoption. Few subjects evoke more emotion and controversy in the child welfare field than that of transracial adoption, in particular when minority children are adopted by white parents. Feelings are strong on both sides, and there is little reciprocal empathy, with high moral claims being made from all positions. The pressures of minority professionals have been strong and have affected adoption practice in significant ways. For example, the traditional agency in the field, the Child Welfare League of America, made the following amendment to its *Standards for Adoption Service* in 1972:

> In today's social climate, other things being equal, we believe that it is preferable to place a child in a family of his own racial background. We however reaffirm transracial adoption as one means of achieving needed permanence for some children. Children should not have adoption denied or significantly delayed when adoptive parents of other races are available.[56]

The minority positions on transracial adoption are not usually so tolerant of the practice. Jones states:

> My basic premise in opposing placement of black children in white homes is that being black in the United States is a special state of being. At a time of intense racial polarity, recognition of this fact is crucial to survival. I question the ability of white parents—no matter how deeply imbued with good will—to grasp the totality of the problem of being black in this society. I question their ability to create what I believe is crucial in these youngsters—a black identity. I suggest that creation of a black identity is a problem for many black parents also; the difference, perhaps, is one of degree.[57]

Many Blacks, professionals and others, feel that transracial adoption has been a convenient substitute for a concerted effort by child welfare agencies to recruit, approve, and maintain a supply of Black adoptive parents. Jones express this point of view:

> The Black Experience—it's the broad sense of family, community, and kinship, blood-related or not, that never has stopped the black community from caring for homeless children, with no regard to adoption as a legal course. It is crucial that solutions to the problems of black people, including homes for black children, be pursued and realized within the context of that community, for certainly at this time in our national development no other solution is viable or acceptable. I suggest that the myth that "no black homes available" is a

social agency cop-out for not devising innovative and creative ways of facing up to the problem—a perfect example of benign neglect.[58]

Billingsley and Giovannoni echo these sentiments and note several reasons for the controversy over the adoption of Black children. They question whether transracial efforts are primarily in the interests of Black children or of white adoptive parents:

> Increasingly Black social workers are voicing strenuous objections to transracial adoptions as being based on ignorance and denial of the Black child's situation. This controversy can be expected to heighten. There are in fact several reasons why agencies should be discouraged from pursuing transracial adoptions on a large scale. To date, transracial adoptions have not made nearly as sizable a contribution to the placement of black children as have placements with black parents. In the agencies which have led in the adoption of black children, the vast majority have been placed with black couples. Those agencies making the highest proportion of transracial adoptions are also agencies that place the fewest black children.
>
> Second, the failure to recruit enough Black adoptive parents for all Black children in need of homes may well relate to the agencies' failure to involve the Black community. Persistent reliance on white couples may only deflect energy away from this basic plan.
>
> Still a third reason arises from past and present undersupply of adoptable white infants. Adoption, as we have noted, originated as a means of serving white couples who wanted children. White infants for adoption are becoming increasingly scarce, and some believe that in the not too distant future there will be very few at all. However, the pressure on the agencies by white couples has not decreased. There is the distinct possibility in such a situation that the white couples' desires will be given priority over the needs and welfare of Black children.[59]

The National Association of Black Social Workers has issued a statement opposing transracial adoption. Its position is that white adoptive parents cannot develop a sense of ethnic identity in the Black child, nor teach him the many defenses Black people have developed to cope with prevailing racism. This statement is cited at length since it reflects the "ethnic identity" ideology of organized Black professionals at the time it was adopted:

> We affirm the inviolable position of Black children in Black families where they belong physically, psychologically, and culturally in order that they receive the total sense of themselves and develop a sound projection of their future. . . . Black children in white homes are cut

off from the healthy development of themselves as Black people, which development is the normal expectation and the only true humanistic goal.

. . . Identity grows on three levels of all human development: the physical, the psychological, and the cultural, and the nurturing of self-identification is the prime function of the family. The incongruence of a white family performing this function for a Black child is easily recognized. The physical factor stands to maintain that child's difference from his family. There is no chance of him resembling any relative. One's physical identify with his own is of great significance.

The historically established and cultivated psychological perceptions and social orientation of white America have developed from their social, political, educational, and religious institutions. Consequently these are the environmental effects they have to transmit and their teachings are not consistent with the realities of the social system for the Black child. He assumes, then, their posture and frame of reference, different and often antithetical to that of his ethnics which can only result in conflict and confusion when he does become aware of the social system in which he lives. Further internal conflict is inevitable by his minority status within his own family.

The socialization process for every child begins at birth and includes his cultural heritage as an important segment of the process. In our society the developmental needs of Black children are significantly different from those of white children. Black children are taught from an early age highly sophisticated coping techniques to deal with racist practices perpetuated by individuals and institutions. These coping techniques become successfully integrated into the ego functions and can be incorporated only through the process of developing positive identification with significant Black others. Only a Black family can transmit the emotional and sensitive subtleties of perception and reaction for a Black child's survival in a racist society.[60]

Although Black people have been the most outspoken about transracial adoption, other ethnic groups have expressed similar feelings. In *Akwesasne Notes,* a publication of the Mohawk Nation, an editorial entitled "American Indian Groups Show Rising Signs of Resistance to Adoption of Indian Children by White Families" stated:

Perhaps we are prejudiced ourselves. But this is not an appeal to white people to adopt Indians. It is an appeal to white people to help their own social agencies to consider Indian applicants. If you, as a person, are truly concerned with the welfare of Indian children, then help strengthen Indian homes and Indian families so that Indian people can look after their own young ones. And if you are Indian, this is an appeal to think about the young ones who need you to teach the language, to take them to the ceremonials and dances, to raise them so they will know the ways, and be Indian in their outlook.[61]

Another Indian newspaper, the *Nishnawbe News,* reported on a lawsuit brought by an Indian tribe in Michigan:

The Wisconsin Potawatomis of the Hannahville Reservation, located in Michigan's Upper Peninsula, have won a landmark decision in Federal Court, Marquette, which may well turn out to be one of national significance to the nation's federally organized tribes. The suit was filed against the Michigan Department of Social Services and concerned the removal of three Indian children from the reservation and their subsequently being sent to Florida for adoption with distant white relatives.

The parents were deceased. The uncle and grandmother of the children—their closest relatives—petitioned for either adoption or guardianship of the children. Reportedly, however, the Michigan Department of Social Services upon receiving custody of the three children sent them to Florida for adoption by a white family because they felt the "reservation was an unfit place to raise children."

U.S. District Court Judge Albert Engel, in a November 16 decision, ruled in favor of the Potawatomi Tribal community, with the Court agreeing that indeed the Tribal community had clear legal jurisdiction involving enrolled children of their tribe. In a 45-page decision the Court held the right of the Potawatomi Reservation to set up their own Court system and Juvenile Adoption Procedures.

Because of other incidents of this nature caused by a rash of adoptions of Indian children into white homes, there has been the formation of an organization known as the Michigan Indian Adoption Advisory Council to inform Indians throughout the State of the problem and compile a list of Indian families willing to adopt or provide foster care. . . .

We are going to say to the Social Service Department, We are the experts—use us. . . . We have to point out that cultural environment may be more important to the child's welfare than material provisions. Low average family income is one of the major reasons why many Indian families have not been considered as having suitable adoptive homes and the Council made the lowering of income requirements one of the first demands. Further it was pointed out that this policy has been accepted for the blacks and that it is high time that it should be for Indians as well.

... To abandon our children to white homes now would be a crime on our parts.... We are already such a small minority and now to lose our children....[62]

". . . and now to lose our children" is a poignant cry from a group that has already lost so much. It also is a universal theme among minorities, expressed for unborn children as well as for born. An example is the resistance of ethnic people to the imposition of family planning and to involuntary sterilization as expressions of genocide.

The moral claim of a group to its children, in which the rights of the group were assumed to supersede the rights of individual members, was most dramatically upheld by the Dutch Parliament after World War II. A decision was taken to return Jewish children who had been cared for by non-Jewish Dutch families during the war to their surviving relatives, even after years of separation. This meant deprivation and loss for many foster families and for children who knew only their wartime caretakers. In discussing this decision, Goldstein, Freud, and Solnit state, "The choice in such tragic instances is between causing intolerable hardship to the child who is torn away from his psychological parents, or causing further intolerable hardship to already victimized adults who, after losing freedom, livelihood, and worldly possessions may now also lose possession of their child."[63]

In deciding to base its ruling on social morality rather than on a case-by-case examination of interpersonal relationships, the Dutch Parliament might have considered the involuntary nature of the separation of children and parents, the hardships and dangers of any other options, and the emptiness of the wartime victory should it result in the more subtle but still devastating loss to Jewish families of surviving children. The situation in Holland differs in degree, but not necessarily in kind, from that of the Indian tribes, the Vietnamese refugees, and numerous other groups at the brink of survival whose children may be regarded as acceptable trade-offs for toleration in the larger society.

If children are central to group survival, then so are child welfare services. And the more threatened the group, the more it is at risk in the larger culture, the more it may seek to have services offered in such a way as not to further undermine group existence. This may be an important factor in the sought-for typology of service delivery to ethnic minorities.

Notes

1. Stanley M. Fong, "Assimilation and Changing Social Roles of Chinese Americans," in *Asian-Americans: A Success Story?*, edited by Stanley Sue and Frank Harry H. L. Kitano, special publication of the *Journal of Social Issues* 29:2 (1973): 118.
2. Stanley M. Fong, "Identity Conflicts of Chinese Adolescents in San Francisco," in E. B. Brody (ed.), *Minority Group Adolescents in the United States* (Baltimore: Williams & Wilkins, 1968), p. 114.
3. Marjorie Sloan Nicol, "Characteristics of Chinese-American Children with Problems," *Smith College Studies in Social Work* 36:3 (June 1966): 254–55.
4. Fong, "Assimilation and Changing Social Roles," p. 119.
5. Pei-Ngor Chen, "Samoans in California," *Social Work* 18:2 (March 1973): 45.
6. Robert G. Hayden, "Spanish-Americans of the Southwest," *Welfare in Review* 40:4 (April 1966): 20.
7. David Ballesteros, "Understanding the Bicultural Child" (Paper presented at the Early Childhood Special Education Manpower Needs Conference in Washington, D.C., December 9, 1971), p. 5.
8. Adolfo Quezada, "Innovative School Losing Pupils." *Tucson Daily Citizen*, October 3, 1973, p. 23.
9. Joe Braswell, "The Concept of Self and Social Work with American Indians" (Paper presented at the National Conference on Social Welfare, Atlantic City, New Jersey, May 27–31, 1973), pp. 8–9.
10. Herbert Locklear, "American Indian Myths," *Social Work* 17:3 (May 1972): 77.
11. Clare Jerdone, "Day Care for Indian Children," *Young Children* 20:3 (January 1965): 145.
12. Jarrold Levy, "Navajo Attitudes Toward Mental Illness and Mental Retardation" (Unpublished paper), p. 4.
13. Charles E. Farris, "A White House Conference on the American Indian," *Social Work* 18:1 (January 1973): 83.
14. An Interview With Carter Camp. *Akwesasne Notes*, published by the Mohawk Nation, early autumn 1973, p. 11.
15. "Culture and Its Relationship to Values in Conflict for Indian People" (Unpublished paper, reprint from the Shiprock, New Mexico, Indian Agency, Bureau of Indian Affairs), p. 5.
16. Jimm G. Good Tracks, "Native American Noninterference," *Social Work* 18:6 (November 1973): 30–34.
17. Ibid., p. 33.
18. Kathryn Polacca, "Ways of Working With Navajos Who Have Not Learned the White Man's Ways," *Navajo Times*, September 8, 1966, p. 1.

19. Hayden, "Spanish-Americans," p. 17.
20. Ballesteros, "Understanding the Bicultural Child," p. 11.
21. Interstate Research Associates, *Approaches for the Institutionalization of Bilingual Bicultural Head Start Programs Serving the Chicano Child,* edited by Frank Carrasco. Washington, D.C.: The Associates, 1972, p. 12.
22. Robert L. Bergman, "Boarding Schools and the Psychological Problems of Indian Children" (Unpublished paper prepared under the auspices of the Bureau of Indian Affairs), p. 3.
23. Fong, "Identity Conflicts," pp. 116–117.
24. U.S. Department of Health, Education, and Welfare, Office of Child Development, *Day Care Handbook Number 2* (Washington, D.C.: Government Printing Office, 1971), p. 25.
25. New York Committee for the Care of Puerto Rican Children, "Recommendations on the Care of Puerto Rican Children" (Unpublished paper), p. 3.
26. Ford H. Kuramoto, "What Do Asians Want?: An Examination of Issues in Social Work Education," *Journal of Social Work Education* 7 (fall 1971): 13.
27. Pei-Ngor Chen, "The Chinese Community in Los Angeles," *Social Casework* 51:10 (December 1970): 591.
28. Nicol, "Characteristics of Chinese-American Children," p. 235.
29. Bok-Lim C. Kim, "Asian Americans No Model Minority," *Social Work* 18:3 (May 1973): 44–45.
30. D'Arcy McNickle, "The Sociocultural Setting of Indian Life," *American Journal of Psychiatry* 125:2 (August 1968): 115.
31. Edward C. Burks, "Indian Home Life Causes Concern," *New York Times,* March 8, 1969.
32. Annie D. Wauneka, "Avoidance of Emotional Disturbances" (Paper for the workshop, "Emotional Problems of the Indian Student in Boarding Schools," Workshop Proceedings, Albuquerque, New Mexico, April 1960), p. 1.
33. Bergman, "Boarding Schools," pp. 5–7.
34. Braswell, "Concept of Self," pp. 7–8.
35. Miguel Montiel, "The Chicano Family: A Review of the Research," *Social Work* 18:3 (March 1973): 25.
36. Ibid.
37. Emilicia Mizio, "Impact of External Systems on the Puerto Rican Family," *Social Casework* 55:2 (February 1974): 77.
38. Ignacio Aquilar, "Initial Contacts with Mexican-American Families," *Social Work* 17:3 (May 1972): 68.
39. Marta Sotomayor, "Mexican-American Interaction with Social Systems," *Social Casework* 52:5 (May 1971): 322.
40. Alejandro Garcia, "The Chicano and Social Work," *Social Casework* 52:5 (May 1971): 276.
41. Mizio, "Impact of External Systems," p. 78.
42. Montiel, "The Chicano Family," p. 23.
43. Daniel P. Moynihan, *The Negro Family: The Case for National Action* (Washington, D.C.: Office of Policy Planning and Research, U.S. Department of Labor, 1965), pp. 5,30.

44. Herbert G. Gutman, *The Black Family in Slavery and Freedom, 1750–1925* (New York: Pantheon Books, 1976), p. 8.
45. Ibid., pp. 8–9.
46. Ibid. Appendix C, "A Brief Note on Late-Nineteenth Century Racial Ideology, Retrogressionist Beliefs, the Misperception of the Ex-Slave Family, and the Conceptualization of Afro-American History," pp. 531–44.
47. Marie Simmons Saunders, "The Ghetto: Some Perceptions of a Black Social Worker," *Social Work* 14:4, (October 1969): 86.
48. Clarence B. Fischer, "Homes for Black Children," *Child Welfare* 50:2 (February 1971): 108.
49. Charles V. Willie, "The Black Family and Social Class," *American Journal of Orthopsychiatry* (January 1974): 50–60.
50. Andrew Billingsley and Jeanne M. Giovannoni, *Children of the Storm: Black Children and American Child Welfare* (New York: Harcourt Brace Jovanovich, 1972), p. 204.
51. New York Committee for the Care of Puerto Rican Children, "Recommendations," p. 2.
52. Shirley Jenkins and Elaine Norman, *Filial Deprivation and Foster Care* (New York: Columbia University Press, 1972), p. 272.
53. Montiel, "The Chicano Family" p. 25.
54. New York Committee for the Care of Puerto Rican Children, "Recommendations," p. 3.
55. Ibid., p. 1.
56. Child Welfare League of America, "Standards on Transracial Adoption," mimeographed (New York, 1972), p. 1.
57. Edmond D. Jones, "On the Transracial Adoption of Black Children," *Child Welfare* 51:3 (March 1972): 157.
58. Ibid., p. 158.
59. Billingsley and Giovannoni, *Children of the Storm*, p. 198.
60. National Association of Black Social Workers, "Position Statement on Transracial Adoption," mimeographed (New York, September 1972).
61. Editorial Comment, "American Indian Groups Showing Rising Signs of Resistance to Adoption of Indian Children by White Families," *Akwesasne Notes*, published by the Mohawk Nation, spring, 1972, p. 6.
62. Mike Wright, "Hannahville Potawatomis Win in Federal Court Decision," *Nishnawbe News*, Marquette, Michigan: Organization of North American Indian Students, late fall edition, 1973, p. 7.
63. Joseph Goldstein, Anna Freud, Albert J. Solnit, *Beyond the Best Interests of the Child*, New Edition with Epilogue (New York: Free Press, 1980), p. 107.

Part II
The United States Field Study

3

The Ethnic Agency Defined

What is an "ethnic agency"? The ethnic organization has been described and classified—there even is a directory for that purpose.[1] Some of the categories are political, fraternal, national, or language. The common denominator for an ethnic organization is a clear statement of goals and an open commitment to a defined group. When an organization is called the National Association for the Advancement of Colored People, for example, there may be disagreements about its policy, but not about its purpose. But if it is called Children's Services, Inc., or the Big Cove Day-Care Center, the matter is not so clear.

The ethnic agency is both a special form of ethnic organization and a special form of social agency. To be functional it must seek a balanced position between both types. It cannot achieve this by posing the goal of services against the goal of ethnicity, nor can it raise ethnic issues at the expense of services. Such an agency must find a way to incorporate both service and ethnic goals in a single delivery system.

Serving the ethnic client is not a new phenomenon for social agencies. With a disproportionate number of Third World people among those who are in poverty, unemployed, poorly housed, and with health problems, it is reasonable to expect that they will makeup a disproportionate number of agency clients. What is new, however, is the concept of public and publically funded agency services that incorporate ethnic factors, not as "problems," but as positive components of service delivery. The research reported here sought to identify programs and agencies where innovative and constructive work was being done with ethnic clients, to analyze the nature of these activities, including "what worked and what didn't work," and to operationalize the definition of ethnic agency.

Target areas in different parts of the United States that had important population concentrations of each of the five ethnic groups in the study were selected for field visits. In San Francisco and New York visits were made to agencies serving Asian Americans; Philadelphia was the target area for Blacks; New York for Puerto Ricans; Brownsville, Austin, San Antonio, and four other communities in southern Texas were visited for services to Chicanos; and Cherokee, North Carolina, and Phoenix and Sacaton, Arizona, were target areas for American Indians. In each setting professional consultants from the particular ethnic group advised the research staff and recommended agencies to visit on the basis of whether they appeared to be incorporating ethnic factors in their child welfare services. More than a year was spent in the field, and visits were made to fifty-four agencies in six states serving approximately fourteen thousand children and their families. Among the agency types visited were day-care centers, foster-care and adoption agencies, residential centers and institutions, programs giving services to children in their own homes, youth services, and multipurpose integrated service centers. Table 1 in Appendix A describes the various settings.

The agencies visited were not representative of all agencies serving children—indeed, they were selected not to be a representative sample but because they were innovative, experimental, and creative and therefore not typical or traditional. The sample is thus "purposive"—chosen on purpose to illustrate a particular type. The national scope was deliberate, to avoid regional parochialism and thus secure information more relevant for national policy. But program types in rural south Texas cannot be generalized to urban Los Angeles, even though Chicano children are served in both. Neither are findings on service programs for children of ten Indian tribes automatically transferable to all Indian people. Since the research goal was to develop a generalized typology for service delivery, applicable in cross-cultural settings, the goal for sample selection was to balance the homogeneity needed to generalize with the heterogeneity needed to compare, and to do this within the practical limitations of time, staff, and funding.

Agency Characteristics and Programs

Agency data were collected in fifty-four extensive interviews with agency directors and in field visits and observations. Areas covered in the interviews include agency structure and staffing patterns, program information, service statistics, reporting on special ethnic needs, cultural content, bilingualism, and ideological approaches to service delivery.

Of the fifty-four agencies visited, five were multiservice and the rest specialized in one or more services to children such as day care, foster care, residential treatment, mental health services, services in own homes, and youth services. Agency auspices was divided, with twenty-five public agencies, nine with private sectarian and twenty with nonsectarian sponsorship. When it came to funding, however, although fewer than half were public agencies, over 94 percent, or fifty-one of the fifty-four agencies, received public funds. In addition, eighteen received private nonsectarian funds and four private sectarian funding. These programs primarily served low-income groups; over half had no fee for services, and the remainder had a sliding scale.

CLIENTS, STAFF, and BOARD

Serving ethnic clients is the first and most obvious measure of the ethnic agency. The data show that almost three-fourths of the agencies in this study served over 95 percent ethnic clients, and no agency served fewer than 50 percent. There were some significant differences in homogeneity of clients by ethnic group. In the Mexican American and Indian programs, 100 percent of the agencies served over 95 percent of ethnic clients. This was true for 64 percent of Black agencies, 50 percent of Asian, and 44 percent of Puerto Rican programs. These differences cannot be attributed to the group, however, but relate to the settings of the programs. The two highly homogeneous programs were in fairly isolated rural areas, and the communities where Black, Puerto Rican, and Asian agencies were visited were large cities with greater neighborhood heterogeneity.

Ethnic personnel is a second important criterion of the ethnic agency. In thirty-one of the fifty-four agencies visited (57 percent) the director was of the primary ethnic group served. White directors were most frequently found in Black and Indian settings. In no case was there a director from a minority group other than the primary group served. Ethnic composition of staff was higher than of administration. In ten agencies all staff was of the primary ethnic group; in twenty-four agencies this was the case for all but a few (under 5 percent). Thus in two-thirds of the agencies 95 percent of the staff was of the same ethnic group as the primary group served. In eleven agencies (20 percent) the staff was mixed, but the majority were of the primary group. In only a handful of agencies were there fewer staff of the primary ethnic group than others.

Ethnic representation on the boards of the agencies was also reviewed. In sixteen agencies (30 percent) all board members were of the primary ethnic group. This was particularly the case for the Indian programs, where it was typically mandated as part of the funding structure for reservation agencies. In fourteen agencies (26 percent) boards were mixed proportionately to clients; thus an ethnic majority was automatically achieved. Black agencies in the study were the only ones in which board members were not in proportion to the clients in terms of ethnic composition. About two-thirds of the agencies had professionals on their boards; this was most frequent for Black and Asian programs. Almost all agencies had community representatives on their boards, and parental representation was highest for Puerto Rican and Indians.

In the agency interview directors were asked about the extent to which they felt there was support for their agencies from the ethnic power structure and/or the ethnic community. About half the directors reported strong support, but the base differed according to group. Highest support from the ethnic power structure was reported by American Indians and Puerto Ricans, least support and highest ambivalence from Asians. This last response reflects some of the differences between the Asian ethnic power in the San Francisco and New York Chinatowns, which represented an earlier migration, and the interests of the social agencies, which must serve new arrivals. The highest support from their own ethnic communities, as distinct from the ethnic power groups, was reported by Black and Mexican American agencies.

ETHNIC PROGRAMS

In any service program, the majority of content is predetermined by the nature of the activity. Four-year-olds in a day-care center, for example, play, nap, eat, toilet, sing, go outdoors, come indoors. Given that pattern, what is distinctive about an ethnic day-care center with regard to program content?

The agency interview asked eleven questions on program content that had direct bearing on ethnic orientation, in addition to the questions on bilingualism, which will be discussed separately. Among the program content items were questions on the use of ethnic food, art, music, history, and celebration of holidays, as well as promotion of ethnic awareness.

An official policy to introduce cultural content in agency programs was reported by 63 percent of all agencies, but by 89 percent of the Puerto Rican agencies. The further step of utilizing program content to develop ethnic awareness was undertaken by fewer respondents—26 percent of all agencies, but 55 percent of Black agencies. There is a significant difference here, with Puerto Rican agencies tending to stress cultural content whereas Black agencies stress ethnic awareness.

Food is often a critical element in cultural programming. Almost one-third of the agency directors said they made regular use of ethnic foods, and another 20 percent said they used ethnic food on special occasions. Greatest use was by Mexican American agencies, which were in more rural areas and had a very homogeneous ethnic clientele. Regular use of ethnic food was reported by about one-third of the Asian agencies, with Indian and Puerto Ricans occasionally having ethnic dishes. Lowest use of ethnic foods was by Black agencies; this may mean that there is less differentiation in urban areas between Black diets and "standard" menus.

Ethnic music was used in programs by almost three-fourths of the agencies (74 percent) with highest use in Asian, Mexican, and Puerto Rican settings. Ethnic art and decorations were used in just under two-thirds of the settings, primarily in Asian, Mexican, and Puerto Rican agencies. The history of the ethnic group was a regular part of the program of only 13 percent of the agencies but was invoked on special occasions by another 44 percent. There was least reported use of historical material by the Black agencies visited. All groups supported ethnic holidays except the Indians.

(This may relate to the interviewers' use of the term *holiday* rather than their asking about tribal or religious events.)

AGENCY IDEOLOGY

Agency directors were asked if they saw their program as supporting a philosophy of "equal treatment," of "recognition of differences" or of "promotion of ethnic identity," the three ideological positions explored in the study. Of the fifty-four agencies, fifteen chose only the last alternative, promotion of ethnic identity, and thirteen chose recognition of differences. Some directors elected a combination of goals. When these combined choices were allocated among alternatives, the weighted results were as follows: 20 percent for equal treatment as an ideology; 40 percent for recognition of differences, and 40 percent for promotion of ethnic identity.

Although the ethnic component has been specifically identified, there were other common denominators in the agencies visited that were not specifically related to ethnicity. Poverty, for example, is neither a sufficient nor a necessary component of the ethnic definition. Yet the five groups selected for inclusion in the study were all economically deprived and had disproportionate numbers among the poor. They all included multiproblem families with substantial services. The commonality here related more to class than to ethnicity, but this variable is hard to separate in the field study because so many of the poor are of these ethnic groups, and so many of these groups are poor.

The common problems of poverty affected agency programs and made for a more integrated approach to service delivery than is usually seen in traditional settings. Of the agencies visited 80 percent sought to meet mental health needs, and 49 percent met child-care needs. But 40 percent also met health and dental needs, 52 percent met nutritional needs, 35 percent gave employment referrals, 20 percent gave housing help, 30 percent helped with migration, 39 percent tried to compensate for poor family patterns, and 37 percent worked to integrate traditional ways with the larger society. In response to a question about what issues concerned the agencies, about equal numbers said "social and political issues," "interpersonal relations," and "ethnic identity." The intermingling of these three areas, in fact, was what characterized most of the agencies. Only 4 percent said they wanted to change "majority" attitudes. Many more wanted to support ethnic identity, strengthen and maintain the ethnic family, and provide growth and leadership for minority children. Strengthening the family was most frequently expressed as the primary goal, noted by 89 percent of respondents and by all ethnic groups. Increasing and continuing involvement of the parents of children served was an important child welfare goal, and a family focus was stressed regardless of agency type. The emphasis on family needs, on developing group strengths, and on integration of services characterized these agencies as much as their interest in cultural content and strengthening ethnic identity.

Ethnic Issues: "Dispelled Myths or New Realities?"

Although the numbers and percentages give some measure of agency activities, the anecdotal reports on problems and programs are what really illuminate the ethnic issues. These responses to the open-ended questions explore the following issues: myths and stereotypes affecting minorities; use of language in programs; appropriate cultural content; positions on separate institutions; and ethnic issues related to the larger community. In addition agency directors were asked to report on "things that worked and things that didn't work."

In ethnic relations, as in any area close to the culture and folk styles of people, myths and stereotypes abound. Some of them interfere with delivery of social services, some put down efforts of groups to prosper, others put down efforts of agencies to be helpful. In response to the interview question about the importance of myths and stereotypes 85 percent of agency directors felt that stereotypes have been dysfunctional for minority groups served. On the other hand, they felt that myths could be used to advance group interests.

There were numerous examples of ways in which sensitive social workers put their knowledge of myths and traditions to good use in delivering services. The concept of "Indian time," for example, was discussed by two therapists on a Cherokee reservation. One therapist, trained in the forty-five-minute-session tradition, expressed frustration and feelings of ineffectiveness in his work because of his Indian clients' avoidance of issues and their habit of making casual references to important happenings on their way out the door after the session. Another therapist, native to the area and empathic to the people, had developed the capacity to "wait it out," accepting the fact that the Indian client would not give fast reactions but when ready was accessible to treatment. She incorporated the concept of "Indian time" in her intervention plan, with substantial success.

Another way in which tribal knowledge was used was in relation to the adoption of an out-of-wedlock Navajo infant. Contrary to patterns in some other groups, for an Indian to give up a baby, whether in- or out-of-wedlock, is against tradition, and for such an act she must secure approval from both family and tribe. In one case, an Indian social worker in a southwestern city worked with a young Indian mother who wanted to give up her out-of-wedlock baby for adoption, against her family's opposition. The social worker went to the tribal council, as well as to the native medicine man, to secure support. He organized a "sing" in which the problem was presented to the tribe. The fact that a plan had been made for the baby to be adopted by an Indian couple of the same tribe was a strong point in favor, and tribal consent was secured and the adoption consummated.

The third illustration occurred on a reservation in the Southwest, where there were many Pima children, and has to do with the myth that a physical handicap may be a punishment. In the tribal mythology such a handicap was described as being "out of tune with balance." The reservation Head Start center was the recipient of funds to establish a pioneer program for handicapped Indian children, but it was feared that this would not be accepted on the reservation because of the negative attitude regarding handicaps. The Indian social workers called together the old women of the tribe, the guardians of tribal history, and spoke with them about the needs and problems of local children with handicaps. Then the older women were asked if they felt these children were being appropriately "punished" or needed and deserved help. Once the issue was made specific to particular children who were known and loved, the response was supportive. The social workers then asked the old women of the tribe to become the spokeswomen for the proposed project and to enlist tribal support. This they did. Through their knowledge of tribal custom, their respect for the involvement of elders, and perhaps a little community organizing strategy, the Indian social workers were able to turn the myth around and allow access to needed services.

For the Asian American group, the major myth the social workers cited was that people from Asia were considered a "model minority," docile, hardworking, and not seeking or needing public services. Asian social workers interviewed gave different interpretations to this myth and its questionable validity. One response was that there were always problems in the Asian community, but in the past they were covered up and handled within the confines of the ethnic institutions. With a changing social climate, people are more free to express needs and even to demand services. Another point was that the accustomed Asian ways of child-rearing—teaching children to be quiet, reserved, and docile—were not functional in today's world. Several Asian workers saw a breakdown in traditional family patterns, including the rebellion of youth, and the loss of older values like respect for elders, which formerly served as an important social control.

Workers also pointed to demographic factors in the changing behavior of Asians, including the substantial rise in recent Asian immigration, with new unskilled workers entering a restricted labor market, and the intragroup conflicts between assimilated Asian youth and new arrivals. Although public welfare is not typically sought by Asian immigrants, this may be explained by the realities of their status and the fear on the part of many newcomers that to admit financial dependency while having alien status could result in deportation. One Chinese social worker on the West Coast summed up the situation when she said, "The Asian community has changed, but it is hard to know what is dispelled myth and what is the new reality."

Black social workers interviewed in ethnic agencies referred more to negative stereotypes than to traditional myths when they described barriers to effective service delivery to Blacks. They reported that whites often equated poverty with Blackness and had lower expectations for Blacks both as clients and as students than for whites. White social workers were often seen, on the one hand, as being afraid of Black children and, on the other hand, of overcompensating by being too permissive. The umbrella use of the term *cultural deprivation* to apply to minority children was criticized. Ethnic culture exists, but it is not white middle-class culture. Furthermore, according to the Black workers, whites did not recognize adaptive behavior needed by Blacks for survival in the white world.

One area of cultural difference reported was in relation to family planning and abortion. One Black worker expressed the feeling that the service system did not comprehend the intensity of antiabortion feeling among many Blacks. For some this negative feeling extended to family planning, seen as being particularly directed to reduce the numbers of Blacks and other minorities.

The stereotype most resented by directors of Chicano agencies was that Chicano children are inferior to Anglos. Some of this was reported to be based on the poor self-image of the Mexican American. One Chicano worker said, "Eighty percent of our problem is to convince Mexican American parents that their children are as smart as Anglos."

Poor self-image of parents was not reported by Puerto Rican social workers, but the stereotype that Spanish children cannot learn was said to be prevalent in the white community. Two other stereotypes that were barriers to service delivery were that Puerto Rican culture is inferior and that Puerto Rican parents are not interested in their children's education. One Puerto Rican social worker said, "The courts think Spanish children are delinquent, the schools think they cannot be educated—and both have given up working with our children."

The responses in the field clarified the differences between stereotypes and myths and their relevance for services. Stereotypes reported were negative, reflecting distorted perceptions of minority peoples, and they generalized from individual pathology to overall groups. They interfered with service delivery and needed to be directly confronted. Myths, on the other hand, arose from historical and cultural backgrounds of people. Although they could and sometimes did interfere with service delivery, they could also be reinterpreted by sensitive ethnic workers, knowledgeable about the culture of their people. Such workers could use and reformulate traditional patterns so that needed services could be delivered without directly confronting historical precedents.

CULTURAL CONTENT

Cultural content in agency problems is one visible way to show ethnic commitment. The celebration of holidays, for example, was widely reported, including some occasions that were religious, some that were national and some that were cultural in origin. Among ethnic holidays frequently mentioned by one or another group were the following: Three Kings Day, Puerto Rican Discovery Day, Mother's Day, El Dia del Arbal ("Tree Day"), Martin Luther King's birthday, Chinese New Year, the Dragon Festival, Mexican Independence Day, Our Lady of Guadelupe Day. For the Native Americans, ceremonial occasions, rather than holidays, were observed.

Several factors affected the use of cultural materials in programs, including the age of clients, the sensitivity and sophistication of workers, and the homogeneity of client groups. Sometimes clients had their own ideas of what was wanted, which might differ from the workers'. Teenagers were reported to have universal devotion to rock music, regardless of ancestry. In some cases it was not the content but the context, or frame of reference, of the ethnic material that was important. A Japanese group leader in San Francisco, for example, said there was strong interest in karate lessons among Japanese youth. He reported that he had searched for months until he found someone who was able to teach karate with a cultural focus, not as a destructive martial art. The latter approach was to be avoided lest the cultural content be used to intensify the street fighting that was prevalent in the neighborhood.

Where therapeutic work was involved, knowledge of family structure and culture patterns was drawn on for use in treatment. Family therapy, for example, was modified in Asian agencies to conform with traditional Asian patterns of what was and what was not discussed between generations. In a mental health center visited all workers agreed that the Chinese psychiatrist who was on staff for supervision was an important asset, since he was able to combine cultural understanding with professional skills. When a Chinese therapist in that setting was asked about the extent to which traditional Western psychiatry was helpful with her Asian clients, she said, "We take something from Column A, something from Column B, and mix with our own particular brand of sauce."

Cultural content was not applied in a mechanical way in the innovative settings. In one preschool program visited in Arizona, the Indian director spoke of the importance of knowing tribal differences in disciplining young children. She had children from ten tribes in her center, and they were accustomed to very dif-

ferent patterns of discipline at home, not because of family differences but because of tribal patterns. In disciplining children
for the same offenses some tribes are permissive, some strict, and
some practice avoidance. Both with the children at the center and
in parent education sessions, tribal membership had to be considered in exercising and discussing child-rearing authority. The director also had to deal with her own conflicts because of the need
to be consistent in center policy, while at the same time avoiding
too wide a gap between practices experienced by children at home
and in school.

On some occasions cultural patterns were in conflict with accepted social work practice. An example is where tribal registration of an adopted Indian baby violated the traditional practice
of confidentiality. There was such a case on a reservation in North
Carolina, where a Cherokee mother was seeking to have her
adopted baby, from another tribe, accepted by the tribal council for registration as a Cherokee. Being on the tribal rolls is
critical for the exercise of many rights, including inheritance, but
if the baby were registered in the tribe of the biological parents
her whereabouts would be known to the natural mother, who
might try to get the child back at a later date. Thus, with the
support of the social worker, the adoptive parents were trying to
have the baby registered in their tribe, which would maintain both
individual rights and tribal rights.

Homogeneity of clients was an important consideration in the
extent to which cultural content was reflected in agency programs. It was obviously simpler to follow cultural patterns where
only one group was involved than in a setting serving different
ethnic groups. Where there was a real mix of children served, as
in the primarily Puerto Rican programs in New York, it was found
that cultural content was inversely related to heterogeneity. This
led to a stronger acceptance of the cultural-pluralism approach in
agency programming.

Use of cultural content was also related to the history of each
specific agency and its program goals. A well-established private
agency serving second- and third-generation Chinese children
and youth in San Francisco was a prototype of the traditional
settlement house model, whether on the South Side in Chicago or
the Lower East Side in New York. Agency goals stressed achievement for the youth and leadership development. This agency was
a busy, active, successful enterprise, which prided itself on not

accepting government funds. But one looked in vain for "cultural content" as a primary component of youth programming. Where ethnic issues arose they were in complaints from parents that children spent too much time away from home, contrary to traditional Asian family patterns. Only in the family-treatment program was a special effort made to employ Asian therapists, as they were considered to be more successful in reaching clients. The one service that "didn't work" in this bustling, exciting house was a program for newly arrived immigrant Chinese youths, who didn't fit with the agency model.

LANGUAGE

Language is one of the components of cultural programming, but its significance differed for each of the study groups. Sixty-five percent of all programs visited were bilingual, over half had bilingual teachers and workers, and one-third used a bilingual curriculum. Language was not a relevant issue for Blacks, although expressions, idioms, and phrases were noted that were unique to Black culture.

The importance of bilingual-bicultural service delivery was emphasized by both Puerto Rican and Chicano workers interviewed. Puerto Ricans in New York stressed the need to make a conscious effort to maintain bilingualism throughout one's life, rather than have the school experience be a transition from Spanish to English, with attendant dangers of loss of cultural patterns and ethnic identity. School age was the most common time reported for loss of native languages. Chicano respondents placed more emphasis on promoting the learning of English in order to succeed in school and as a way to maximize opportunities. The families served in the programs visited in Texas were primarily Spanish-speaking, and the rural setting was less of a threat than was total exclusion from that culture. Thus a group's attitudes toward bilingualism were affected by how strong the group was in the subculture and how isolated or integrated it was in relation to the larger society.

For the Asian community, language issues reflected both length of time in this country and identity questions. For recent immigrants, there was strong pressure from parents for children to learn English as soon as possible, in order to succeed in school. This parental attitude sometimes came into conflict with culture-oriented social workers. In one day-care center in San Francisco, for example, Asian workers were urging recent Filipino immigrants to continue to speak Tagalog at home so that their children wouldn't lose all native language content. The parents, on the other hand, were urging Filipino teachers to speak only English in school in order to help their children adjust to their new life in the United States.

The most impressive handling of language differences was observed in a day-care center, also in San Francisco, where children spoke three Chinese dialects: Mandarin, Cantonese, and Tonshaniese. The program was designed to help these newly arrived youngsters of four and five years prepare for entry to the public school system. There were teachers who spoke each of the three dialects as well as English, and in addition there was an American-born Chinese who was to provide a role model as a "nonaccented" English-speaking teacher. Several group discussions were observed in which each child spoke in his or her own dialect and was answered in the same and then in English; the child responded in both English and dialect and was answered in dialect and English. Throughout the exchanges teachers adjusted the extent to which they used English in their responses according to the length of stay of each child in this country and his or her language capacity. As a child became ready to leave for public school the amount of English dialogue increased.

A very different issue arose when Asian respondents defined language as an identity question. This was raised primarily by Asian workers who were young adults, many of whom had English as their basic tongue. They reported a movement of Asian students back to school to learn their national languages. This occurred for political and social reasons, and involved Japanese and Korean youth who wanted better communication and more contact with their parents' native lands. Age was a significant variable in Asian attitudes toward language—the old people seemed content with their foreign tongue, the very young needed English for acculturation, and the young adults wanted to revive a native tongue or to introduce bilingualism.

Language issues were important matters to the Indian workers. The early official U.S. policy toward Indian languages, one of total obliteration, left scars not easily healed. Several middle-aged Cherokees told of their experiences in boarding schools, to which many Indian children were and still are sent. As youths they were not allowed to speak one word of their native language; if they did, their mouths were washed out with soap. This policy has now changed, but a whole generation grew up with no knowledge of its mother tongue. Now that they are parents, they are determined that their children should know the tribal speech, and so native languages are being introduced in the schools. It is thus the very young and the very old who know the native Indian languages, and the adults in their middle years who express feelings of deprivation and frustration.

One problem in promoting bilingualism among Indians is that of communication among themselves. There are hundreds of different tribes, each speaking somewhat differently. In Arizona alone five basic Indian languages are spoken. So English becomes important not only for work opportunities and mainstream activities but for intertribal business. In spite of this the revival of Indian languages is an important issue for many Native Americans, not as a substitute for English but as a way of ensuring continuation of the culture of their forefathers.

SEPARATE INSTITUTIONS

A controversial issue in social services is whether or not there should be separate institutions for different ethnic groups, if such was their choice. In the field interviews each agency director was asked his or her position on this issue; 41 percent supported separate institutions and 55 percent opposed. The reasons "for" and "against" differed for different groups.

In the Asian community, for example, those directors who supported separate institutions stressed the unique language needs of their people and the special problems of mental health work, which require understanding of culture, client, language, and custom. One respondent said, "Separate programs are a reality for us, and have been for a long time. The traditional child welfare system has ignored the Chinese child, and we have had to create our own system." A worker in another agency said, "A separate system would be a dream come true—but it is not likely to happen as long as we have to relate to the public agencies." The majority of Asian directors, however, came down on the negative side in relation to separate institutions, expressing their concern that such a service system would further isolate Asians from the larger society. One worker said, "I like the idea of integration—

there is much that different groups can learn from each other." Another worker gave as an analogy the special taste of an Irish stew: "My carrots remain carrots and my potatoes remain potatoes—but together they make a terrific dish." A stronger negative feeling from some Asians was that separate institutions were discriminatory, and that agencies should respond to the needs of all persons in the community, regardless of ethnic group.

Chicano agency heads who supported separate institutions took a more political stance, seeing them as an avenue to power and community control. One director who supported separate institutions said, "They should be staffed by Mexican Americans to ensure that the needs of our people are really met." Those Chicanos who opposed separate institutions gave two main reasons. One was the feeling that such agencies would be discriminatory—a Chicano worker said, "Our children should never be allowed to believe that they are an inferior group. That would be the message if you had separate institutions." Several directors gave administrative reasons for their opposition: the belief that separate agencies would waste time and money by duplicating services and would only mean that "too many people are trying to have a share of the same pie."

Puerto Rican agency directors were divided along some of the same lines. There was strong feeling that only ethnic leadership could ensure that services would be directed to meet ethnic needs. Community survival was also an issue. One director said, "In looking at the history of the Puerto Rican community in New York we had to develop some Puerto Rican agencies for the survival and development of our community." Another said, "Each group should be able to provide the needed services to its own community. We think the quality of each program would improve." On the other hand, there were Puerto Rican workers who feared segregation. One said, "It would mean the separation of our people. It would only polarize our society even more." A third said, "Racial problems would emerge and everyone will start fighting for a share."

Directors of Black agencies who supported separate institutions based their support on their perceptions of the role of social services in the community. One director said, "In order to realize the meaning of democracy there must be a recognition of differences. Separate institutions are likely to be more creative and innovative in meeting the special needs of minority children."

Another said, "There should be neighborhood institutions—if an area is Black, the institution should be Black."

The majority of Black agency directors, however, expressed negative feelings about the prospect of separate institutions. One said, "The real world is mixed—we should prepare children to live in the real world." Another said, "It would be a cop-out not to prepare children for a multiracial society," and another said, "Separate institutions would further alienate people from each other. The direct interaction of different kinds of people in small group settings is a vehicle for dispelling myths and furthering understanding." A third position taken by directors of Black agencies was that there should be room for both separate and integrated institutions. One response was, "Some Blacks need ethnically solid services, others can benefit from an integrated experience. Both should be available."

For the Indian tribes, separate institutions were not a new idea but reflected the traditional pattern of reservation life. The directors and workers were concerned with the impact of that separation on individual and group development. Two points of view were expressed. One was that separate institutions, under Indian direction, were the only route to self-realization and independence. In mixed settings Indian leadership is rarely allowed, and ethnic needs are not recognized. Separation was seen by some as the only chance for group survival.

On the other hand, others expressed real concerns about the effect of the removal of Indians from the mainstream of American life. One respondent said, "I believe some of the hardships faced by Indians are due to lack of competence. Better training can be secured off the reservation, and more integration would help Indians compete in the world." A second expression of this point of view was that there is a danger of "reservation mentality" in which people can do well only in the shelter of the reservation, but not away from it in the open community.

LARGER ISSUES

The majority of agency directors expressed interest in "larger issues." Some specified these issues as "family, not just child," whereas others spoke of poverty as the major problem.

For the Asian agency directors concern with larger social issues was a new phenomenon, reflecting changing social patterns of their ethnic group. A major issue for the San Francisco Asian community was busing; Chinese residents took a strong position against having their children bused out of their neighborhoods. Busing was perceived as a threat to ethnic identity, with the prospect that it would result in less rather than more services. Chinese and Japanese language classes, Asian studies, and bilingual teachers are provided in schools with high Asian enrollment. The result of busing would be to scatter Asian students around the city and destroy the base for special services. This is an example of how a larger issue, school desegregation, looks different from the perspective of two different ethnic groups.

Directors of Black agencies felt that their child-welfare task was made more difficult by lack of support in the larger community for the Black family. An issue of concern for one respondent was the pressure on pregnant Black women to have abortions or to surrender out-of-wedlock infants. This pressure was attributed to the lack of comprehension on the part of whites of the significance of children for the Black family.

It was among the Indians that "larger issues" were most prominent on the agenda of the ethnic group, reflecting the social structure on the reservation. Tribal councils were concerned not only with social and child welfare but with land rights, housing, education, and employment. They were also involved in issues involving legal rights of offreservation Indians and intertribal conflicts. Respondents were also concerned about potential conflict on the reservations between those defined as "white Indians" and the half- to full-blooded members of the tribes. It was expected that both groups would unite if threatened from the outside, but within their own settings the issue of blood had increasing political significance. It also had economic meaning for tribal members, since inheritance rights were involved and a defined percentage of Indian blood was required for formal inclusion as a tribal member. It was reported that this issue has resulted in subtle pressure to "marry up in blood" to ensure continuance on tribal rolls.

What "Worked" and What "Didn't Work"

In the field interviews directors were asked to discuss program and policies that had "worked" and those that had "not worked," in terms of agency goals. These were analyzed across groups, and the major areas of success and failure are as follows:

Agencies expressed most satisfaction with the following:

1. Bilingual–bicultural programs
2. Career development for parents and leadership development for youth
3. Supports to families to care for their own children
4. Recruitment of minority parents for foster care and adoption
5. Utilizing traditional cultural and/or tribal patterns to effect change

On the other hand, the following didn't work or were problems:

1. Use of groups for therapy or treatment, especially for teenagers
2. Efforts to have the community accept group homes and/or deinstitutionalization
3. Handling of interethnic relations between their group and others
4. Conflicts between new and old arrivals, or between more and less acculturated members of the group
5. Persistence of some dysfunctional cultural patterns, particularly of bilingual programs

The most general enthusiasm expressed in the ethnic agencies was for programs involving bicultural–bilingual learning. This was expressed by all groups except Blacks, where it was not relevant. For the Puerto Rican and Chicano directors, and for the majority of the Asian Americans, such programs were considered to be the core of their effectiveness, and the major way in which they differed from traditional service agencies. One Puerto Rican respondent, for example, said, "Clients seem to be at ease when they are referred to our program and find out the staff is from the same ethnic background and speak both English and Spanish."

Use of languages other than English in children's services does not follow any single model but depends on both goals and situations. Where there is an immigrant or migrant group, such as the newly arrived Chinese and Filipinos in San Francisco, or migrant workers from Mexico in south Texas, there is pressure on agencies to help clients learn English so there can be an easier transition in schools and on jobs. At the other extreme, where groups have been purged of native languages and speak only English, as with some Indians and some third-generation Asians, the ethnic group may seek to recapture its own tongue, often in order to strengthen its political base. Finally, there is the position often expressed by Puerto Rican groups who seek the development of bilingual–bicultural learning that asserts that an entire people can be literate and functional in two languages. There are numerous examples from Europe and Canada and also from "white ethnics" in which families are fluent in the ethnically based language, as well as in the tongue of the majority people.

Some of the programs visited were outgrowths of the War on Poverty and had been exposed to "maximum feasible participation of the poor" as a project goal. Thus many of the key people in the innovative agencies felt that the career development of parents through training programs was one of their best accomplishments. More than one respondent told the interviewer that she had "been a Head Start parent" and introduced teachers and group leaders who were former welfare clients. The director of one Puerto Rican agency reported that the center had been a laboratory for career development, and that ten people who had begun as parent-users of the program were now full-time staff members. A different but related aspect of development was of youth leaders who had formerly been agency members. One settlement house, serving third-generation Chinese youth, said they regarded the numbers of youth who went to college as one of their best measures of success. This agency stressed acculturation and "making it" in the larger society.

The majority of agency directors, representing all ethnic groups, reported that giving supportive services to families to help them care for their own children was one of the most important programs that "worked." This was accomplished in a variety of ways. An Asian American agency reported monthly parent meetings and discussions of program materials with parents. An Indian group illustrated ways in which parents were encouraged to make decisions about their children's education. One Black agency maintained a parents' workroom and encouraged parents' involvement by drawing them into all aspects of the program. Another Black agency said its single biggest success was the family counseling program. This agency reported that it places priority on preservation of the natural family and sees child placement as a last resort. One Chicano agency encourages visits of parents and seeks to strengthen parental confidence in the educational capacity of their children. Another Chicano agency reports that staff works with parents so they will be able to continue in the home some of the special training given children at the center.

A number of agencies, in discussing stereotypes, reported that traditional agencies acted as if few minority people were prepared to function appropriately as foster or adoptive parents. Yet programs to recruit such families were reported to be very successful, high among the activities that "worked" for the ethnic agencies. One Puerto Rican agency was involved in the recruitment of Spanish-speaking foster parents, which resulted in the placement of several hundred Puerto Rican children in foster homes of matching culture and language. Indian agencies both in the Southeast and the Southwest reported success in recruitment of Indian foster parents and adoptive families. Intertribal adoptions were being undertaken, with due reference to tribal relationships.

The last major area of reported success was in dispelling stereotypes and turning around traditional myths to allow for needed services. This is an area where respondents feel ethnic agencies "work" because of their knowledge of cultural background.

Turning to things that "didn't work," agency directors tended to report first on many of the general problems faced by almost all social agencies—lack of funds, need for staff, increasing client needs, and fragmentation of services. They were then encouraged to report more specifically on "what didn't work" in the context of the ethnic agency.

There were frequent references by respondents to their view that "groups," whether for therapy or other treatment, did not work for minority people. This was said to be particularly the case for teenagers, many of whom were nonverbal, very shy, and unable to share in group communication. One director in a Black agency said, "Our girls come from families where they are told to be quiet." A director of a program for Asian youth said, "It is hard to motivate our youth to be self-directed . . . they are not geared to decision-making but to accepting the authority of their fahters." A director of a Puerto Rican agency said, "Adolescents are not an easy group to engage in therapeutic efforts to modify their behavior, and they are even less willing to do so as a group." Finally, an Indian agency director said, "Groups don't work; it's better on a one-to-one basis."

For adults as well, work with groups was not satisfactory; privacy and shame often stood in the way of communication. One Chinese respondent said, "We have to develop almost individual treatment plans for each family to account for their degree of traditionalism, their degree of acculturation, and the severity of the emotional disturbance." This finding on resistance to group treatment cannot be generalized to ethnic settings under all circumstances. The skills and knowledge of the therapists and the agency investment in such a program must also be considered. These were primarily innovative settings with young workers, many of whom did not have formal training as therapists. With more experience and better trained staff the situation might change. But the negativism manifested in the field visits was widespread and strongly expressed, and it cut across all groups and settings.

Problems in securing community acceptance for group homes are not unique to ethnic agencies but are experienced wherever clients with special problems move into neighborhoods. But when the proposed client group is composed of minority children, the resistance may be even stiffer. A Puerto Rican director said his agency had tried to establish a group home in a community composed primarily of older citizens and intact families and had been told that teenagers were not wanted in the neighborhood, especially "those types of teenagers."

There were a few examples of interethnic problems discussed by agency directors, and some agencies reported trying programs with other groups that "didn't work." One example was given by a Japanese youth leader in San Francisco who was struggling with conflicts between Black and Japanese teenage street groups. Their neighborhood "turfs" were contiguous, and there were constant arguments about territory. But on the whole, little interethnic conflict was reported. On the other hand, there were almost no reports of interethnic cooperation among agencies— each group defined its needs in relation to its own members. Although ethnic workers were aware of the issues and struggles of other groups, they tended to move in parallel rather than merging paths.

Intraethnic conflicts were mentioned more frequently than

problems between groups. These related primarily to generational differences, differences in degree of acculturation, intermarriage, and timing of migration. The field interviews were completed in a year of substantial immigration of Chinese from Hong Kong, and these new arrivals caused disruptions and changes in existing patterns of life in the Chinatowns of both New York and San Francisco and created new needs for new services. A long-established settlement house in San Francisco with a record of successful work with generations of Chinese adolescents, for example, reported, "Our outreach effort for immigrant adolescents was a failure because of the reputation the agency has for serving the American-born. There is a lot of animosity between the American-born and the Chinese-born youths in Chinatown." Another example of intraethnic strain was expressed by some Indian respondents, who referred to present and potential differences between full-bloods and Indians who were the products of intermarriage. The latter were more likely to be identified with official policy of the Bureau of Indian Affairs and they appeared to have more options in making lives for themselves both off or on the reservation.

Although, as has been noted, myths were utilized by some ethnic agencies and could be reformulated to meet current needs, there also were situations in which rigid traditionalism was the reason some programs "didn't work." In a day-care center for Chinese children, for example, the director reported that free choice of activities "didn't work" for children who were culturally accustomed to structure; adjustments had to be made so that teachers helped children to decide on activities. In another Asian center the director wanted to introduce sex education to the children, but the parents objected and nothing was done. Some of the agencies reported resistance from parents to more modern concepts of child-rearing. Chicano parents expressed different ideas on discipline than teachers and often considered children's agencies to be "too permissive." The director of a Puerto Rican agency with a training program for mother providers reported that not one Puerto Rican mother in the program would allow children to fingerpaint in her apartment, saying that the activity was "too messy."

Agency directors complained that their best efforts often came to nothing when clients left the agency orbit and went to the larger community. In particular, ethnic agencies saw the public schools as not meeting special needs, and as settings where the positive effects of bicultural–bilingual programs were lost. One reaction to problems in program effectiveness was expressed by an Indian social worker on a reservation who said, "Probably the biggest problem was wanting so much, and trying to do too much."

Operational Definition of the Ethnic Agency

To give the concept of ethnic agency general validity, it is necessary to go beyond the descriptive and anecdotal material and move to quantitative analysis of the interview data. If a way can be found to measure the ethnic commitment of an agency, the measurement instrument can be applied in a variety of settings and thus can contribute to the comparative study of ethnicity and service delivery.

The agency interview was lengthy and included both closed and open-ended questions. It explored a series of issues in the following areas: agency programs, client characteristics, service delivery, administration and staffing, ideology and policy, and parental and community supports and involvement. From the extensive data collected and analyzed, thirty relevant items, drawn from all topical areas, were selected. Each item referred specifically to some question of ethnicity. Responses to these items were tabulated, scored, and factor-analyzed to see if there were identifiable components.* Three sets of items emerged from this procedure with high factor loadings related to their core dimension. Examination of the content of these items led to naming the three factors as follows: "Culture," "Consciousness," and "Matching." (See Table 2, Appendix A).

The next statistical procedure was to test each of the three sets of factors for validity and reliability. This was done by means of item-criterion correlations, in which each item was tested against the composite index of which it was a part, excluding the item to avoid autocorrelations. Upon inspection of results five items were dropped and new sets of item-criterion correlations were run for

---

*Factor analysis is a statistical procedure in which the relationships among a set of variables are studied by means of intercorrelations in order to identify a smaller number of "factors" that best account for the interrelationships. The procedure followed a principal-components analysis followed by rotation according to the Varimax Criterion.

each of the three indexes. Individual items correlated at sufficient levels with their respective indexes, and the Cronbach Alpha measure showed sufficient strength to indicate reliability.* (See Table 3, Appendix A.) Since each of the three factors represented a separate measure of commitment, for purposes of analysis it was decided to retain the three indexes rather than combine them in a single measure. Thus the operational definition of the ethnic agency is an agency that scores relatively high on all three parts of the agency ethnic commitment instrument, "Culture," "Consciousness," and "Matching."

AGENCY INSTRUMENT

The twenty-five items on the three-part ethnic agency instrument are shown below, together with a scoring plan. The scoring shown was used for the fifty-four agencies in the study but could be altered or adjusted within items, as long as each item is equally weighted in relation to all others. When the scoring indicates "mentioned" or "not mentioned" this means that the ethnic position was or was not spontaneously stated by the respondent, rather than being an answer to a direct question. In the field study the twenty-five items listed were embedded in a much longer interview schedule, applied in a two- to three-hour session with agency directors. To secure a full picture of agency operations, open-ended questions as well as the commitment scale should be used.

The three parts of the instrument reflect the three factors that emerged from statistical analysis of the interview data. Part I, "Culture," has as its core the use of ethnic materials such as foods, art, music, holidays, history, and one item of a different order but with a strong statistical association, the ethnicity of the director. Part II, "Consciousness," refers to the ideological position of the agency. Items ask about support of ethnic institutions, leadership on ethnic issues, pride in ethnic culture, the development of separate ethnic institutions, and the level of ideological commitment based on the continuum from "equal rights" to "cultural pluralism" to "ethnic identity." Finally, Part III, "Matching," in-

*The procedures used are described in C. Bohrnstedt, "A Quick Method for Determining the Reliability and Validity of Multiple-Item Scales," *American Sociological Review* 34 (1969): 542–48.

cludes items on the percentage of ethnic clients, the ethnic composition of staff, the preference on staff composition, and agency policies on recruiting and matching of staff and client.

COMMITMENT ITEMS AND SCORING PLAN

PART I—CULTURE

1. Is the agency director of the same ethnic group as the majority of clients served?
   (3 = yes   0 = no)
2. Have you made efforts to develop cultural content in your program?
   (3 = yes, successfully   1.5 = some, not enough   0 = none)
3. Do ethnic staff participate in programming?
   (3 = yes, the majority   1.5 = some   0 = none)
4. Do you use ethnic foods?
   (3 = regularly   1.5 = sometimes   0 = never)
5. Do you use ethnic art or decorations?
   (3 = yes, mainly   1.5 = sometimes   0 = no)
6. Do you use ethnic music or folklore?
   (3 = yes, regularly   1.5 = sometimes   0 = no)
7. Do you teach ethnic history?
   (3 = yes, regularly   1.5 = on occasion   0 = never)
8. Do you celebrate ethnic holidays?
   (3 = yes   0 = no)

PART II—CONSCIOUSNESS

9. Does your agency support ethnic institutions?
   (3 = mentioned   0 = not mentioned)
10. Do you give leadership on ethnic issues?
    (3 = mentioned   0 = not mentioned)
11. Do you get support from the ethnic power structure?
    (3 = substantial   1.5 = some   0 = none)
12. Do you get support from the ethnic community?
    (3 = substantial   1.5 = some   0 = none)
13. Do you train to develop ethnic consciousness?
    (3 = mentioned   0 = not mentioned)

14. Do you seek to develop pride in ethnic cultural institutions?
    (3 = mentioned   0 = not mentioned)
15. Do you support ethnic identity as a larger issue?
    (3 = mentioned   0 = not mentioned)
16. Where do you see your agency's ideological stand on the ethnic commitment scale from "equal rights" to "cultural pluralism" to "ethnic identity"?
    (3 = ethnic identity   1.5 = cultural pluralism   0 = equal rights)
17. Do you support the establishment of separate ethnic agencies?
    (3 = yes   2 = yes, conditional   1 = no, conditional   0 = not at all)
18. Do you have minority representation on your board proportional to your clients?
    (3 = all minority   2 = mixed proportional   1 = mixed, not proportional   0 = none)
19. Do you feel you have been successful in your use of ethnic content?
    (3 = mentioned   0 = not mentioned)

PART III—MATCHING

20. What percent of your clients are ethnic minorities?
    (3 = over 95%   2 = 80–94%   1 = 50–79%   0 = under 50%)
21. Would you prefer to have minority staff?
    (3 = all minority   1.5 = mixed   0 = no preference)
22. Do you have agency policy on matching staff and clients on ethnic grounds?
    (3 = policy to match   1.5 = respond to requests   0 = no policy)
23. Do you have a policy on recruiting ethnic staff?
    (3 = policy to hire minority   1.5 = prefer but no policy   0 = no preference)
24. Have you had success in use of matched staff?
    (3 = mentioned   0 = not mentioned)

25. What is the ethnic composition of your staff?
    (3 = all same ethnic group   2 =
    majority same group   1 = mixed staff,
    not majority   0 = no minority staff)

If the scoring plan is followed, the potential range of mean scores on each part is from 0 to 3. For the fifty-four agencies visited mean scores were as follows: Culture, 1.76; Consciousness, 1.14; Matching, 1.43. Thus the sample agencies score higher on ethnic commitment on cultural items, lower on matching, and lowest on consciousness or promotion of ethnic identity.

An analysis of variance was undertaken to see if there were any significant differences among different groups in terms of commitment scores. (See Table 4, Appendix A.) No such differences were found on Parts II or III, but there were highly significant differences on Part I, "Culture." Ethnic agency scores were significantly higher on the "Culture" part for the three groups whose first language was not English—Asians, Chicanos, and Puerto Ricans. This is of particular interest since there were no specific questions on language among the "Culture" items. This finding can be interpreted as giving external validity to the instrument, since it can be hypothesized that groups whose native languages are other than English would be further from the mainstream in cultural matters and would see maintaining cultural differences, including language, as part of group survival.

To Sum Up: The Utility of the Ethnic Agency

The task of defining the ethnic agency could have been approached deductively. That is, the ethnic group would be described and then deductions would be made about what kind of institution would serve its needs, so that model of an ethnic agency would be created. In the research reported here, the inductive method was chosen. Actual operations of fifty-four selected agencies which were reputed to be doing innovative work related to ethnic needs were studied. From the field visits and extended interviews with directors, twenty-five items relevant to ethnic commitment were abstracted and factor-analyzed. They were found to be distributed on three main dimensions, "Culture," "Consciousness," and "Matching." The instrument that was developed, based on these three indexes, was tested for reliability and validity. Thus the definition offered to describe the ethnic agency is empirically derived, and the instrument makes it possible to operationalize the concept.

An important limitation is that the data are based on a purposive and not a representative sample. The field visits included fifty-four agencies in five states, located in target areas with important representation of each of the five minority groups. They were delivering a variety of child-welfare services to approximately fourteen thousand children, and were under both public and voluntary auspices. Almost three-fourths served over 95 percent ethnic clients, and none served fewer than 50 percent. Given these limitations, the findings represent a beginning effort. The ethnic agency concept and related instrument on ethnic commitment need further testing and wide application in a variety of settings for appropriate validation.

The majority of agencies visited made special efforts to introduce ethnic cultural content. Culture, especially bilingual aspects, was stressed by the Puerto Rican agencies interviewed. Ethnic awareness on identity issues was more characteristic of Black agencies. Use of ethnic foods, music, art, history, and holidays were commonly reported. Most agencies tried to meet a wide spectrum of family needs and saw strengthening the family as a logical aspect of giving support to ethnic social institutions. Ideologically 20 percent of agency directors opted for the "equal rights" concept, and 40 percent each were for "cultural pluralism" and "ethnic identity."

Ethnic issues have been described in a series of anecdotal reports, organized around the main themes of myths and stereotypes, use of language, cultural content, positions on separate institutions, and on larger ethnic issues. Program efforts that "worked" and "didn't work" were also reported.

All groups suffer from negative stereotypes—some minority members were reported to accept the negative view held of them by the dominant culture, and agencies worked to dispel self-contempt and to build pride in ethnic institutions. Myths can interfere with change, but creative ethnic workers have taken traditional beliefs and made them work in behalf of their clients.

Cultural content was integrated in most aspects of programming for minority children, but sometimes traditional social work practice was in conflict with traditional ethnic ways and had to give way. Bilingualism was a subject of major interest to ethnic agencies, but the forms it took differed according to whether an old language was being revived, a new one learned, or the goal was to maintain both old and new.

There was some support for separate ethnic agencies, but not by the majority of directors. Several of them expressed concern that if their agencies were separate they would be removed from the mainstream of American life, and there were dangers of increased segregation. On the other hand other respondents saw separate agencies as the only way to establish ethnic power. For the sample as a whole, opinion was divided. Although not enthusiastic for separation, the majority of agency directors did express interest in "larger ethnic issues." However, this was defined in rather narrow terms, primarily as family and community.

Ethnic agencies in child welfare do not see themselves as "child savers." Instead the main emphasis is on supports for families to help them care for their own children. This is an area in which agencies say programs have "worked." Other successful efforts have been in bilingual–bicultural programs, career development for parents and leadership for youth, recruitment of minority foster and adoptive parents, and utilizing culture patterns to effect change. Unsuccessful efforts included use of groups for therapy with adolescents, placement of group homes in the community, combatting some kinds of traditionalism in cultural patterns, dealing with inter- and intra-ethnic differences, and lack of follow-up programs.

This chapter began with the question "What is an ethnic agency?" It was suggested that it is a special form of the ethnic organization, and a special form of the social agency. The data analyzed provide an operational basis for defining the ethnic agency in terms of the scores obtained on the three-part instrument that incorporates "Culture," "Consciousness," and "Matching." Such scores have more than theoretical interest and can be useful for the field in several ways. They make it possible to view agencies and differentiate among program, policy, and ideology, since the index has shown that agencies can score differently on these separate factors. Knowing the nature of ethnic commitment can aid decision-making on funding, referrals, and student training. These decisions would be made in reference to another set of goals—e.g., whether high, low, or average commitment was considered desirable for the particular purpose. But a tool is provided to assist in decision-making.

A broader question than the definition of the ethnic agency is its utility for social service delivery. In the original conception of this study, it was hypothesized that the bureaucratization of services that occurred as they moved from self-help groups to the public sector meant that the needs of ethnic minorities were not being met. The growth of the ethnic agencies has been seen primarily as a political response to movements for minority rights, but it can also be interpreted as a way of remedying serious deficits in traditional methods of service delivery. The state may act *in loco parentis,* but is it adequate to act in such a role with Black or Puerto Rican children, for example?

Many of the examples of "what worked" in the ethnic agencies refer to primary-group functions. The ethnic agency stresses family supports, encourages parents to accept responsibility for their own children and to maintain their own languages, provides career advancement for its clients, accommodates traditional myths to meet service needs, and recruits minority adoptive and foster parents. All of these activities can be interpreted in terms of extending primary-group goals to large numbers of people, thus supporting the hypothesis of Litwak and Dono.[2] Furthermore, the anecdotal material has numerous examples of meeting unexpected needs and multiple contingencies, characteristic of the primary-group function. This was certainly the case with the Chinese therapist who spoke of using some techniques from column A, some from B, and her own brand of sauce, and the Native American day care director who considered which of 12 tribes her three- and four-year olds came from before she disciplined them.

The findings from the field interviews extend our understanding of the utility of the ethnic agency beyond the interpretation that it is a political response to minority pressures. It suggests that the ethnic component serves to mediate between the primary-group and bureaucratic functions, thus facilitating the task of delivering services. Under this interpretation the ethnic agency becomes the efficient way to deliver services rather than the expedient way.

Notes

1. Lubomyr R. Wynar, *Encyclopedic Dictionary of Ethnic Organizations in the United States* (Littleton, Colorado: Libraries Unlimited, Inc., 1975).
2. Eugene Litwak and John Dono, "*Forms of Ethnic Relations, Organizational Theory and Social Policy in Modern Industrial Society*" (Unpublished paper, Columbia University, December 21, 1976).

4

Worker Attitudes:
A Dual Approach

The way services are delivered to clients depends to a great extent on the attributes and attitudes of the service deliverers—the on-line social workers. In spite of training and professionalization, it is expected that the attitudes of social workers will vary on ethnic issues. To test this, an extensive survey of worker attitudes on ethnic commitment was undertaken in both traditional and innovative settings. The findings show significant differences between workers in the two main samples on twenty-eight of the thirty questions asked. The differences in attitudes are related both to the ethnicity of the workers themselves and to their work settings. This points to a dual approach in practice on issues of ethnic significance.

In developing the attitude survey instrument, strength of ethnic commitment was measured along the three ideological dimensions that were used in the agency study. These were "equal rights," a "color-blind," or melting-pot, ideology; "cultural pluralism," implying recognition and acceptance of ethnic and cultural differences; and "ethnic identity," which advocates support for ethnic distinctiveness and tends to be separatist rather than integrationist.

Issues in service delivery that arose in the agency field visits as well as the literature search were incorporated in the attitude study. Questions were asked about "mixing or matching" of clients and staff along ethnic, cultural, or language categories; inclusion of cultural content in programming; and minority-group input in decision-making and policy formulation, including the power to control agency programs. Worker attitudes were explored on a range of services for families and children, including services in own homes, day care, foster care, institutional care, and adoption.

The study instrument was designed to offer the respondent a series of socially acceptable alternatives, each of which could be chosen by a professional concerned with children's needs. (See Appendix B.) The choices made by respondents reflected the importance they placed on recognizing ethnicity in service delivery, and their scores were considered to represent ethnic commitment.

There were five parts to the survey. The first was composed of ten forced-choice items, with one option representing a "traditional" approach to practice and the other a more "innovative" approach with an ethnic emphasis. The second part was also composed of ten items, each with three possible answers, related to the three levels of ethnic commitment already discussed. The ten items in the third part referred to specific issues affecting each of the five ethnic groups in the study, two items per group. Responses here were given on a four-point scale that measured the level of agreement with each item. In addition the instrument included the five-item Srole scale, which secured a measure of alienation or anomie. Finally there was a section incorporating demographic data on workers and characteristics of their employing agencies. The instrument was pretested, revised, and reviewed for appropriate reliability and validity.

Characteristics of Survey Samples

To see whether there would be the anticipated duality in attitudes of social workers, the instrument was applied to two groups. One was composed of members of the National Association of Social Workers; they were considered to be the "traditional" sample. The comparison group were workers in the fifty-four innovative agencies visited in the field survey. These two groups of respondents will hereafter be referred to as the "national sample" and the "ethnic agency" sample.

NATIONAL SAMPLE

The national sample was obtained through a mailing to the entire membership of the National Association of Social Workers who identified their field as primarily "child welfare." There were 2,733 such social workers in the continental United States, and 1,606 of them (approximately 60 percent) responded to the mailed survey. Certain limitations were encountered in testing the representativeness of the sample, since the NASW maintains confidentiality of its mailing list and detailed characteristics of nonrespondents were not available. It was possible, however, to determine that the returns showed an appropriate sex balance: The total mailing list included 35 percent males and 65 percent females, and the responses came from 33 percent males and 67 percent females. A further analysis was done by geographical region of respondent, as determined by postmark, with the results showing that the distribution of returns was almost identical with the distribution of the mailings for all six regions in the United States. (See Table 5, Appendix A.) Thus on the two criteria of sex and region, the national sample is representative of the entire NASW membership, which identifies itself as child welfare.

A few of the main characteristics of the national sample will be noted here; others are referred to in Table 6, Appendix A. The median age of respondents was forty-one years; 88 percent were white and 6 percent black; Protestants were 48 percent of respondents; 57 percent were married; half of them had children; 89 percent had M.S.W.'s or had done further academic work; and the median family income was $18,377. Over half the respondents worked in public agencies and the rest in sectarian or nonsectarian voluntary agencies. Just over half were in administrative and supervisory positions, and just under one-third identified themselves as caseworkers. They were a group with solid experience; the median time in practice was ten years, four months. About half had more experience in working with white children than with ethnic children, and one-third had equal experience.

About half of the national sample respondents worked in cities, but only one-third in the inner city, with the remainder in medium cities or less populous areas. There was a wide range of agency settings, with protective services being the modal group, employing 30 percent, and foster-care and childrens' institutions following. Over half the agencies where they worked served fewer minority than white children, and where the agencies did serve minority children, they included children of two or more ethnic groups.

ETHNIC AGENCY SAMPLE

The contrast group, called the ethnic agency sample, was derived from a different base. Workers in the fifty-four agencies visited in the field interviews agreed to respond to the attitude instrument, and 583 mailed responses were obtained. Since the agencies had been selected because of their special programs with ethnic groups, staff members who responded were actually a purposive sample of workers in innovative programs designed to meet ethnic needs. Ethnic diversity was achieved in this sample. Respondents were as follows: Asian Americans, 11 percent; Blacks, 26 percent; Mexican Americans, 11 percent; Indians, 12 percent; Puerto Ricans, 11 percent; and whites, 29 percent, including 2 percent who were non–Puerto Rican Hispanics. Thus 73 percent of the 583 respondents were from the ethnic groups included in the study, and in no case was there fewer than sixty workers from each ethnic group, thus enabling interethnic comparisons.

Selected demographic characteristics describing the ethnic agency sample are shown in Table 6, Appendix A, where they can be compared with the national sample respondents. Some of the key variables follow. Respondents from the ethnic agencies were younger by ten years than those in the national sample, with a median age of thirty years. More were female, 73 percent; 45 percent were Protestants and 32 percent Catholics, and their marital and parental statuses were like those of the national respondents. There were major differences in income, education, and experience between the two samples. The median annual family income of respondents in the ethnic agency sample was $10,545, only 17 percent had graduate social work degrees and only 17 percent were administrators or supervisors. The median years in practice were four years, nine months, and 81 percent had worked "only" or "more" with minority children. The agency sponsorship for these workers was like those in the national sample, but the type of program was different, with 34 percent in day-care settings. Two-thirds of these settings had only minority clients, and most of them served children of one minority only.

Comparison of Samples: Alienation Scores

The two samples showed obvious differences in such demographic characteristics as ethnicity, income, years in practice, and education. Another important difference was on their scores on the five-item scale measuring alienation. Workers in the ethnic agencies scored significantly higher than workers in the traditional agencies (p < .001) on the Srole scale for anomie. (See Table 7, Appendix A.) However, when workers in each setting were compared in terms of their own ethnicity, a continuum emerged. Highest alienation was ethnic workers in ethnic agencies; next, ethnic workers in traditional settings; next, white workers in ethnic agencies. Lowest scores on alienation were achieved by white workers in traditional settings. An analysis of variance showed ethnicity was more important than setting in explaining the level of the alienation scores.

The group data on the two samples were subject to statistical manipulation, so that analyses could be done that would hold constant some of the demographic variables and reveal the separate effects of such factors as age, credentials, income, and ethnicity. But in a way these analyses beg the question. It is clear that traditional child-welfare settings are directed by older, better-paid, primarily white professionals, and their attitudes do contrast with prevalent views in the innovative, minority-run programs, where ethnic personnel are younger, less experienced, with less formal education, and less well paid. The study goal was to contrast ideologies; thus, if the initial analysis held all demographic variables constant it would undercut the realities in the field. Those realities point to valid differences in ethnic attitudes between workers in traditional and innovative settings.

Analysis of Responses: The Two Samples

The responses to the attitude study provide baseline data on where workers stand on sensitive questions of ethnicity. By comparing responses from traditional settings with those from ethnic agencies, the significant differences in ethnic commitment are identified. Furthermore the relationships between such factors as worker training or ethnicity and ethnic attitudes can be measured. Such a measure could lead to prediction of ethnic commitment, based on knowledge of respondent characteristics.

ISSUES OF MIXING OR MATCHING

A major issue of ethnic interest is the conflict between "integrationist" and "separatist" positions. "Separatist," as used here, is distinguished from "segregationist." It implies that the decision to be with one's own group is made by the ethnic minority itself and it not imposed by the white majority. In relation to the delivery of social services, this issue has been labled "mixing or matching." This refers to whether policy at any level is directed toward mixing persons or toward matching persons of the same background. Items to test responses on this issue in a range of situations, with socially acceptable alternatives, were included in the study instrument. Four forced-choice items with percentage responses to each alternative from both samples are shown in Table 4–1.

Although in every instance a substantial majority of respondents opted for the "mixing" alternative, in the national sample from 9 to 21 percent opted for "matching" on these four items, and in the ethnic agency sample from 19 to 38 percent. The differences were statistically significant ($p < .001$) on all four items and were in the direction of matching in the ethnic sample. The question with the smallest difference in responses between samples was on children's experiences in relating to other children. The largest difference was on the item that posed the relative importance of credentials versus having a worker of the same group as the client.

In the second part of the study instrument there were five items on mixing and matching, with three choices for each (Table 4–2). On two issues, selection of the best therapeutic milieu for an adolescent and selection of the agency with the best reputation, the majority of social workers in both samples opted for an "equal rights" ideology, regardless of ethnic group. Differences did occur, however, in the percentage of each group at the other extreme of the continuum, those who chose a separatist position. The alternatives of "allowing boys to group themselves by race in a treatment center if they wished" and "selecting an agency run by

Table 4-1. **Responses on Mixing–Matching, Part I, by Sample**

ITEM[a]	PERCENT RESPONSES	
	National (N = 1606)	Ethnic Agency (N = 583)
The most important thing about a homemaker is		
a. that she love children	91	80
b. that she be of the same ethnic group	9	20
A social worker is more likely to be helpful		
a. if the worker has a degree	79	62
b. if the worker is of the same ethinic group	21	38
The child in an institutional residence		
a. does better by mixing with all kinds	88	81
b. feels more secure with his/her own group	12	19
With regard to adoption		
a. there is more sense of belonging in adoption, even if transracial, than in foster care or an institution	89	74
b. a minority child can rarely experience a sense of belonging with parents of another group.	11	26

[a] Items have been reworded for brevity, using key concepts. For original statements, see Appendix B.

your own group" were chosen by only 4 and 3 percent, respectively, of the national sample, but by 11 and 13 percent of the agency sample. This finding was reinforced in the responses on the key issue of transracial adoption. Only 5 percent of respondents from the national sample, but 18 percent from the ethnic agencies, said they would not approve the adoption of a black child by a white family.

The one low "matching" response from the ethnic sample was on the effectiveness of the minority worker. Here 69 percent of ethnic agency respondents chose the option that said "minority workers could work well with all groups, but had a special understanding of their own," and only 5 percent said the "minority workers could be most effective with children from their own groups." One interpretation is that the minority workers felt the first statement could lead to reverse discrimination in that if a "matching" policy were instituted their caseloads might be restricted to clients of their own group.

Table 4-2. **Responses on Mixing–Matching, Part II, by Sample**

ITEM[a]	PERCENT RESPONSE	
	National (N = 1606)	Ethnic Agency (N = 583)
Assignment in residential treatment		
a. choose best therapeutic milieu	61	61
b. recognize race, but not as main consideration	35	28
c. allow boys to group by race if they wish	4	11
Criteria for agency selection		
a. select agency with best reputation	65	57
b. select agency where members of your group have been served	32	30
c. select agency run by member of your own group	3	13
Effectiveness of minority worker		
a. work well with children from all groups	14	26
b. work well with all groups, but special understanding of own group	85	69
c. be most effective with children from own group	1	5
Transracial foster care		
a. take note of race-ethnicity, then place child with best-rated parents	35	43
b. give importance to ethnicity and race in placement, but not as determining factor	54	43
c. only place child with foster parents of same race or ethnic background	11	14
Transracial adoption		
a. approve the adoption	46	49
b. allow adoption only if no black homes are available	49	33
c. do not approve the adoption	5	18

[a] Items reworded. See Appendix B.

CULTURAL CONTENT

Ethnic differences are most obviously reflected in differences in cultural content, and it was anticipated that this area would be the least controversial and that cultural variety would be widely accepted. In general this was the case, but there were some unanticipated findings from ethnic respondents. Cultural questions were raised in all three parts of the instrument. Responses to

Table 4-3. **Responses to Cultural Content, Part I, by Sample**

	PERCENT RESPONSE	
ITEM[a]	National (N = 1606)	Ethnic Agency (N = 583)
Bilingualism for a young child		
a. is confusing	16	15
b. is an advantage	84	85
Lunch in a day-care center		
a. should be a balanced meal	40	52
b. should include foods served at home	60	48
Values of ethnic groups		
a. are basically all the same	29	35
b. different cultures have their own values	71	65

[a] Items reworded. See Appendix B.

items in Parts I and II are reported in Tables 4-3 and 4-4, respectively, and will be discussed together.

The broad acceptance of bilingualism as an advantage rather than a disadvantage represents movement from traditional attitudes, and there is no difference here between the two samples. Similarly, over half of the respondents in each group supported the need for program personnel with the linguistic backgrounds of children served. On the issue of ethnic food to be served in a day-care center, there was an unexpected finding. Just over half the workers in the ethnic agency sample (52 percent) chose a balanced meal over serving foods like those the child eats at home. This was the choice of only 40 percent of workers in the national sample. In this case, respondents in the national sample favored the presumed ethnic-oriented option more than workers from ethnic agencies. One explanation may be that the choice of foods "like those the child eats at home" may reflect an idealized concept of ethnicity; ethnic workers, who may know more intimately the poverty of the people, are more ready to choose the balanced meal option for their clients.

Items on cultural content in Part III of the study instrument were developed from references in the literature to major myths, stereotypes, or issues with special meaning for each of the five minorities. Responses to the four-point Gutman scale were grouped for purposes of analyses into those who agreed or who

Table 4-4.   **Responses to Cultural Content, Part II, by Sample**

ITEM[a]	PERCENT RESPONSE	
	National (N = 1606)	Ethnic Agency (N = 583)
In celebrating holidays in an institution with children of different backgrouds the staff should		
a. celebrate only traditional American holidays to avoid friction	1	7
b. have children from all groups celebrate all holidays	76	73
c. help each cultural group celebrate its own holidays	23	20
When a client expresses machismo as a cultural value, the worker should		
a. try to change the attitude	7	16
b. discuss cultural differences among people	74	63
c. accept it as a cultural attitude and not challenge it	19	21
A program serving children of different linguistic backgrounds should		
a. encourage all children to speak English	8	15
b. allow children to speak whatever they wish	41	32
b. be sure there is some time when children can speak their own language	51	53

[a] Items reworded. See Appendix B.

disagreed, whether "strongly" or "slightly," as reported in Table 4–5.

For Asian Americans, respondents in both samples rejected the myth of their being a model minority. On a major controversial issue, that of busing Asian children to schools out of their neighborhoods, opinion was almost evenly divided in both samples. This was an item with special significance for Asians, whose position was very different from that taken by Blacks. Thus there was no clear-cut "ethnic" position on busing because of interethnic differences.

The two items relevant to Puerto Rican needs had to do with making Spanish compulsory in social worker education and with preferences for placement of Puerto Rican children. On the first, there was substantial difference of opinion, with only 23 percent of the respondents in the national sample as against 57 percent in the ethnic agency sample supporting required Spanish courses. On the placement issue, there was an unanticipated response. Staying with relatives with problems in preference to foster care for Puerto Rican children was chosen by 73 percent of the national sample respondents as against only 62 percent of the ethnic agency sample.

Another unanticipated finding was with regard to the Indian child. The majority of respondents in both samples did not feel that life on the reservation meant cultural isolation, but agreement was stronger in responses from the national than the ethnic agency sample (70 percent versus 64 percent). And the statement that the Indian child must learn to compete even if this conflicted with traditional tribal values was endorsed by a higher percentage of respondents from the ethnic agency sample (71 percent) than the national sample (66 percent). As with the question on a bal-

Table 4-5. **Responses on Cultural Content, Part III, by Sample**

	PERCENT AGREEMENT	
ITEM[a]	*National* *(N = 1606)*	*Ethnic Agency* *(N = 583)*
Asian Americans have fewer problems	10	18
A Puerto Rican child is better off in a good foster home than with relatives	27	48
Isolation on the reservation does not mean cultural deprivation for an Indian child	70	64
Belief that there is no illegitimacy stigma in the Black community has rationalized lack of services	62	51
Permissive day care can undermine discipline of the Mexican child	53	51
Busing Asian children could do more harm than good	50	47
The Indian child must learn to compete	66	71
The Mexican American child can adjust in a center where English is spoken	75	73
Spanish should be compulsory in schools of social work	23	57
Good practice is important; there is no such thing as Black practice	89	79

[a] Items reworded. See Appendix B.

anced lunch, the national response on these four items may reflect an idealized stereotype, whereas the ethnic response may be based on a stronger sense of reality and service needs.

There was close correspondence between both samples in responses to the items related to Mexican Americans. About three-fourths in each sample felt the Mexican American child can be helped to adjust to Anglo society in a day-care center where he experiences a cultural pattern other than his own. About half of the respondents in each group felt that a permissive day-care center could undermine traditional home discipline for these children. A higher percentage of respondents in the national sample than in the ethnic agency sample (62 percent versus 51 percent) agreed with the ethnically oriented statement that the stereotype that there is no illegitimacy stigma in the Black community has rationalized the lack of services for Black unwed mothers.

ISSUES OF DECISION-MAKING AND ETHNIC POWER

The third content area in the attitude study was the role minorities should play in making decisions on policy and service delivery. Part I of the questionnaire had three such items, and the responses from workers in both samples are shown in Table 4–6.

Opinion was divided in both samples on the importance of having most of the board of the same group as clients, with a majority in each sample supporting ethnic board membership as being crucial to serving client interests. With regard to accountability and pressures, there were more differences of opinions. Forty-five percent of respondents from the ethnic agencies but only 31 percent from the national sample emphasized the role of community representatives in securing services for their own group. Furthermore, 27 percent of ethnic agency respondents but only 13 percent from the national sample said there was no difference between the interests of minority clients and those of the community to which they belong.

Two further items in Part II of the questionnaire related to policy issues. One asked about the desirability of separate ethnic programs, and the other questioned who should make policy decisions in day care. Workers' responses to these items are shown in Table 4–7.

On these two issues, significant differences emerged between respondents. Only small numbers in each sample were for dis-

Table 4-6.   **Responses to Issues of Decision-making and Power, Part I, by Sample**

ITEM[a]	National (N = 1606)	Ethnic Agency (N = 583)
	PERCENT RESPONSE	
Composition of board versus staff		
a. Unless majority of agency board is of same group/race as clients, cannot be sure clients' interests will be well served	54	59
b. If majority of staff is ethnically the same, composition of board doesn't matter	46	41
Public agencies		
a. Public agencies are accountable first to families they serve, secondly to public at large	69	55
b. Representatives of community and of minority groups should see that their own group gets services from public agencies	31	45
Ethnic issues		
a. Sometimes ethnic issues in social work are raised that serve the interests of the total minority community, but not necessarily of the clients being served	87	73
b. There is no difference between the interests of minority clients and their community	13	27

[a] Items reworded. See Appendix B.

couraging separate ethnic programs. The difference that emerged was with regard to the use of public funds. Both encouragement of separate programs and the use of public funds for such programs were approved by 51 percent of national sample respondents and 65 percent from ethnic agencies. Although the latter response is significantly higher, both figures testify to broad acceptance by social work respondents for publically supported separate institutions if based on minority choice.

RESPONSES BY ETHNICITY WITHIN SAMPLES

In addition to the significant differences in attitudes on ethnic commitment between workers in the two samples, there were also

Table 4-7.   **Responses to Issues of Decision-making and Power, Part II,
by Sample**

	PERCENT RESPONSE	
ITEM[a]	National (N = 1606)	Ethnic Agency (N = 583)
Separate programs		
Members of minority groups who wish to run separate programs for their own children should		
a. be discouraged	19	16
b. be allowed, but not given public funds	30	19
c. be encouraged and given public funds	51	65
Decision in day care		
Decisions in day care should be made primarily by		
a. teachers and social workers only	25	17
b. parents, with input from teachers and social workers	32	30
c. representatives of the community with input from teachers, social workers, and parents	43	53

[a] Items reworded. See Appendix B.

differences within each sample on a number of items, depending on ethnicity of workers and credentials, or level of professional training.* In the national sample, responses of ethnic and white workers differed significantly on the issue of transracial adoption. Only 10 percent of white workers but 20 percent of ethnic workers said a minority child can rarely experience "belonging" with parents of another race. Another important difference was on bilingualism, with only 9 percent of ethnic workers in the national sample believing bilingualism to be confusing for a child, as compared with 17 percent of white workers.

Some of the items on decision-making and power also drew significantly different responses from ethnic and white workers in the national sample. Twenty-five percent of ethnic workers said there was "no difference between the interests of minority clients and the community to which they belong," a response given by

*Credential is defined as an M.S.W. degree. A separate analysis was also done using the B.A. or B.S. degree as a base for defining credentials.

only 12 percent of white workers. A higher percent of ethnic than white workers, 53 percent versus 43 percent, opted for community involvement in day-care decisions. With regard to separate programs for minority children, however, setting superseded ethnicity as a decisive factor. Ethnic workers in traditional agencies were significantly less supportive of separate programs than were ethnic workers in ethnic agencies.

Although the majority of workers in the ethnic agency sample were from the five ethnic groups included in the study, there were enough white workers to allow for comparisons between ethnic and nonethnic respondents. Transracial adoption was again a key issue, with 31 percent of ethnic workers from the ethnic agencies, as compared with only 15 percent of whites from the same settings, feeling the minority child could rarely experience "belonging" with parents of another race. Furthermore, 22 percent of ethnic workers in ethnic agencies, but only 8 percent of white workers, would not approve adoption of a black child by a white couple as not being in the best interests of the child.

Overall there were more differences between ethnic and white workers in ethnic agency responses than in the national sample, with significant differences on four of the five mixing–matching items. Several of the differences were at the extremes of the choices offered. For example, from the ethnic agencies 16 percent of ethnic workers but only 4 percent of white workers would give highest priority in choice of an agency to one run by members of their own group. Support for the existence of an ethnic practice was expressed by 24 percent of ethnic workers in ethnic agencies but only 13 percent of white workers in the same settings. On decision-making issues such as the involvement of community in securing services for minorities, the identity needs of minority clients and their own groups, and public support for separate programs, ethnic workers in ethnic agencies were more apt to support the ethnic option than were the white workers.

Responses by Worker Credentials

In addition to contrasts according to ethnicity of worker, there were numerous items where significant attitudinal differences were found between trained social workers and those without credentials. In the initial analysis the M.S.W. degree was used as the "credentials" criterion. In the national sample, noncredentialed workers were more likely than M.S.W.'s to feel that being of the same group as the client was more important than having a graduate degree. They did not follow the ethnic position on transracial adoption, however; 60 percent of the noncredentialed workers but only 44 percent of credentialed workers approved adoption of a Black child by a white couple, without question. Credentialed workers supported this position only if no Black homes were available.

Of all the items dealing with cultural content, only one, the issue of Spanish in schools of social work, brought significant differences in responses from credentialed and noncredentialed workers in the national sample. Support for compulsory language teaching was higher among noncredentialed respondents. On items related to decision-making and power there were no significant differences related to credentials in the national sample. Thus, mixing–matching was the only area where credentials really made a difference.*

In the ethnic agency sample, credentialed respondents felt more strongly than noncredentialed ones that minority workers had a special understanding of children from their own groups (84 percent versus 65 percent). Credentialed workers also took a more ethnically oriented stance on the issue of transracial foster care. Placement with the "best-rated" parents regardless of race was the choice of 47 percent of noncredentialed but only 29 percent of credentialed workers. In addition, a higher percentage of noncredentialed workers than of credentialed workers (52 percent versus 40 percent) expressed approval of transracial adoption. Credentialed workers expressed stronger belief in an "ethnic practice." On almost all issues of power and decision-making, such as the role of community in securing services for their own groups, and support for the development of separate ethnic programs, workers with credentials were more strongly committed to an ethnic position than their noncredentialed colleagues. Thus 74 percent of credentialed workers in the ethnic agencies, as compared with 62 percent without the M.S.W., felt that separate ethnic programs should be encouraged and funded.

This analysis has shown that credentials, defined as the mas-

---

*Reanalysis with B.A. or B.S. as the credentials criterion produced only two item changes in the national sample, moving from the .05 to .01 level of significance.

ter's degree in social work, are more significant in differentiating among worker attitudes in the ethnic agencies than in the national sample. With the exception of one item, the credentialed workers in the ethnic agencies support a position of stronger ethnic commitment than their noncredentialed colleagues.

Because of the large number of non-M.S.W.'s in the ethnic agencies the responses were reanalyzed using the B.A. or other college degree as the credentials criterion. When this was done in the national sample there were very few differences. Among workers in ethnic agencies, however, a number of changes emerged. The impact was to strengthen the finding that credentialing was associated with higher ethnic commitment for ethnic workers.

This analysis of credentials and ethnic commitment in the ethnic agency speaks to the issue of training and the minority worker, since most of these respondents are themselves members of the ethnic groups in the study. The paraprofessional in the ethnic agency appears to have less ethnic commitment than does the credentialed ethnic worker, whether B.A. or M.S.W. These findings may reflect the fact that the items in the study instrument are based on the professional literature, as formulated by ethnic writers, and the credentialed worker may be more familiar with the "ethnically approved" answer. Furthermore, the trained ethnic worker has more options for employment than the paraprofessional. If he or she chooses to work in the innovative ethnic agency there is a strong element of self-selection and preexisting commitment. But nonetheless, in the setting studied, the data show the trained worker to be in the leadership on ethnic issues. This may be a reassuring finding for academic settings offering degree programs for minorities, which are hopeful that the students' ethnic commitment will not be "trained out" by professional education.

RESPONSES BY INTERETHNIC DIFFERENCES

The national sample of 1,606 included only 147 ethnic members, of whom two-thirds were Black, which was not sufficiently representative to test differences among ethnic groups. The ethnic agency sample, however, had a much broader diversity of workers of all five groups, none of which had fewer than 60 respondents. Since there was a proportionately greater number of Black social workers, the totals for each of the five ethnic groups were weighted to ensure that each contributed equally to the overall results. Analysis of data was then made by comparing responses of each ethnic group to responses of all other ethnic workers. Significant differences between each group and "all other ethnics" were noted, as well as the direction of the difference, which could be "more" or "less" in ethnic commitment.

Workers in the Puerto Rican agencies expressed relatively more ethnic commitment than respondents in all other groups on both the mixing–matching items and those dealing with cultural content. Agreement among groups in general was highest on mixing–matching issues, low on cultural issues, and lowest on decision–making and power items.

With respect to the relative importance of a social worker's race versus training, for example, Black respondents placed significantly greater importance on the worker's having a professional degree than did other minorities. On the issue of assigning adolescent boys to cottages in a residential treatment center, Black workers placed great emphasis on placing boys together in what one would consider the best therapeutic milieu. Finally, in selecting an agency Black workers were significantly more likely to look for an agency with the best reputation for high-quality services and least likely to look for an agency run by members of their own group.

Asian American workers placed greater emphasis on the ethnic background of the social worker and were more likely than other minority workers to select an agency because it was run by members of their own ethnic group. With respect to the effectiveness of the minority group social worker, Asian American workers were most likely to feel that the ethnic social worker could be most effective with children from his or her own group. However, they were less likely to disapprove of the transracial adoption of a Black child by a white couple than were other ethnic workers.

The level of ethnic commitment of Chicano workers was comparatively lower than that of the combined group of other ethnic workers on transracial adoption, on the criteria for placement of adolescents in residential treatment, and on effectiveness of the minority social worker. Only two of nine mixing–matching items elicited significantly different responses from Indians as compared to other ethnic workers. They were considerably less in favor of transracial adoption, but they took a more middle-of-the road position on the issue of racial and cultural matching as a criterion for cottage assignment in residential treatment.

Among the numerous differences among groups on cultural issues was the above average ethnic commitment to bilingualism on the part of Asian Americans, Chicanos, and Puerto Rican respondents, and less than average by Blacks and Indians. When the item related specifically to the use of Spanish, however, it was strongly supported by only Puerto Ricans and Chicanos; Asian Americans switched their position to less commitment than average.

On some items specific to one ethnic group, only that group expressed strong support. Asian Americans, for example, agreed to a significantly higher degree than others that the myth that they were a model minority hindered service delivery. Indians were significantly stronger in their belief that life on the reservation was not deprivation. Puerto Ricans were significantly more committed to the idea that children in day care should be supported in speaking their native language. Issues of power and decision-making brought forth strongest ethnic support from Asian Americans. The concept of separate programs was most strongly supported by Asian and Puerto Rican respondents.

The data on interethnic differences need to be interpreted with caution, since the respondents are not a representative sample, and their particular settings as well as the regions they come from undoubtedly affect attitudes as well as their group membership. For example, the Chicano workers were rural, not urban; the Puerto Ricans were urban, not rural. The findings, therefore, can not be generalized, but they do suggest certain hypotheses with regard to the central question of whether there is an "ethnic position" in service delivery, and they help challenge ethnic stereotypes.

Issues of mixing–matching and cultural content do emerge and receive significant ethnic support, but the extent of support varies with the particular relevance that the issue has for each group. Language is important for the three groups for whom English is not the mother tongue—but when the item specifies Spanish the ethnic commitment on language falls off for the Asian Americans, but stays strong for Chicanos and Puerto Ricans. On the overall instrument credentialed workers in ethnic agencies had higher total scores in favor of ethnic commitment. than did noncredentialed workers, but on the specific item of social work training Blacks diverge in the direction of less commitment than other minorities. The lack of extreme support by Blacks for race as against credentials for workers was unanticipated, but can be understood. Black workers in the sample hold far more credentials (e.g., professional degrees in social work) than do other minorities. Thus many of these respondents represent a group socialized into the profession.

On cultural items related to each group, commitment also tended to be specific. Thus, any generalized instrument on ethnicity for use with different groups should avoid specific examples and focus on broader principles. What may be an ethnic issue for one group in one setting—for example, bussing—may have different implications for another group in other settings, depending on historical factors, alliances, geographical locale, and political goals. The interethnic differences in no way obviate the need for a general policy recognizing ethnicity in service delivery. What they do show is the need for a flexible formulation that accommodates to the way in which each group defines its own issues. This would avoid the danger of replacing an old stereotype with a new stereotype.

WORKER ATTITUDES AND AGENCY SCORES

Since the worker attitude instrument and the ethnic agency interview, reported in Chapter 3, incorporated many of the same questions on ethnic commitment, it was possible to compare scores of agencies with scores of workers in those agencies on ethnic commitment. To sharpen the analysis, the ethnic agency sample was divided into two groups: the 375 workers whose ethnicity matched that of the agency where they worked, and the 208 workers in ethnic agencies who were either white or from ethnic groups other than the dominant one in the agency. In both the matched and the nonmatched groups each worker had two scores: a score on the worker attitude instrument, and an assigned score of the agency in which he or she worked. The agency score had three parts, with separate measures for culture, consciousness, and matching. Comparisons were then made of the average level of agency and worker scores for both groups. In all cases, both agency scores and worker scores showed higher ethnic commitment for the matched than the nonmatched group, as shown in Table 8, Appendix A.

Further analysis derived measures of correlation between the ethnic commitment scores of workers and their agencies, as well as intercorrelations among the three parts of the agency scores. These measures were calculated separately for the matched and nonmatched groups; e.g., the workers who worked in agencies of their own ethnic groups, and workers in ethnic agencies not of their own ethnicity. The correlation coefficients, shown in Table 9, Appendix A, also show increased correspondence in commitment in the matching situations. For matched agencies and workers, all correlations were highly significant ($p < .001$), including intercorrelations among all three parts of the agency index and with worker attitude scores. Corresondence for the nonmatched group, however, was not that high and not that comprehensive. The conclusion is that the more homogeneous the setting, including matching of worker and agency, the more correspondence will be found on ethnic commitment in all respects. Whether this results from self-selection of settings by workers or the influence of the setting on the worker cannot be answered by this study. But the findings do show that when the ethnic workers is in a matched ethnic agency, homogeneity and commitment appear to reinforce each other.

The Ethnic Commitment Scale

The attitudes of child-welfare workers toward ethnic issues in service delivery had not been systematically studied prior to the present survey, and no standardized instrument was available for use. The findings that have been reported describe responses to the thirty-item questionnarie developed for this research. The analysis then proceeded to determine the reliability of the new attitude instrument and the extent to which certain independent variables explained the variance found. It was also necessary to see how differences among respondents on demographic variables affected their scores.

Results from the initial survey show some of the problems of developing an attitude scale appropriate to different groups. There were significant differences in responses to twenty-eight of the thirty items from the ethnic agency and national samples. But there were also significant differences between respondents in each sample, e.g., traditional and innovative agency workers, on almost all of the demographic and other independent variables, such as income, age, education and ethnicity. For this reason it was decided to analyze data for the two samples separately, since they obviously represented very different populations. Three statistical operations were conducted: item-criterion correlations to test the validity and reliability of the attitude instrument; multiple regression analysis to see which variables contributed most to the variance; and study of the distribution of the scale scores to observe their direction and skew.* These tests were applied to two subsets from the larger instrument, a nine-item group and a five-item group. As a result the nine-item combination scored higher in reliability as measured by Cronbach Alpha scores, and there was little difference in validity, as measured by interitem intercorrelations. Based on these findings, the nine-item scale is recommended.

The items included in the Modified Attitude Scale on Ethnic Commitment are listed below. In terms of content, the major relevant dimension is that of mixing or matching.

MODIFIED ATTITUDE SCALE ON ETHNIC COMMITMENT
(one choice for each item)

1. a. If you need help from a social worker, you are more likely to get it if the worker is of the same race or ethnic group that you are.
   b. A trained worker with a social work degree is more likely to help you with problems than one without a degree.
2. In placing a child in foster care, after studying the child and evaluating the foster parents, the worker should
   a. give importance to ethnicity and race in placement, but not as the determining factor
   b. take note of race and ethnic background, then place the child with the best-rated parents
   c. only place the child with foster parents of the same race or ethnic background, even if it means extensive recruitment
3. If a white couple wants to adopt a Black child, you would explore motives and evaluate the home, and if both are acceptable

*Details of these statistical procedures are reported in Appendix C.

    a. approve the adoption
    b. allow the adoption only if no Black home is available
    c. not approve the adoption as not in the best interests of the child

4. If you are a mother seeking services for your child you would
    a. look for a good agency run by members of your own group, since then your needs would be met and you would be understood
    b. look for the agency with the best reputation for high quality services
    c. look for a good agency where members of your group have been served

	AGREE		*DISAGREE*	
	Strongly	*Slightly*	*Slightly*	*Strongly*

5. The important thing in a child-welfare agency is to have a good practice; there is no such thing as "white practice" or "Black practice." _____ _____ _____ _____

6. a. One good thing about institutions where there are children from different races and backgrounds is that a child can learn to make friends and get along with different kinds of people.
    b. If a child is in an institution where there are children from different races and backgrounds, he will feel more secure if he makes friends primarily with children who are like himself.

7. In assigning adolescent boys to cottages in a residential treatment center, you would
    a. allow the boys to group themselves together by race and ethnic background, if they wished
    b. place boys together in what you consider will be the best therapeutic milieu
    c. assign boys recognizing race and ethnic background, but not as the main consideration

8. a. Unless the majority of an agency board serving minority children is of the same race or group as those children, we cannot be sure the clients' interest will be well served.
    b. If the majority of an agency staff working with minority

children is of the same race or group as those children, then the ethnic composition of the board does not matter.

9. a. A minority child can rarely experience a real sense of belonging with parents of another race or ethnic group.
    b. A child gets more sense of belonging in adoption than in foster care or an institution, even with parents of another group.

MULTIPLE REGRESSION

In order to determine the relative importance of several demographic factors in explaining ethnic commitment of the workers, a multiple regression analysis was undertaken. The dependent variables in the regression procedure were the two subscales of the larger thirty-item attitude questionnaire, one with five items and the other with nine. The independent variables were nine demographic measures, which were entered in the equation as regressors. They were selected on the basis of data obtained and relevance for the study, and were entered in the following order:

1. Alienation score of worker (Srole scale)
2. Ethnicity of worker
3. Setting of worker's agency
4. Region of country in which worker resides
5. Credentials of worker
6. Professional status of worker in agency
7. Type of area in which worker resides (rural/urban)
8. Age of worker
9. Income of worker

The analysis showed that, after controlling for the effects of the other regressors, age appears to be the most important factor in determining degree of ethnic commitment as measured by both scales for workers in the national sample. There is a consistent negative relationship between age and ethnic commitment. For the nine-item scale alienation also emerged as a relatively important factor.

With respect to workers in the ethnic agency sample there were five regressors that emerged as relatively important in determining degree of ethnic commitment as measured by the nine-item scale. It appears that minority workers in a day-care setting would have higher predicted ethnic commitment scores relative to workers in other settings, followed by workers in mental health settings. This would be particularly the case for those ethnic workers residing in the southern states, and for those who are relatively more alienated. All nine regressors, however, explained only 18 percent of the variance in ethnic commitment scores as measured by the nine-item scale.

DISTRIBUTION OF SCALE SCORES

The difference between the ethnic agency and national samples in the variance explained in the multiple regression analysis led to a further examination of the distribution of scale scores for each sample. Figures 4-1 to 4-4 show that there was a range of responses on both scales, even though a pronounced skew was observed. Because of this, it was decided to proceed with a further regression analysis, using the square roots of the scale. This would help in normalizing the distribution, and then a further regression analysis could be completed using the scale scores as a base.

The results of the regression analysis using square roots of scale scores were very similar to the analysis of raw scores. Age was the most important variable for the national sample, and it was inversely related to ethnic commitment. For the ethnic agency sample, day-care and mental health settings, southern residence, and alienation scores were highly related to ethnic commitment. In addition, older age and higher income were associated with lower ethnic commitment.

A multiple regression analysis was done for a combined sample using the raw scores on the nine-item scale as the dependent variable. Sample affiliation was entered as a dummy variable in order to assess its relative importance in explaining ethnic commitment scores. There were three variables that emerged as significant with beta weights over .10. These were age, which had a negative beta weight, day-care setting, and sample affiliation. In effect the two variables that predominated for the separate sample regression (i.e., day-care setting for the ethnic agency sample and age for the national sample) emerged as the most significant in the combined sample regression analysis. In addition, the significance of sample affiliation shows important differences between the two samples with respect to attitudes on ethnic issues in

Figure 4-1.   Ethnic Agency Scores on Nine-Item Scale.

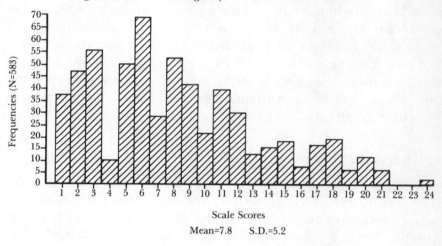

Mean=7.8   S.D.=5.2

Figure 4-2.   National Sample Scores on Nine-Item Scale.

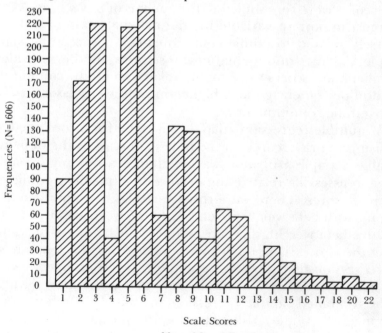

Mean=6.2   S.D.=4.1

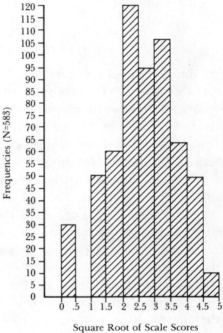

Figure 4-3. Square Roots of Ethnic Agency Scores on Nine-Item Scale.

Figure 4-4. Square Roots of National Sample Scores on Nine-Item Scale.

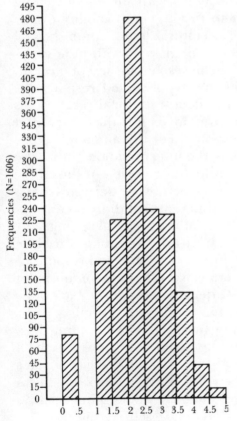

child welfare. This supports the initial hypothesis of the research, that there is a duality of social work attitudes on ethnicity as between traditional and innovative ethnic settings.

FINDINGS ON ATTITUDES

For the responses analyzed, the findings clearly show where different groups of child-welfare workers stand on a series of delivery questions. On ideological issues the field as a whole takes a position somewhere between "equal rights" and "cultural pluralism," with a recognizable but small response for "ethnic identity." Workers in ethnic agencies are further in the direction of ethnic commitment than are respondents from the national sample.

On contextual issues, items dealing with cultural content do not discriminate as strongly as do items with mixing–matching dimensions. This is due in part to the higher reliability of the mixing–matching questions. As for cultural items, some showed substantial acceptance by workers in all groups, with little variation. Bilingualism, for example, achieves broad acceptance. In other cases there is a reversal of the hypothesized response. A balanced meal at lunch, assumed to be a traditional response, is chosen by ethnic agency workers over foods like those served at home, assumed to be an ethnic response. For this and a few other items, such as learning to compete, the interpretation is that the hypothesized direction assumed a romanticized view of the ethnic position. Since the items for the instrument were derived from a review of the ethnic literature, it is apparent that there is continuing need to test out ideological material in empirical settings.

In a series of analyses where various demographic variables were held constant, there are significant differences in responses. One finding is that the highest overall level of ethnic commitment is from ethnic workers with M.S.W. degrees who worked in ethnic agencies. They outscore their ethnic counterparts among paraprofessionals significantly, indicating that social work training does not negate commitment. It should be noted that there may be a self-selection process at work—the trained ethnic social worker usually has job options, and when the choice is to work in an innovative ethnic agency it can be assumed that the commitment is already there. Nonetheless, such workers do achieve higher commitment scores than their nonprofessional colleagues. It may be that the trained ethnic workers have a clearer conceptualization of the problems and a sharper definition of the issues.

When interethnic differences are analyzed, they show that although there is a similar underlying structure of responses, issues are often perceived in different ways depending on how specific they are to the experiences of each group. Blacks, for example, with their significantly higher numbers of credentialed workers, are relatively less committed to choosing ethnicity as against training than are other groups; Chicanos, Puerto Ricans, and Asian Americans are all heavily committed to bilingualism, but when Spanish is specifically referred to, the Asian American group defects. The interpretation is that there is an across-the-board ethnic commitment on the part of the ethnic agency respondents, significantly different from the national sample, but that interethnic differences do exist, related to specific issues experienced by the group in question. The responses reflect situations, needs, and historical referents of each group.

Item-criterion correlations are presented to evaluate validity and reliability. Responses of the ethnic agency sample produce positive although low levels of validity, satisfactory for this type of diverse content. The national sample is more heterogeneous and fewer items show appropriate validity. However, there are sufficient numbers of items that appear in both trials to allow for the development of two modified subscales. One of these incorporates nine items, and the other is further reduced to five items. Statistical analysis including multiple regression was done on both. The overall finding is that the reduced scales of both five and nine items have sufficient validity, but that the nine-item scale has substantially higher reliability, and it is therefore the preferred measure. The items it includes stress mixing–matching issues, with only one cultural issue relative to ethnic practice and no items on power or decision-making.

Findings from the regression analysis show a higher percentage of the total variance accounted for in the ethnic agency than in the national sample. Among the regressors with significant beta weights in the ethnic agency sample are alienation scores, age, ethnicity, and day-care and mental health settings. For the national sample, alienation and age are the only significant predictors of commitment. In all cases age is inversely related to ethnic commitment scores.

Further inspection of scale score distributions shows a skewed distribution, leading to utilization of the scale score square roots to improve the potential for analysis. A final multiple regression based on the scale score square roots shows additional relevant regressors for the ethnic agency sample. For the ethnic agency sample high commitment is related to youth, ethnicity, and working in a day-care or mental health setting. In the national sample the youth of the respondent and, secondarily, the alienation are the best predictors of high ethnic commitment.

As an overview, the survey shows that cultural issues are not particularly controversial, and there is broad acceptance in the child welfare field, at the attitudinal level at least, of an approach close to cultural pluralism. On power and decision-making issues, there is a small but defined ethnic identity position. The real arena where attitudes can be identified and measured is that of mixing and matching, and a nine-item Ethnic Commitment Scale, with appropriate reliability, is recommended. Scores will not be fixed but will shift over time on the basis of social climate and social conflict.

5

Parents' Perceptions of Ethnic Issues

Social workers and social planners may have very different perceptions of client needs and attitudes than the clients themselves, and the issue of ethnicity is no exception. For this reason, in addition to exploring attitudes of workers and positions of agencies, the research investigators went directly to clients who were the consumers of services to learn how they felt about ethnicity and its role in service delivery. This was done by means of group interviews with parents whose children were receiving services from programs in the agency study. Ten agencies were involved, in Texas, Arizona, North Carolina, Pennsylvania, and New York, two in each of the five ethnic categories. Interviews were conducted in English, Spanish, and two Chinese dialects, Mandarin and Cantonese. Each parent group was made up of from four to eight members. For all groups the interview was tape-recorded, translated if necessary, and transcribed so that interaction as well as responses could be analyzed.

The Nature of the Parent Interviews

The interview was in two main parts. It began with the general question, "In your experience with social services, have you been treated in a way that did not recognize or respect your background as a _____? [Interviewer inserts minority group—Asian American, Black, Chicano, Indian, Puerto Rican.] Please tell us about it."

The second part of the question guide was made up of the ten items social workers had been asked in the initial attitude study. These were mainly issues dealing with culture and with mixing or matching. Because the same questions were raised, parent responses can be compared to social worker responses to see if they agree or differ, and, if they differ, in what ways.

The group interview was selected as a procedure for data collection for several reasons. It could be conducted and completed in a shorter time and more inexpensively than individual parent interviews. Since the group interviewer was of the same ethnicity as the respondents, this neutralized the possibilities of interviewer bias or parent concealment because the leader was from another group. All interviews involved agencies that had participated in the earlier agency phase of the study. Thus the arrangements were facilitated because they were built on both agency and worker knowledge and commitment to the research.

Perhaps the major advantage of the group interview, as opposed to individual interviews, is in the group process generated among the members. They stimulate each other, both to agree and to disagree, and help in recall and recognition of relevant experiences. The careful study of transcripts also shows how the same incident can be interpreted differently by people; what one parent attributes to a conscious racial slur another may attribute to ignorance or stupidity or bureaucracy. These differences are useful in gaining perspective on parent perceptions and help to challenge the sterotype that there is a solid ethnic position on all matters.

There were fifty-four parents involved in the ten group interviews. They were invited to participate by agency workers. The main selection criteria were that they had children in agency programs, were concerned with the issue of services and articulate in responding to questions, and belonged to the ethnic group served. Members were mostly mothers. There were eight interviewers, all social workers. One was Black, one Puerto Rican, two Chicano, two Indian, and two Chinese.

In their initial responses parents expressed strong feelings about being poor, being clients, and being single parents if that was the case. They spoke against bureaucracy, the welfare and health system, indifferent workers, and routine. It was the system that seemed oppressive rather than the ethnic component. With added probing, issues of language surfaced, and then many examples of problems in being understood were given, especially by Hispanic and Asian respondents. Later in the interviews, in discussing specific areas of service, the parents began to identify ways in which ethnic needs were ignored. But the burden of parental complaints was against the social service system itself and the families' sense of powerlessness in dealing with it.

Client Complaints

Some of the clients' complaints were against members of their own ethnic groups who were in the bureaucratic or "caring" roles, such as foster parents, social workers, or hospital attendants. The resentment was against lack of sympathy, superior attitudes, and exploitation of children. A number of clients complained that children in foster care were getting poor food and limited activities, and that discipline was harsh.

Complaints against the health system generally cut across ethnic groups and were expressed against lack of services and lack of responsiveness in the system. Few clients argued for separate ethnic health services, since in the experience of several parents better care was delivered where services were integrated. One Puerto Rican mother, for example, expressing an opinion about a private health insurance plan, said, "Their centers are not designed for minorities, but if you look at it they are composed of minorities, and you just don't get the service you are paying for. It's next-next-next, that type of thing." In response, another member of the group said that it depends on the center. She changed from a center serving only Blacks and Puerto Ricans to another center in a different neighborhood. She said, "It's a mixed center and is patronized by Hispanics, Blacks, and whites and everyone. I don't know what the ratio is but there is a mixture of races and the service is very good." When asked how she explained this, she said, "I think that the whites as a whole put more pressure for a better quality service and Hispanics and Blacks don't."

Although the burden of being clients in an unresponsive service system seemed to be based on substantial experience, some of

the interview content raised another question: Were the clients'
expectations of the system appropriate? Were their demands
realistic? Four examples can be cited.

One client complaint was by a Black mother in Philadelphia
who had placed her daughter in foster care because the girl stayed
out late, was unmanageable, and was too difficult to keep at home.
The mother complained that the foster mother was too strict and
dealt out heavy punishment to the girl. A second client, an Indian
mother in Arizona, complained of lack of dental attention for her
three-year-old. When she took him to the dentist to have his teeth
cleaned the child fidgeted, jumped about, and wouldn't sit still.
The dentist gave her fluoride tablets and told her to come back
when the boy was four and he would do a professional cleaning.
In the third case a Puerto Rican mother in New York said she had
taken her child, who had 102-degree fever, to a hospital emergency room. She complained that the doctor examined the boy,
said he had measles, gave her medicine, and told her to take the
child home and care for him. Another Puerto Rican mother who
wanted to take some courses put her child in family day care. She
complained that when she came to pick up the youngster he was
watching a television program. She thought there should have
been educational play activities in the day-care home.

In these and some other cases the nature of the client complaints seemed to reveal unrealistic expectation of services.
Perhaps a youngster placed for difficult behavior needs strong
discipline; a three-year-old who can't sit still can wait until he is
four for a professional dental cleaning without harm to his teeth;
a child with measles is better cared for at home than in a hospital;
and a foster mother should have the same freedom to turn on the
TV set as a biological mother. When otherwise acceptable activities occur as part of a paid service delivery system they may be
perceived as punitive or inappropriate. These complaints are not
necessarily ethnically based but seem to arise from an under-
standable lack of clear boundaries between what is a professional
service and what is a parental responsibility.

DEFICITS RELATED TO ETHNICITY

There were three areas where parents reported deficits in services
that were specifically related to ethnicity. The first was what they
perceived as condescending or stereotypical behavior by workers,

the second was discrimination by agencies, and the third was based on community ignorance of cultural patterns.

Several Indian parents reported feeling that professionals spoke to them in condescending ways; as one mother put it, "Surface sweet but 'Ah, poor thing' underneath." An Indian mother said her child went to a Head Start program with Black children and the teachers were amazed at her son's behavior. He talked a lot and was very active, and the teachers said they were surprised because Indian children were supposed to be shy and quiet.

The feeling of being bullied or put down in services was also expressed by many of the parents. A Chinese mother said that when she goes for food stamps the *lo-fan** (non-Chinese) break in the line and get served first. An Indian father complained that the policy in the schools is not to be Indian but to be American— just American, not American Indian. An Indian mother objected bitterly to the family-planning services. She said, "They are so afraid another Indian is going to be born, they push you to birth control. They shouldn't pull their white attitudes on me."

Ignorance of their cultural patterns on the part of others was the most common complaint of Chinese parents, and sometimes the lack of understanding went both ways. One issue raised by several Chinese mothers was the way the doctors and nurses draw blood samples from their children. One mother said, "The Chinese do not like to draw blood from their body. But no matter how much we tell them that they still do it." Another mother complained that her son was anemic, but every time she takes him to the doctor he draws blood. "If my boy doesn't have enough blood," she asked, "why do they take some away?"

Several Chicano parents recalled that in their own youth efforts to teach Spanish children English were punitive and harsh. The typical procedure reported was to charge each child a penny for every Spanish word he spoke, even in grade school. Perhaps the greatest frustration relating to language was reported in relation to a parent-counseling program that served Chicano clients (some of whom spoke some English) and used Anglo counselors (some of whom spoke some Spanish). Because of scheduling difficulties, inevitably there would be an occasional match between a Chicano parent who spoke no English and an Anglo counselor who spoke no Spanish. And if they couldn't find anyone to inter-

*Lo-fan means "barbarians" or, more practically, "non-Chinese Westerners."

pret, it was reported that parent and counselor would just sit and look at each other for the assigned hour.

VARIATIONS IN FOOD HABITS

Food habits and tastes varied among the parents interviewed; some of the differences reported were cultural, some regional, and some were based on income. A Puerto Rican mother, for example, said, "When I just came here I thought for the longest time that steaks were paper thin. When I was a teenager I was taken out to dinner at a classy restaurant. I ordered a steak and expected a real paper-thin steak, with onions and garlic and sauce. They brought me this two-inch steak. I didn't know what to do with it. I didn't know how to cut it. I said, 'My God, it's a monster.'"

On occasion differences in food habits were used to "put down" children of different groups. One mother reported that when she was a child in sixth grade, the only Spanish girl in the class, she had a home economics assignment to make a menu for a week based on the food her mother prepared for the family. She made the menu out and failed the assignment. Her menu was rice and beans every night, and the teacher said, "This is junk food" and ridiculed her in front of the class. The parent respondent said, "I didn't know everyone doesn't eat rice and beans every night. I felt like a dumb fool, like someone from another planet."

Although food habits were matters of interest to all groups, most parents did not consider it important that ethnic foods be served in day-care centers or children's institutions. Parents were more concerned that their children have good nutrition and a balanced diet. In this respect, their position was closer to that taken by the social work respondents in the ethnic agency attitude survey. Fifty-two percent of that group, as compared with 40 percent of workers in the national sample, opted for a balanced meal against the alternative of food like that served at home.

Several parents from different groups felt it was important for children to be exposed to a variety of foods, so that when they got older they could make a better adjustment. A Chicano mother said, "We're not in Mexico now—they have to learn the other cultures too." A Chinese mother said, "They're in America—you can't get Chinese food everywhere." In response to a question about the desirability of having ethnic food on the day-care menu, another Chinese mother said, "Not if there is no Chinese cook. How can a non-Chinese cook Chinese food? When they do my son won't eat it; he says it tastes awful." Lack of cultural understanding was reported by Indian parents, who criticized the practice of serving frozen fish on Fridays to the children in the day-care center. "Our people like fresh fish," she said, "and they catch it themselves. The children won't eat stale old fish. If you want to know what children eat, look in the garbage cans."

ETHNIC PREFERENCES IN HELPERS

Parents were asked whether, if they had to choose, they would prefer to seek help from a person of their own ethnic group as against one with a social work degree. Only two or three parents among the fifty-four in all groups expressed preference for the trained social worker. The rest were divided between those who said it depended on the individual and those who preferred a member of their own group.

Equivocation in responses and alternative answers were more possible in the parent group interview that when the social work respondents answered the "forced choice" items in the attitude instrument. Some of the parental discussions showed considerable insight into what is expected of a helping person. One Chicano mother, for example, said, "I want the most qualified person, and qualification means not just a degree but feelings and being sensitive to the job." An Indian father said, "You don't want someone who is too 'in' because then they know your past too well and can't be objective."

A majority of the articulate parents opted for a helping person of their own group. Three main reasons were given related to language, prejudice, and cultural awareness. Language was particularly important for the Chinese parents, even more than for the Hispanic respondents, probably because more white workers were likely to know some Spanish than to know any Chinese. Black workers expressed particular concern about prejudice. One Black father said he preferred a Black worker because "You can never tell when a white will be prejudiced against you just because you are Black."

Cultural factors were considered to be important in delivering services in terms of both knowledge and empathy. A Black mother said, "I want a worker of the same group. Maybe he or she is going through what you are going through." An Indian father said, "Choose the one that understands your problems and lives with them. The one from outside has got a lot of book learning, but it would be hard for him to catch on to what you're trying to tell him."

A worker of the same group may have insight into problems because of special ethnic experiences. A Puerto Rican mother who was a paraprofessional said she saw a girl in the agency who she was told was "real sick"; she had been diagnosed as schizophrenic because she said she saw things and heard voices. The mother said, "The social worker told me to get in there and give her therapy. Now I knew this girl's mother was a medium, and she believed in spiritualism. Being Puerto Rican, this is part of my culture, and even if I don't believe it, it was real for this girl. So I took her to a medium, who said, 'You have this and that, and this is what you should do.' She stopped seeing things but the only way I was able to help this kid was because I was in the culture. If I was American I don't know if I would have understood it, but I was brought up as a Puerto Rican and this was part of the underground."

Although no comparisons can be made that can be quantified, the parent respondents in the group interviews appeared to place more stock in having a worker of their own group than did the social worker respondents to the attitude questionnaire in either the traditional or innovative settings. Only 21 percent of social workers in the national sample, and 38 percent in the ethnic agency sample, chose "own group" over training.

CARE AND ADJUSTMENT OF CHILDREN

The next interview question was, "If a homemaker came to the house to care for your children, would the most important thing be that she be of the same group or that she love children?" The fifty-four parental responses were almost unanimous—the homemaker should love children first. The only qualification was that, for older Spanish-speaking children, it is also important that she understand their language.

The tenor of expression was the same in all ten group interviews. An Indian mother said, "She should love children, I don't care if she is red, black, yellow, brown, or white." A Puerto Rican mother said, "Love children, whether white, black, Chinese,

Jewish, or Irish doesn't matter." A Chinese mother said, "I'd rather have a *lo-fan* who loves children than a Chinese who doesn't." Furthermore, there was at least one parent in each of the ten groups who spontaneously commented that there are people in all races and groups who do not like children—also in their own group. To illustrate her position a Puerto Rican mother said that the fact that even whites who were prejudiced in the Old South had Black women to take care of their babies showed that race had no bearing on taking care of children.

The social worker responses to this question were 91 percent for "love children" in the national sample and 80 percent in the ethnic agency sample. Thus ethnic parents placed relatively more stress on "love" as opposed to "own group" than did ethnic social workers.

There were three questions in the interview about the adjustment of children in different ethnic situations. The issues were whether the minority child will adjust better in later life if in a day-care center with children of other groups; whether children in institutions are better off with others of their same group; and whether children whose parents can't care for them are better off in foster care or with relatives who have problems of their own.

There were real differences of opinion among parents on the first of these three questions. On the one hand, a number of parents in all ethnic groups felt that the young child gets a stronger sense of identity and belonging with those of his own group. On the other hand, an almost equal number of parents felt that their children's later adjustment would be helped by broader exposure, and the issue of belonging could be dealt with at home in the family. All parents agreed that children needed to know who they were and to have a group identity; the disagreement was on whether the day-care center was the place to develop it or a beginning step for the child to the wider world.

Social workers were also divided on this issue, with about 75 percent of workers in both national and ethnic agency samples being more supportive of the idea that the minority child can adjust better later on if exposed to an integrated day-care center.

Parents were next asked whether children placed in institutions should be grouped together by ethnicity and/or race. A few responded that it would help children to establish their own identity to associate mainly with others like themselves. A Puerto Rican mother said, "I want mine with her own until she can walk in any place and say 'I am me.' The problem is that children are wonderful but adults mess them up." She was an exception, however; the majority of parents spoke about the benefits of intergroup contacts and wanted their children to mix freely with members of all groups. One Indian mother said, "My son was telling me about his friends, and I said, 'Are they Indian?' He said, 'I don't know, they're just my friends!' I was embarrassed to have asked."

Among the advantages cited for mixing were better attitudes, better educational opportunities, and a better chance for future adjustment. In each group there was at least one parent who said, "This is America. It isn't—Mexico, or China, or Africa, or Puerto Rico, or only the reservation." One Black mother said, "Children should mix. If you keep them only with their own they will have their own prejudice." A Chinese mother said, "I don't mind any race, as long as they behave." And a Puerto Rican mother said, "How else will they learn to get along?"

Although the questions were asked about children and their relationships, in several of the interview groups parents began to discuss their own feelings about mixing. There was a good deal of ambivalence. Some of the conflicts were expressed around the issue of whether it is better to be comfortable where you are or struggle to get where you want to go.

The response of one Black mother illustrates the problems faced in a transitional society. This woman said, "I feel more at ease around someone of my color. I have more in common with them. . . . My husband is a Puerto Rican and I've met his people. But I still have more in common with my own people because I'm Black." Not discussed was whether she felt things in common with her husband, who was not of her group, and, considering her own ambivalence, with what group her children identified.

Parental responses on this question were very close to social worker responses. Preference for children mixing with others was stated by 88 percent of workers in the national sample and 81 percent in the ethnic agency sample.

The last question on child adjustment was whether, if parents couldn't care for them, children would be better off placed in a foster home or with relatives with problems of their own. The purpose was to see how strongly parents felt about extended kin. Some of the responses challenged stereotypes and showed that even feelings about relatives can be "relative."

Most of the parents said it would make a difference what kind of problems the relatives had, and how good the foster home was. Disappointment with the performance of relatives was expressed by a number of mothers. A Chinese woman, for example, said, "Your relatives have to be 'close' because they are relatives. But sometimes they are not really close and sometimes they don't keep their promises." A Chicano mother said her relatives wanted to divide her children up when she was sick, and she said, "If you can't take all, don't take any. I would rather have all of them together in a good foster home."

Other parents said they would rather have children with relatives unless the problems were drugs or drinking. An Indian father said, "It's better to stay with your own: Even the dear Lord didn't mix deer with goats." One Puerto Rican mother said, "It depends on the problems. But it shouldn't depend on money. I would rather my kids be with my family and eat what they eat and listen to their fights—they are my people." Another Puerto Rican mother said, "With your own. Foster homes are a pisser."

Although there was division of opinion, on the whole more of the parents opted for the foster home than for relatives with problems. This can be compared with social worker attitudes and it reveals an interesting continuum. For the national sample, 73 percent of social workers chose relative placements. In the ethnic agency sample, this dropped to 52 percent. Although no comparable quantitative figure can be derived from the ten parent group interviews, the analysis shows that the majority of the parents favored foster care over relative care. It appears that the closer the respondent is to the actual situation, the more doubt is expressed on the suitability of relative placement. One explanation may be that the social work professional is responding to the children's needs, whereas the mothers may be responding to their own problems in relationships with extended family. On the other hand, the parent respondents may know some things about their relatives that the social workers don't know.

INTERGROUP RELATIONS

The last group of questions in the parent interviews were broader in nature, dealing mainly with intergroup relations and the structure of services. The issues related to values of groups, ethnic practices of agencies, funding for separate programs, and separate agencies.

Parents had a difficult time with the question on whether or not all people had pretty much the same values, or different groups had different values. The difficulty was that it was hard to differentiate "values" from "culture." They agreed that there were different manifestations of behavior but were unsure whether this meant that people really felt differently about basic matters. Some areas where they did identify differences were around issues of money, self-sufficiency, and respect for elders.

One of the Indian fathers interviewed, for example, said, "We are a proud people. I know some of us have taken the white man's side and come to welfare. But we still have a lot of people on the reservation who would rather starve to death than take welfare." And a Chinese mother expressed shock at a Jewish family in her building that pays the grandmother to baby-sit for their daughter. She said, "For us Chinese it would be unthinkable for a grandmother to ask for money to look after a grandchild." Another Chinese mother said, "We Chinese emphasize thrift and think of the future. *Lo-fans* think only of the present."

These observations refer only to a few individuals, and they are not backed up with empirical data. Many Indians do receive one or another form of welfare, and many *lo-fans* also are concerned about the future. But the parents in the interview perceived these to be examples that describe the values of their own groups, and that is why they are of interest.

Several parents said groups differed in the extent to which they stuck together for common goals or sought individual gain. One Black woman said, "Black jealousy is a problem. They are like a bunch of crabs in a basket. As soon as one pulls up, the others pull him right back down." One value area in which the Chinese claimed to be different from other groups was in their respect for older people.

On the other hand, about as many parents who commented on differences commented on similarities among groups. A Chicano mother, for example, said, "We may do things differently, but we all want the same things." A Black mother said, "Everyone wants to succeed, wants their children to have things better than they did."

In every interview at least one parent made the point that you can't generalize to all people in any ethnic group, and that there are differences among people, tribes, and locations. A Chicano mother summed it up when she said, "Cultures are different, but not necessarily values. We pierce our ears—some people in Africa pierce their noses."

When the social workers responded to this question, 29 percent in the national sample said values were about the same, and 71 percent said they differed by groups. The social workers in the ethnic agency sample were less sure of differences; 35 percent of them said values were about the same, 65 percent that they differed. Although no comparable quantitative figure is available from the group interviews, the qualitative analysis shows parents appear to be more evenly divided on this issue, about half and half.

STRUCTURE OF SERVICES

The next group of questions deals with organizational and structural issues in service delivery. Although the questions brought some reactions from parent respondents, they were not of as much interest to them as the direct service issues. The questions ask whether parents would prefer agencies run by members of their own group, whether they believe there is an "ethnic practice," whether they think government should fund agencies run by ethnic groups, and, finally, whether there should be separate agencies for separate groups. These issues are related, and there is a good deal of overlap in the parents' reactions. Some of the responses, however, are of interest because they identify areas where clients may take positions different from those taken by many professionals in the field.

Among the parents who said they would prefer going to agencies run by their own groups were a few who said they would feel more at home in such agencies. An Indian mother said that at the Indian center she never felt that she was just a number. And a Chicano mother said, "At least I wouldn't wonder if I was being discriminated against." A Puerto Rican mother gave a more political reason. She said, "We should support places run by our own. That's what other groups do."

The conviction that better service would be received if the agency was run by one's own group was not universally expressed. A number of parents cited experiences in which they had received good services in agencies run by other groups. One Puerto Rican mother said that it depended on what the needs were. "If I had a toothache," she said, "I'd go to any dentist to cure it." Asked whether language would make a difference, she said, "I could point to where it hurts."

In the social worker attitude survey three alternatives had been offered for choice: to go to an agency with the best reputation; to one where members of one's own group had been well served; or to one run by members of one's own group. The last alternative, "run by your own" was chosen by only 3 percent in the national sample and 13 percent in the ethnic agency sample. On the basis of the interview responses this choice would rate higher, but not much higher, among ethnic parent clients than among workers in ethnic agencies.

The question of whether or not an ethnic practice can be defined presented a difficult concept to professional social workers and was even less comprehensible to parents. Responses were hard to obtain without a prior definition of ethnic practice. The concept was finally said to be helping people according to the life experiences of their groups. Even this formulation was regarded as vague, but it assumed reality when there were concrete illustrations of such activity.

Chinese mothers, for example, noted that the Chinese way of child care is different from the Western way. Moral education is important in traditional teaching, and even when children are very small they are taught manners, filial piety, and respect for teachers. The mothers suggested that this is how a Chinese child-care worker could carry out a "Chinese practice."

The assertion that there is a valid ethnic practice for each group was agreed to by only 11 percent of workers in the national sample and 21 percent in the ethnic agency sample. It was not too well understood by parents, who had a difficult time in the interviews separating out what agencies offered from the methods of service delivery.

When it came to the final question on whether or not ethnic groups who wanted to do so should be allowed to run their own services and receive public funds, parents interviewed were almost all supportive of this proposal. A number of parents in all groups said they were not dumb, and that if other groups could run services, why not theirs? With regard to the use of public funds, several parents said, "Why not? Aren't we taxpayers too?"

Although parents strongly supported the right to have separate programs, they were very divided on whether they themselves would prefer separate services. A Chicano mother expressed the feelings of some parents of all groups when she said, "The best thing would be one place for everyone—with equal treatment. The reality, though, is that our kids don't get a fair shake where there is the Anglo concept." An Indian father said, "It depends on getting a fair shake. In Cherokee it's not bad, out West it's different." Some spoke of geographic realities. A Chicano parent said that her town of nineteen thousand was 94 percent Mexican American with about fifteen Black families. How realistic is it to suggest separate agencies in that setting?

A few parents said that separate agencies would give their children a chance to know their own groups first, before they moved out in wider society. Chinese parents in particular referred to the need for young Chinese children to be in a setting where they are understood. But even Aisian parents said that sooner or later their children would have to be with the majority, and if they don't know how to deal with them they will "fall flat." A Puerto Rican mother said she felt that if children were separated early in life they would later have an "inferiority complex." And a Black mother said, "They would get the idea that they would always have to be with their own race or group. That's not healthy." This was a more frequent response than the need to develop identity.

Several parents who objected to separate agencies expressed their own struggle against segregation in the past and their fears that separate agencies would, as one Black mother said, "be the very thing that we have been trying to overcome for years." Finally, one Chicano mother said, "It could be good or it could be bad. . . . It depends who wants it and how it is done."

Once again the parental ethnic position was stronger than the social work attitude. The alternative of giving minority groups public funds to run their own programs if they wished to do so was chosen by 51 percent of social workers in the national sample and 65 percent in the ethnic agency sample, as against nearly all of the parents.

The fixed alternatives in the attitude survey, however, did not allow for equivocation, and the discussion of the parents in the group interviews opened up a new area. A group may support its right to restructure services along ethnic lines, but not necessarily the desirability of doing so.

Parents and Workers: Summary of Positions

Very different methods were used to explore the attitudes of social workers and parents on ethnic factors in service delivery. Workers answered a forced-choice mailed questionnaire; parents participated in group interviews. But they both responded to the same questions, and there appears to be consistency in the differences observed in their positions on ethnic commitment.

There were ten questions on which comparisons can be made. In seven of them there were important differences in the responses of social workers in the national sample and the ethnic agency sample, and in all cases ethnic parents gave responses closer to the ethnic agency responses than the national sample, but further along the continuum. For example, the preference for placing children with relatives with problems over foster parents was stated by 73 percent in the national sample, 52 percent in the ethnic agency sample, and by less than half of the parents who spoke. Preference for an agency run by members of one's own group was stated by 3 percent in the national sample, 13 percent in the ethnic agency sample, and by about one-quarter of parent respondents.

In one case, the choice of the main criterion of a homemaker—one of one's own group or one who loved children—there was an exception. Parents all opted for a homemaker who loved children. This option, and the discussion on the other issues, helped to identify some of the factors involved in making choices. There were two main variables involved—situations and alternatives.

In response to the question of whether parents preferred a trained worker or one of their own group, "own group" was chosen. The situation here was "going for help," and the alternative was a higher credential, which apparently did not have strong appeal. But when the situation was a homemaker coming to the house, and the alternative to "own group" was "loves children," "own group" carried less weight than the other option.

The same set of vectors appears in the discussion of choice of agency. The woman with a toothache wanted a dentist—"own group" was not a factor in her choice in that situation. And the positions on balanced meals as against food like what one has at home, or on relatives as against foster-care placement, both show that there cannot be a simple determinism in prediction of the ethnic response. People will make ethnic commitments in relation to their situations and their alternatives. Both factors need to be considered in developing a typology that incorporates ethnicity in service delivery.

Part III
Cross-cultural Testing

6

Israel: Melting Pot
or Cauldron?

A typology for an ethnic service system should apply not only to different ethnic groups in one country but to ethnic groups in other countries as well. To test whether the principles derived from our study of services to minority groups in the United States were applicable to similar services in other countries, visits were made to Israel and England.

In Israel, the diversity of peoples and multiplicity of origins create a microcosm of cultures. Israelis call themselves a country of immigrants, and the Law of Return, which establishes the right of all Jews to immigrate and settle, legitimizes this diversity. It is also the basis of the state's assumption of responsibility for newcomers. Jews have come to settle in Israel from all over Europe, North America, South America, New Zealand, Australia, Africa, and India. The population includes people formerly known as Moroccans, Yemenites, Iranians, Egyptians, Tunisians, and Ethiopians, as well as Poles, Russians, Americans, and British. The issues of service delivery to new arrivals involve not only personal adjustments and absorption of large numbers of newcomers in the national economy but also problems of modernization in which gaps of centuries need to be breached.

But this is only part of the Israeli picture. Arab people who have lived in Israel for centuries, and in particular those in East

125

Jerusalem and other occupied areas, are also in need of social services. The cultural and language differences are extreme, but even these are overshadowed by political issues. Problems of service delivery for Arabs assume a different configuration than for Jews, and although issues of ethnicity exist, they arise in a context where the options are defined primarily by the political dimensions. They bear separate discussion.

Ethnic Cohesion: Ethnic Diversity

Although diversity in the origins of peoples within Israel's borders is widely acknowledged, there is still some question as to whether or not the Jews in Israel actually comprise different ethnic groups. The answer depends on the definition of the concept of ethnicity and the relative emphasis on its components, such as national origin, religion, language, sense of shared past, and consciousness of kind. It is also a question with political and social overtones and has been a controversial issue almost since the state was founded. In 1955 Shumsky wrote, "Five years ago, open discussion of ethnic group tensions and differences was very unpopular and uncommon in Israel. But today the question of ethnic group relations has become a front-page issue. The feeling is widespread that the nation is divided—that there are two Israels: Occidental and Oriental."[1] In 1949-50 Shuval studied immigrants in the first year of arrival during the inauguration of the policy of free, unrestricted entry, a policy that resulted in the doubling of the population of the State in the first three years of its existence, with considerable ensuing social and economic strain. She reports, "A theme which runs through the analysis of almost all the problems . . . is the salience of the ethnic reference group during [the immigrant's] early period in the new country. I assume that, apart from his immediate family, which in many cases has not been preserved intact in the course of immigration, the most critical reference group for the immigrant is the ethnic one."[2] Shuval adds, "Many of the most affectively toned attitudes and behavior patterns have their roots in the complex of the ethnic culture. Such patterns concern food habits, child-rearing practices, family relationships. These are among the most tenacious culture traits of immigrants and are least likely to change quickly in a new social environment."[3]

This emphasis on ethnic cohesion was not unexpected in a country settled with successive major waves of immigrants. As Willner says, in contrasting the formation of Israel with other newly pronounced national entities, "Israel . . . is a new society as well as a new state."[4]

In her study of the resettlement of Moroccan Jews from the Atlas Mountains, Willner implies that new culture norms were stressed for nutrition, health, work, and language, and old culture norms were pretty much allowed to persist for family structure, child-rearing, and traditional observances, unless they came into conflict with Israeli law.

Time did not necessarily mitigate ethnic differences—in fact some prejudices tended to harden over the years. In a report on ethnic strain, for example, Shuval compares three studies done in 1950, 1953, and 1959 on rejection of a specific group as neighbors. She states, "The percentage rejecting North Africans has risen systematically over the nearly ten-year period from a low of 5 percent to a third of the population. . . . We have reason to suspect that the still prevalent ideological norm acts as a brake to the full expression of hostile feelings on the part of an even larger segment of the population."[5] In her study of stereotyping of North Africans by the medical bureaucracies, Shuval found the extent of stereotyping was related to the size of the physicians' practices and the strain they felt in coping with patient needs.[6]

Our interest here, however, is not in ethnic diversity but in its relevance to the service delivery system. In Israel, as in the United States, data on poverty and pathology tend to be intermingled with data on racial and ethnic groups. Israeli social statistics show significant differences in deprivation between Ashkenazi (Western or European origin) and Sephardic (Eastern or Oriental origin) Jews. This is true for poverty, overcrowded housing, educational deficits, and social pathology, and it is difficult to separate out the ethnic variables from the class and income data. One Israeli social work study used three variables to identify social deprivation: low income, many children, and overcrowded housing.[7] Furthermore, an analysis of urban Jewish families in Israel by degree of deprivation reported that 90 percent of those designated as "deprived" were Asian- or African-born, 6 percent were European- or American-born, and 4 percent were Israeli-born.[8]

This combination of ethnic grouping and deprivation inevitably results in a high concentration of social service clients with

Sephardic, or Oriental Jewish, background. In adoption, for example, Jaffe states that "the dominant pattern in Israeli adoptions is one of Sephardic children being adopted by Ashkenazi parents."[9]

The phenomenon of institutional care for dependent children is widespread in Israel, and has been since the early days of settlement when institutions were the primary response to caring for homeless, orphaned youth. This pattern has changed, however, and a study by Jaffe in 1964 showed a disproportionate number of Sephardic children living in institutions. He notes, "There has been a shift in recent years towards utilizing children's institutions for the housing and education of low-income educationally deprived Israeli children of Middle Eastern origin."[10]

Field Study in Israel

In Israel, as in the United States, even the traditional child-welfare fields of adoption and institutional care must cope with issues of ethnic diversity. Our research sought to identify at first hand how ethnic differences were accommodated in the Israeli system, and whether the factors of culture, mixing–matching, and decision-making and power were as relevant to service delivery in Israel as they had been found to be in the United States. The Israeli agency visits were not a systematic national review but rather constituted a purposive sample of a range of programs comparable to those studied in the United States.*

Twenty programs were visited in three intensive months of field work in Jerusalem, East Jerusalem, Haifa, Ashdod, Ashkelon, Bethlehem, and Afula. In selecting agencies for visits a wide range of services for children and families were covered: foster care; day care; adoption; "predelinquents"; young pregnant girls; compensatory work for "deprived" children of all ages, including toddlers, preschool, and school-age youngsters; community work with parents; and day and institutional care of handicapped children. Children served were mainly of Oriental Jewish or Arab background. Program visits were usually in two parts—interviews

*The visits were made over a three-month period in 1978 during which the writer was visiting professor in child welfare at the Paul Baerwald School of Social Work, Hebrew University, Jerusalem.

with directors and staff, using the agency instrument developed in the United States study, then actual observations of program activities including talks with clients, including mothers and children, and with students.

Although generalizations must be made with reservations, certain patterns did emerge in response to the study instrument. Agency directors tended to take an equal rights position with a strong melting-pot component to program goals. Exceptions were found to some extent among the few Sephardic social workers who leaned more in the direction of cultural pluralism. Where services for Arabs were under discussion, separate institutions were seen as inevitable by the majority of both Arab and Jewish workers, except for the occasional token client.

Responses to the issue of ethnicity in service delivery on the Israeli scene were varied. On the one extreme some traditional social workers totally rejected an ethnic approach, stating that their concern was with individual needs and the psychoanalytic dynamics of the problems presented. At the other extreme was the highly political response, which regarded the issue of ethnicity as a "romantic slogan"—a smoke screen that would divert the attention of the poor from the basic class issues. The more the service issue involved community issues and new settlers, rather than adoption and foster care, the more attention was paid to cultural and ethnic components. Use of ethnic factors, however, was frequently seen as a divisive and potentially disruptive choice rather than as a positive way to develop strengths and supports for eventually integrated programs.

Visits to Jewish Agencies

Each service visited was an example of how the society tried to cope with a particular social problem. Thus in each case some discussion of the social needs is necessary as background for the special attention given to ethnic issues. Visits and social needs were viewed on a continuum from the most personal services, such as to the young woman pregnant out of wedlock, to foster care, day care, compensatory education, and finally community-based services for neighborhood development.

Ethnic issues emerged in adoption services in three areas: the population of unwed pregnant women, the shelter environment, and the placement of babies. Out-of-wedlock births are not a major problem in Israel, but the numbers are growing. Approximately six hundred such births are reported a year, and since workers estimate that about 40 percent of the girls who receive counseling have abortions, a rough estimate can be made of approximately a thousand known pregnancies. In Israel abortion is an acceptable alternative for the pregnant girl. Where this does not occur placement in a shelter or foster home is possible. Although counseling for these young women is supposed to help them make decisions on their future, it was apparent from interviews with the social workers that the approved behavior involves surrender of the babies. Israeli society does not offer extensive supports for the single unmarried mother, and if the pregnant girl chooses to keep her child, she must also accept the burden of making arrangements for housing, support, and child care. Without family help, this is an overwhelming burden. The alternative of foster care for newborns is not approved, since it could place the babies "in limbo" for years, and permanency for children is the goal.

A shelter for unmarried pregnant women was visited in Jerusalem. It was housed in a private home in a residential area, surrounded by trees, and unmarked from the street—thus seeking to be inconspicuous and avoid neighborhood attention. The shelter had facilities for twenty women, whose ages mostly ranged from seventeen to twenty-one, and an apartment for a counselor who lived there with her family. The staff included two other counselors, a social worker (incidentally also pregnant), and three social work students. Many of the residents were "in hiding" from their families or villages and planned to return once they had delivered and surrendered their babies. Nineteen of the twenty women were Sephardic, and of these sixteen were from Morocco. The cook was Oriental, and the food was prepared to Oriental (Middle Eastern) taste—highly spiced, with much oil used. The music played was "teenage" music. The social worker responded to questions on cultural difference by identifying only food as characteristic, reporting that other characteristics of the women are "more socio-economic or class level than ethnic."

Social workers experienced with this population were asked in interviews to speculate as to why out-of-wedlock pregnancies appeared to be more characteristic of the Sephardic than the Ashkenazi population, although the actual numbers involved are small for both groups. The response obtained from workers, however, reveals as much about their own attitudes and preconceptions as it does about the phenomenon of illegitimacy. One Ashkenazi worker said the Moroccan out-of-wedlock pregnancies may reflect the negative impact of the French influence on the Jewish community in Morocco. Modernization was introduced, but family values were not considered important, and thus the traditional Jewish family life was undermined. Although most of the pregnant clients in the shelter visited were technically Sabras, having been born in Israel, they were raised by mothers who had been exposed to continental values and tended to be more violent and highstrung, thus providing an atmosphere of high tension for their children. The contrast was drawn between the life of these families after immigration—when they lived in crowded facilities, were exposed to sexual acts, and were at all kinds of risks—and the life of the early settlers, who were motivated by certain ideals of socialist pioneering and Zionism, ideals that did not impact on the Oriental immigrant families.

A second interpretation given by another Ashhenazi worker related to the class composition of the immigrant group from Morocco. She speculated that the upper-class Jewish population went to France, and the lower-class and village Jews came to Israel. Family factors were also involved; in Morocco the father was a strong authority figure; in Israel in the absorption process he lost his role and function. In addition, the worker suggested that the Moroccan girl gets double messages about sex in her home. On the one hand virginity and traditional behavior are highly prized; on the other hand this worker reported that Moroccan women tend to behave in a seductive manner, stress femininity, and are provocative with men. The girls report that their mothers are always telling them not to get pregnant and then closely follow the calendar to check their menstrual periods, as if always expecting the worst. Fertility is highly prized, and Moroccan women resist taking the pill because they are afraid of infertility. One superstition is that things injected in the body will travel and go to the heart—hence the opposition to intrauterine devices.

The mixing–matching issue in the shelter was raised in relation to staff and to placements. The agency position was clearly negative in terms of the matching concept. Except for the Oriental cook, who cooked "to the girls' taste"—a cultural variable—staff and placement decisions were related to professional criteria and sustaining the therapeutic milieu. The social work supervisor said that in recruitment they look for people who are sensitive to client needs rather than seek to match staff with clients on ethnic grounds. There is no special search for Oriental social workers, although a few are employed. One worker said she felt that the pregnant girls who are Oriental are less accepting of Oriental workers than they are of Western workers.

The question of matching was pursued with regard to placement of babies, and the answer was that there is a definite policy of *not* matching. Placement decisions were based on meeting the needs of the infants, and each case must be worked out individually. Thus in terms of the continuum developed in the ethnic factors research, the policy for adoption in Israel followed a color-blind, equal rights, melting-pot approach. The emphasis was on meeting individual needs, ethnic factors were not taken into account, and the service system supported an ideology appropriate to developing a unified national state. The differential incidence of out-of-wedlock pregnancies among Sephardic women was acknowledged but was explained in terms of ethnic pathology or class variables.

In Israel foster-home care has not been the principal way of providing substitute care; instead institutions have accounted for over 80 percent of child placements. More recently, however, there has been concern with the impact of years in institutional placement on young children, and there have been efforts to develop foster homes as an alternative placement service. One voluntary children's agency that was visited is involved in a pilot program that stresses home as against institutional care. This agency gives extensive help designed to keep children in their own homes. If that is not possible, then carefully selected foster homes are used and given supportive services.

Although this voluntary foster-care agency is based in Jerusalem, the new program is concentrated in development towns, serving almost entirely Sephardic families, mainly Moroccan and Indian. It also works with recent Georgian immigrants. When asked if the program was bilingual, workers said that the Indians speak English, the Moroccans speak Hebrew, the Georgians speak only Georgian, and some foster mothers from North Africa speak Arabic. "Bilingual" doesn't begin to describe the language problems.

When asked about the policy on mixing or matching of foster parents and foster children, the agency director said the practice was to disregard the background of the child. As long as a child is

Jewish, it can be placed with any good family. The one kind of differential policy is based on how religious a family is. A child from a family that is not religious can be placed with either a religious or a nonreligious family, but if a child is from a religious background it must be placed with a religious family. There is no ethnic component in placement, however. As with adoption, the emphasis is on individualized services and the ideology is that of the melting pot or equal rights.

A field visit to the foster-care program in the development town of Ashdod confirmed the impression that ethnic factors, although not an explicit part of the service delivery, did exist and differentiate among clients. The majority of foster children are Oriental Jews, including Moroccans, Egyptians, Tunisians, and Indians. The new emphasis on trying to help children in their own homes brings the workers in the agency into closer contact with various culture patterns. This creates new issues of worker acceptance of a range of child-rearing practices that differ from the Western experience and requires a lessening of a judgmental approach.

A home visit to a foster mother who was caring for Moroccan children showed the intensity of cultural as well as class differences. This foster family had migrated from Tunis; her parents had gone to Paris but her husband's parents went to Israel, and so they followed the latter. The Tunisian background had been middle class, but the migration lowered the social status of the family and two incomes were needed. Work for the wife outside the home was not approved by the husband, so foster care became the way to earn income for needed extras, such as dental work. The Tunisian foster mother was a warm and capable woman who spoke with affection for both her own children and her foster charges. Her resentment was for the Moroccan biological mothers of the children in care, most of whom she regarded as "violent and tough." Her attitudes reflected some of the feelings brought from Africa—when asked to compare Tunisia and Morocco, for example, she made a characteristic gesture and said, "Even our Arabs were better than their Arabs."

This foster mother offered strong family life to the foster children in a small but well-kept apartment. This was a two-parent setting with an employed father, and there was close involvement of foster and own children. It is ironic that the own son of this foster family was in a boarding school program for "disadvan-

taged" children because he had scored well on national achievement tests. Being "disadvantaged" is synonymous with having
Oriental parents, and the boarding school program, which will be
described later, was designed to provide educational opportunity
for Sephardic children in schools primarily attended by
Ashkenazi. When the foster mother was asked if she wanted her
own son to continue to university, her answer was, "Please God, I
would scrub floors if my son would go to university." The example of this one family illustrates social stratification among
Sephardic Jews, as well as the danger of stereotyping. This stable
Tunisian family was sheltering children of unstable Moroccan
mothers at the same time that their own son was labeled disadvantaged and lived away from home to integrate with Ashkenazi.

A number of factors contribute to the growing interest in day
care in Israel: the need of working mothers, large family size, and
the new concerns with overinstitutionalization of children. There
is no distinction by ethnic group in eligibility for day care, but
neighborhood centers tend to serve children who live nearby, and
housing clusters tend to reflect ethnic homogeneity. In the city of
Ashkelon, for example, Ashkenazi and Sephardic families for the
most part live in different sections of town. Three day-care settings were visited in the Sephardic area, including a babies house
and one religious and one nonreligious center for two- to four-
year-olds. Almost all the children served were Sephardic, because
of the cachement-area principle of service delivery.

In the day-care center under religious auspices, there were
sixty children, fifty-nine Sephardic, mostly Moroccan and Iraqi,
and one Ashkenazi. This center has a sliding scale for tuition;
most of the families are on welfare, and for them tuition is paid.
The one family that pays full tuition is Ashkenazi. The program is
basically designed to help mothers who have many children cope
with family responsibilities. Most of the mothers don't work outside the home; the average number of children is seven to eight
per family.

This day-care center is meeting the needs of large families,
who are primarily Sephardic. Cultural content is mainly religious;
parent education is geared to raising standards of child care and
"getting them to behave according to Western norms," according
to the director. She went on to say that the center tried to serve
food the children like—for example, rice is served rather than
potatoes because that is what Moroccans are used to. "However,"

she said, "our standards are Israeli standards and they hold for everybody." Next to the religious center on the block was a non-religious day-care center, also serving Sephardic children, including one Fallachin boy whose family was from Ethiopia.

A day-care home for babies in the same community cared for forty children from three months to two years. All the families served were Sephardic, and all were on welfare. The need for care was not because mothers worked out of the home but because of the size of families. One Iranian baby who was getting special help was one of fifteen children in her family. One baby of thirteen months was there because she had a two-month-old brother. In the babies home, as in the two day-care centers visited, the directors were Ashkenazi and the staff was Sephardic.

Issues of ethnicity are not explicitly involved in day care in Israel. Groupings of children are affected by many of the same factors that affect population constellations of day-care centers in New York—welfare status and proximity in housing rather than a policy on ethnic minorities. In the three centers visited in Ashkelon these factors resulted in differential grouping of children of Sephardic background. The ethnic implications were implicit in that children were there because the mothers had large families, and child-care norms in the homes were considered not to be up to Western standards. Positive cultural content was minimal, and an equal rights ideology prevailed.

Programs for compensatory education in Israel need to be reviewed against the demographic background. The mass immigrations from eastern countries brought large populations unexposed to Western technology, education, or living patterns, and the high birth rate for these people accelerated the problems of modernization. The use of Hebrew as the language of the State was a major unifying force for all immigrants, but even the single national language and religion did not mean that the Israeli society would achieve instantaneous homogeneity. Thirty years after the establishment of the State there were still substantial gaps in achievement between Ashkenazi and Sephardic children, even among those who were Israeli-born. Recognition that the gaps were not being closed through the normal educational process has encouraged Israeli leaders to initiate programs at all levels, from infancy through university, to seek to compensate the disadvantaged by promoting social integration. Although the primary impetus for these programs is the educational system, family and social factors are also involved, and the line between educational services and social services is hard to draw. Some of the problems result from poverty, some reflect cultural and ethnic differences.

Israeli scholars have varying views of the origins of what is called cultural disadvantage, some of which are summarized by Peleg and Adler in a review of compensatory education in Israel.[11] Frankenstein described this phenomenon in terms of "ethnic characteristics," or collective elements specific to particular groups. Among these he identifies faulty perception of time, poorly developed individual autonomy, and failure to assume responsibility for making judgments. Other scholars emphasize language usage and differences between oral and literary societies. Sociologists stress economic factors, family life, and problems of integration. Some have pointed to problems of immigration and modernization, citing differences between Western immigrants from industrialized countries who come for ideological reasons and those from Jewish communities in less developed countries who had been targets of discrimination and seek improved personal status.

Structural factors in Israeli society also affect immigrant status. Inbar and Adler studied dyads of brothers of Moroccan descent who immigrated—one to France and the other to Israel. Their findings show that in all areas of social achievement, but especially income and employment, the brother who went to France fared better than the one who went to Israel.[12] Thus it is not ethnicity *per se* that is the only critical factor, but the reception of the ethnic group by the host country. There are other studies that explore these factors, but class is not well discriminated from ethnicity, making it impossible to differentiate the variables. The theoretical work has affected the content of the compensatory programs, but the designation of who is disadvantaged, to determine who is eligible for compensatory education, is basically an empirical task. The Israeli Ministry of Education has developed an index to determine which students should receive the special programs for the disadvantaged, and the three factors included are country of origin, father's educational level, and family size.[13]

Although ethnicity, as measured by country of origin, was a significant variable in the designation of disadvantage, ethnic content was not a significant component of the compensatory programs at any level. The programs thus primarily reflect the melting-pot approach and do not support an ideology of cultural pluralism. When applied in the field, however, it is impossible to ignore cultural differences, and mixing–matching issues are increasingly raised. Issues of decision-making and power, however, are rarely discussed.

There are different points of view on where to intervene with compensatory programs. One position is the earlier the better—and HATAF (Home Activities for Toddlers and their Families) is a new pilot effort in Israel that grew out of the Home Instruction Program for Preschool Youngsters (HIPPY). Both programs, for different ages, seek to use mothers to foster the intellectual growth of their children by providing a highly structured sequential series of cognitive tasks to be given in the home. In discussing their target population, the interim report of HATAF states,

> The children of the Asian and African immigrant families of the 1950's, who comprised the bulk of the disadvantaged school population in the past decades, are now young parents. Most of them have completed eight years of school. However, there is no evidence as yet that these young parents provide their children with the kinds of experiences that seem to be necessary for school success and the development of intelligence.[14]

Families for the toddler program were selected on the basis of five criteria: a firstborn of eleven to thirteen months; young intact families without major physical or social problems; both parents of Afro-Asian origin; both parents Israeli-educated; and the mother at home as major caretaker. Central to this project is the wish to learn more of the parenting patterns of young Sephardic mothers.

The popular HIPPY program, from which the toddler program developed, was designed to provide compensatory instruction for preschool youngsters of four, five, and six years of age.[15] The criterion for admission is being from a deprived or disadvantaged family—defined as being of Oriental or African background. The highly structured program, heavily influenced by the American Head Start and Home Start programs, began in a small way in neighborhoods of Sephardic population in one city, but then was taken over on a national basis by the Ministry of Education. The rationale of using mothers to develop cognitive capacity with children is based on the results of experimental trials that show better achievement for youngsters in home-based instruction than in teacher-based nurseries. Country-of-origin dat१ of parents in one report show over 75 percent of the families served to have been born in Iraq, Iran, Yemen, Syria, or elsewhere in Asia, with another 18 percent being Israeli-born. Fewer than 7 percent came from Europe. There is no ethnic content in the curriculum that strictly prescribes educational tasks designed to aid in learning potential. We learned, however, that a mirror game had to be eliminated because it was perceived by some mothers as bringing bad luck. One difficult aspect in the execution of the program that was reported was trying to limit the role of the paraprofessional when she visits the family with educational materials. Social, health, and family problems arise and must be handled by referrals rather than by direct service.

Although the population served is almost entirely Oriental, and families are involved, cultural content is not present in programs with either toddlers or preschoolers. With regard to issues of mixing–matching, the professionals in both programs tend to be Ashkenazi, but the aides and paraprofessionals, who enter the homes and work with the mothers, tend to be Sephardic. Issues of decision-making and power were not discussed. As with adoption and foster care, the ideology followed was that of the melting-pot or equal rights position, with Western-style cognitive achievement as the primary outcome measure.

When it comes to the older group of high school age, the compensatory education program takes a different turn. Instead of the emphasis on the home and family, as with the young ones, able disadvantaged children who test above a specified score on national examinations are offered the opportunity to leave home and live in boarding schools that are attached to regular well-rated day high schools, attended primarily by Ashkenazi children. Thus the integration occurs in the classroom, since the Ashkenazi children live at home. In their extracurricular time the Sephardic youth receive compensatory work, tutoring, cultural opportunities, and a supervised group living experience.

In describing this work Smilansky and Nevo show how the program for gifted students from "culturally disadvantaged strata" developed and how it relates to the ideology of the integrated state.[16] They refer to three stages in the development of the educational system. The first stage was "formal equality," when the state was established and a national educational system was organized. This lasted about ten years. It soon became apparent that differences in background and culture meant that formal equality would not result in equality in outcome, and a second stage of "compensatory education" was entered, also lasting about a decade. Here the aim was to foster opportunity for equality of all ethnic groups through special programs for culturally disadvantaged. The third stage, under discussion, is the "reform" stage. This calls for complete reorientation of the educational system rather than special compensatory programs.

Two boarding schools with special programs for disadvantaged youth were visited, one religious and one nonreligious. Both are attracted to excellent academic high schools. In the nonreligious school there were eight hundred pupils of both sexes, one-third in the boarding school and two-thirds city youth who lived at home. Admission to the boarding school depends on scores on national standardized tests—there is a national cutoff point for the entry to the program by the disadvantaged, and there is further subcategorizing so that the top group can have entry to the higher rated academic schools. Thus there is a rough approximation in scores between boarding and day students. The ratio of 1:2 seeks to avoid a "tipping point" at which the disadvantaged group might predominate and the day students withdraw. At this point the strong academic program attracts the Ashkenazi day students, and the opportunity factors and high motivation brings the Sephardic disadvantaged.

The high school principal was asked how this effort meets ethnic needs, and he said that the program gives status to the Oriental Jews. It shows them that in class they can do as well as or better than the Ashkenazi students, and it also shows the Ashkenazis that Sephardic children can be as bright as or brighter than they. Where special help is needed for the disadvantaged children it is provided through tutoring, supervised study, and skills training. Counselors are available, and the children are exposed to books and concerts, hoping to make them better future consumers of culture. Ties with families are maintained. Sephardic children may call home whenever they wish, and they go home every third weekend and for holidays.

With regard to cultural content, the principal reported that there is slow but growing recognition in Israel of the need to broaden the Western-based conception of education. In 1970 special materials were introduced in the high school curriculum on problems of Sephardic Jews, and there was an effort to bring in teachers who knew more of Oriental history and the history of

Zionism among the North Africans. A special survey was done of Sephardic pupils in this school in the eleventh and twelfth grades, and the students asked for curriculum revisions so that the content would deal less exclusively with Western culture. As a result a special course in Oriental studies was introduced. In addition a project to learn about the contributions of different tribes of Israel was undertaken by the students, and a Yemenite dance group performed at the school.

In response to questions on mixing–matching, the principal said if he had two applications with the same qualifications he would prefer a Sephardic over an Ashkenazi teacher. The reason he gave is that the Sephardic teacher would have a greater understanding of student problems and more knowledge of habits, food, history, and culture of Oriental Jews. Such a role model, he believes, is needed for Sephardic youth to support their feelings of identity and give them a sense of status. By comparison, no such special need is seen for recent immigrant Hugarian youth because they are European in background, know their own culture, and have a strong sense of their own status.

The other high school visited was religious in orientation and for girls only. It had the opposite ratio of boarding to day students. There were 160 Sephardic girls in the disadvantaged group and only 80 in the day program. We were told that there are problems because religious families are less ready to send their girls away to school, and there is concern about sending girls to this school because of the large number of Sephardic girl students. The principal said some people had told him they would send their daughters to the day school if he would have separate classes for Sephardic and Ashkenazi girls, but his answer was negative; the whole purpose of the school was to get them to mix.

This is one of the few settings where the leading figure was Sephardic—the principal was a Yemenite man—and we were told that the school attracted many Yemenite families for that reason. Perhaps because the authority figure was Sephardic, as were the majority of girls, there was a more open sense of cultural pluralism in content and ambience. The principal set as one goal helping the Sephardic girls to have a sense of identity and to be proud of their culture. For example, we were told a Yemenite scientist from the Weitzman Institute was invited to speak and one of the girls said with astonishment, "You are a Yemenite, and you are a professor!"

The boarding school gives special help to girls, extracurricular activities, and study skills. It also seeks to strengthen religious commitment. Cultural content is not overlooked; the director spoke of some beautiful customs of Moroccans and Yemenites that some girls feel are primitive, but that the administration supports and tries to help the girls to appreciate.

Academic outcomes for both high schools visited are good; they retain the students, and the disadvantaged youth graduate in significantly higher numbers than would be expected if they had not been in special schools. Other outcomes are less easy to measure, such as relationship with families, social mobility, and cultural confusion. In the nonreligious school promising Sephardic youths are in the minority (one-third) but with enough peers to avoid a sense of tokenism. The education is Western-style with minimal recognition of cultural background, such as the course in Oriental studies. Since all eighteen-year-olds enter the army after graduation, there is a deferred period for outcome data in academic terms. The principal reports that follow-up studies show good results both in University attendance and vocational goals.

For the girls in the religious school, social factors enter that alter the outcomes. Religious girls can secure exemptions from army service, and many make career and life decisions right after high school. There is family pressure for early marriage and child-bearing, but when the Sephardic girl with a good education returns to her village, she often has problems in accepting the local males, who have traditional views on the role of women. The educated male Sephardic youth has more freedom and opportunities; girls are expected to remain at home until marriage. These are some of the by-products of the compensatory education program, probably inevitable when social mobility is introduced for one group in a traditional culture.

More basic is the issue of "creaming," and whether the compensatory education phase is still appropriate in a society where about 55 percent of the population fall into the disadvantaged Sephardic group, based on country of origin. Smilansky and Nevo, in evaluating this program for the Szold Institute, note several assumptions on which it is based. One is that the fact that the majority of Jewish children from Middle Eastern ethnic groups do not attain appropriate norms for secondary education does not mean limited potential ability. Another is that resocialization is possible, especially in adolescence, by moving a person from his sociocultural equilibrium. A third is that in order for this to be effective the more able of the culturally disadvantaged should receive preferential fostering.[17] To prepare Sephardic youngsters for the boarding school program, enrichment was given to the upper 30 percent of students in elementary schools who were labeled culturally disadvantaged. Furthermore it was decided that 80 percent of places in the boarding schools were to be for children of Middle Eastern origin. The rest were reserved for children of new immigrants from eastern Europe. Thus the selection process leads to a creaming of Sephardic children of superior ability from their communities and their removal from their local high schools. Attendance at the boarding schools is voluntary, but it is regarded as a special opportunity and has a high status value. What the impact of this process is on the 70 percent of Sephardic children not identified as potentially gifted is hard to evaluate. Would community-based enriched education achieve as good academic results? The proponents of this program would argue that it would not, because the key element of the integration would be absent. It is the argument that says separation cannot be equal. But what is the cost to the regular schools of the annual siphoning off of the most able students? Is there differential ethnic treatment if the very able Ashkenazi youth can live at home and be educated but the very able Sephardic youth must leave home for the same education? This program has done well by the students who have participated, but as the Sephardic youth become the majority in the country different models are being explored that suggest broader national educational reforms.

Ethnic issues were more prominent in compensatory education than in substitute care, such as adoption and fostering. But they were even more important in programs for community-based services. Where workers entered the homes of families and were concerned with neighborhood issues and relationships among groups, they were forced to work out ways of dealing with cultural diversity. Differences were not only along the Ashkenazi-Sephardic axis—each ethnic group among the Sephardim had separate customs and culture. This was as true, of course, in the case of Western Jews as of Eastern Jews—the difference is that the Eastern Jews are more likely to become clients of the social service system. Thus how to work with different cultures becomes a policy issue for service delivery.

A new housing development of approximately ten thousand people in a formerly occupied area was visited, since it was a good example of how the service system tries to cope with differences. This was mixed housing, and included new immigrants, resettled slum dwellers, young families, and welfare clients. The attempt was to develop ethnic as well as economic integration. The actual population mix was one-third Russian, one-third "Anglo-Saxon" (meaning Western) and one-third resettled slum dwellers, primarily younger Sephardic families of Iraqi, Moroccan, and Yemenite background. Social workers from the university conceptualized a service system to support integration. One of the first decisions was not to be associated with welfare, so no welfare office was included in the service center.

In old temporary quarters on the site of the modern new housing there is a community center, very lacking in space and facilities. There are three main programs: work with individuals and families, work in the center (including a small day-care group), and outreach neighborhood work. Central to the plan is that there is an integrated corps of social workers from many different agencies who work together to give services rather than having clients referred from one agency to another.

A new development in the program is family day care, which is working well although reaching a small number. Because of the lack of services for very young children of working mothers, a plan was developed to have women in the project who are good in mothering trained to look after a small number of children in their own homes. When visited, the program included ten mothers caring for a total of forty children, and efforts to recruit another ten were under way. There were some problems of supervision and level of compensation for caretaker mothers, as well as handling their attitudes to the children's natural parents, but these were being worked out by the program director.

Because this community effort was so consciously directed toward integration of culturally diverse groups, the issues of ethnicity were easier to raise. As far as mixing or matching, the director of the center is Ashkenazi, and so are all the senior people, except for the youth leader, who is Moroccan. There are efforts to integrate staff, and social workers are of both Ashkenazi and Sephardic backgrounds. Having workers of ethnic backgrounds is no assurance of cultural comprehension, however. One worker said the Moroccan youth leader, who was known to speak freely about how hard it was for him when he was young to give up his own culture and become Israeli, now himself gives orders to children in ways that do not recognize their special ethnic needs. For example, a Bukharan boy was told he must remove his embroidered jacket and little hat before he could play ball, but the boy refused. The leader did not recognize that this special jacket and hat were the symbol of the boy's group, and he was not yet ready to part with it.

The center workers were asked specifically if they seek to develop ethnic awareness. The response was that although the basic goal of the community is integration, it must be done in a pluralistic way because the ethnic communities are very separate. On Independence Day, for example, instead of everyone's going to town to participate in the big national celebration, the center is planning an ethnic carnival in the community and a fair. Each ethnic group will have a booth and show native foods, handicrafts, and dress. At the center of the fair will be Israeli films and Israeli dancing to symbolize the national State.

The decision on the fair was taken only after much consideration. In the community center there is substantial controversy over whether recognition of differences is a necessary phase in the ultimate goal toward a unified national State. For example, there was a difference of opinion about a local neighborhood newspaper where items were written in different languages to facilitate reading by different groups. After much discussion it was decided to print all items in easy Hebrew. This excluded some who didn't know Hebrew, but it tended to be a unifying factor for those who did. The worker interviewed, however, freely stated that she didn't know which was right. To sum up their own ideology, these workers said they believed it was necessary to begin service with an approach of cultural pluralism and then work to strengthen each of the groups toward the goal of integration.

One program not concerned with integration but rather with direct supports for Sephardim was "Bridging the Gap," based in Haifa. Supported by a major university, this activity involved about six hundred students of Oriental origin from development towns and underprivileged areas that were engaged in educational and social programs for Sephardic Jews. Among the activities are identification of promising youth, encouraging higher education, training of future leaders, and self-development for families in Sephardic communities. The program has strong ethnic components, including encouraging leadership from Sephardic people themselves. It fits all three criteria developed in the ethnic agency study: cultural content is stressed, matching is consciously pursued, and there is recognition of the need for decision-making and power by the ethnic people themselves.

Two Sephardic Jews involved in this program challenged the whole concept of "cultural deprivation," as used in compensatory education. One Egyyptian Jewish man said, "I do not feel deprived—with my cultural background from Egypt I have much to give and not only to take." A Moroccan woman, a leader in the program, said, "Because a culture is not known does not mean it doesn't exist." Both speakers called for research and study on the history and culture of Sephardic Jews. They were impatient with programs such as HIPPY, which works with preschoolers, saying that will take too long to get results. A Moroccan youth, a student at the university, was one of the few Israelis interviewed who raised issues of decision-making and power. He saw both the economic gap and the social gap between Ashkenazi and Sephardim as widening rather than narrowing. He defined the aim of the program to ensure "that social problems will not become ethnic problems." However, this student felt Sephardic people must be trained for leadership and decision-making. His reason was that unless Sephardic Jews move into positions of power in politics, where they can vote money to alleviate deprivation, there is no chance to close the gap.

This position was also expressed by the head of a large national association of Sephardic Jews, who stressed the demographic facts. He noted that not only are the majority of the people in Israel Sephardic, but because of the higher birth rate of Sephardic Jews and large private school population of Ashkenazis, the percent of Sephardic children in the public schools is now from 70 to 75 percent. In the interview special problems of Sephardic youth were discussed, such as high dropout rates. The problem of housing is very serious; it was stated that immigrant families who were allotted housing when they had one or two children may be in the same quarters with six or seven. And since buying rather than renting an apartment is the pattern in better Israeli housing, poor families are in a double bind. The labor unions, according to this Sephardic spokesman, are "unions of those who are strong," not of all workers. His organization is concerned with preserving songs, history, and culture of Sephardic Jews and seeks to have this material recognized in the school curriculum. The issue is seen as a "communal" one, rather than an ethnic one, and cultural pluralism is the preferred ideology.

Not all Shepardim agree with the emphasis on cultural differences. A Sephardic social worker involved with the streetwork program in Jerusalem took a very different approach. His work was with about a thousand youth, with about 40 social workers trying to relate to alienated youngsters with special problems. About 60 percent of the workers were Sephardic, 40 percent Ashkenazi. The teenagers in trouble are almost 100 percent Sephardic.

Although working with Sephardic youth, and being himself of Moroccan background, this social worker did not wish to discuss ethnic differences, saying that ethnicity was "a romantic approach of the West," not likely to solve the problems. The issue, as he sees it, is class struggle, and class issues in Israel tend to be hidden behind other factors, such as the religious question and relations with the Arabs. He agrees that the Asian-African immigration to Israel introduced people at a different level of technology. However, he states the problem is one of rich and poor, and the need is not for social services, even ethnically based services, but for basic improvements in living standards. As for the kibbutz and the socialist principles of sharing, this social worker noted that only from 3 to 4 percent of the population live on kibbutzim, and he said that anyway to him the kibbutzim are like monastaries in the West—they are run by dedicated people who live by certain principles but whose style does not affect the basic national economy or structure.

Reference was made by this worker to the so-called Black Panther group of youngsters in Israel who had expressed dissatisfactions with social services and were involved in social action. He maintained that the influence of the American social work system in Israel has been negative in that Americans concentrate on the subsystem of welfare and do not deal with overall national problems. Separate ethnic institutions for Sephardim were not approved by this informant, since his goal was to involve people in the broader Israeli scene.

The denial of ethnic needs on the part of Israeli social workers came from two extremes, those who saw social problems as entirely related to class and poverty and those who saw entry into the mainstream of Israeli life as being unrelated to group origin. An example of the latter point of view was seen in a visit to an absorption center, where the sharpest ethnic differences were observed. The visit was to a group of sixty Fallachian, African Jews recently arrived from Ethiopia. They included babies, children, teenagers, and adults; none spoke Hebrew, a few spoke English or French, all spoke Amharit, the Ethiopian language. They were agricultural workers from primitive villages who had lived in remote places in Ethiopia and preserved their Jewish culture and religious tradition for some two thousand years. They said that in Ethiopia they were not actually persecuted, nor did they suffer severe discrimination. However, there was strong pressure from the Christians there to convert, and some intermarriage was occurring. Thus behind the drive to emigrate was the desire to maintain Jewish culture and tradition.

The process of absorption in Israel is particularly complicated for this group—they must change their style, their language, their housing. In Ethiopia they were used to straw houses, no electricity, no running water, and they worked their fields according to their biblical ancestors, Abraham and Jacob. The women's roles were sharply differentiated from the men's, and their tasks were in the house. The Fallachian have special problems with social workers in Israel, it was reported, since they are not used to dealing with women "as bosses."

There are other serious problems in the acculturation process. The teenagers, who wish to continue with their education, will probably make the best adjustment. For the adults studying Hebrew, however, the problem is not just learning another language but basically that they are illiterate and have no experience at all with reading or writing. The area of medical care is also complicated. The Fallachian tend to resist modern medicine, yet they lacked immunization and have been exposed to diseases not typical in Israel, thus creating a potential health problem. Native culture and art were in danger of being entirely lost. In Ethiopia the Fallachian did embroidery and pottery but it was reported that they did not bring their pottery tools. As for music, only one man brought his own drums. The spokesman for the group said the immigrants agreed to forget what had been in the past and do the new things that should be done in Israel.

When asked whether the group still identified as Blacks and Africans, as well as Israelis and Jews, the response was that what they had in common with other Jews was more important than the

African tradition. They do not wish to create new ghettos in Israel; if there is contact with others, differences will be overcome, and the prediction was that Fallachian will intermarry and take their part in Israeli life. In reality, however, the settlement program tries to send people where they will do well, and this means the immigrant group will probably go to development towns where other Fallachian live and to villages where they can have open spaces and where discipline over the children can be sustained.

Loss of culture was also experienced by another set of Jews of distinctive background who emigrated from India. These comprise two separate groups, Cochin Jews from the south of India and the Bene-Israel from the Bombay area. From the point of view of the anthropologist, these two categories represent different ethnic groups—they differ in customs, traditions, language, and geographic area of settlement. In Israel both groups deliberately abandon traditional patterns, partly in response to the concept of the homogenous national State. Culture is lost, songs and legends are not being transmitted orally, wedding customs are being modernized. Food patterns change, and it was reported that the new generation even scorns the traditional spices. Saris may be worn by older women but not by the young.

In any mass migration it is inevitable that immigrants, especially the younger members, will seek to conform to new culture patterns. Much of the old is no longer functional in adapting to the new society. But the process of social change is more complicated than simple adaptation. One relevant question is whether recognition of ethnic factors and support for cultural differences do not facilitate the absorption process, rather than impede it, in that each group can maintain pride in its own background and in its potential to contribute to the new society. A second question is more pragmatic—historical evidence in many countries has exposed the false illusions of the melting-pot process for new immigrants. The Jewish experience itself proves that culture persists beyond geographic displacement, as do prejudice and discrimination. Successful adjustment to a new society is a multifaceted problem, and religion is not the only factor. Class, race, education, and skills are also relevant. Ethnic factors are being considered in the reception of groups of different background, such as the Fallachian, although they are not part of the planning for their new life-style. But culture tends to persist, and as long as one man brought one drum from Africa, it is likely that the past will not be entirely forgotten.

SERVICES TO ARAB CHILDREN

There are at least three contexts for services to Arab children. If they are residents of Israel proper, they may be "token" clients of Jewish agencies. If they live in East Jerusalem or other occupied areas they may receive services from government-supported programs, delivered primarily by Arab workers. Or they may get help from private voluntary agencies, a number of which are supported by foreign sources. Visits were made to programs of all three types.

Early in the investigation it became apparent that the service needs of Arabs and of Jews had to be conceptualized in different terms. Not only are service problems relating to Arabs affected at every turn by political issues, there are also sharp cultural differences between Arabs and Jews in language, custom, religion, and life-style. Although the preferred ideology for dealing with Sephardic Jews is that of the melting pot, where Arabs are concerned respondents of both Arab and Jewish groups strongly opted for separate institutions and a dual set of programs to meet the separate needs.

The situation of unwed motherhood and adoption is a good case in point to illustrate different cultural orientations. Being pregnant out-of-wedlock is totally unacceptable in the Arab culture, and punishment by death is still known. The shelter for pregnant girls in Jerusalem has had an occasional Arab girl, typically "in hiding" from her parents. We were told of one Arab girl who spoke perfect Hebrew who entered the shelter pretending to be Jewish. After some weeks, she told the girls she was not, and she was well accepted. The shelter had housed a girl from a Druze family who was returned to her parents after she delivered her baby. The father told the social worker that everyone in his village thought he would kill his girl, but since she was "not right" (lame and slightly retarded), he decided the trouble she was in was not her fault and he let her live.

Such retributions, however, apparently still take place, although documentation is difficult. In an interview with a Bedouin student at the university he reported that a sixteen-year-old girl from a village next to his got pregnant and delivered at home.

The mother threw the baby on the road, and the father and brothers told the girl they were going out for a few hours, and if she were alive when they returned they would kill her by cutting her in pieces. The girl found a well and drowned herself. The Bedouin student went on to say that the young putative father of the baby was arrested by the Israeli authorities and jailed for two years, presumably for his own protection. But on release he will face trial by a Bedouin court, and the punishment could be either death or financial compensation to the girl's family.

These are extreme incidents, reportedly happening to village people. In the cities there may be different solutions. Abortion is preferred, and is available through the state. A hidden confinement, delivery, and surrender are also possible. Although the number of Arab babies who survive out-of-wedlock births is not large, they constitute a special problem since adoption by nonrelatives is not a part of the traditional Arab culture, with its heavy reliance on blood lines and family inheritance. In cases of infertility, copulation for conception may be arranged with other relatives rather than going outside the family or settling for an adopted child.

In spite of the negative feelings on adoption, a few such cases have been handled by the regular adoption services. One was to an educated Arab family in a progressive Arab town. Another was to a woman who pretended pregnancy to friends and neighbors, both verbally and in appearance, and after the appropriate nine months left her village to "deliver." She returned with the adopted infant and presented it as her own.

If adoption is not widespread, what happens to the Arab out-of-wedlock baby? Abandonment is one outcome. One foster-care agency with a babies' shelter reported that it was providing temporary care for a two-month-old male infant who was found after birth as a bundle in the desert by an Israeli driver. The question is whether the infant is Jewish or Bedouin. The matter has gone to the rabbinate for decision. If declared Jewish, the child will be put up for adoption; if Arab he will be "sent away." In the meantime the infant is in an institution rather than a foster home since the worker said a Jewish mother would "feel uncomfortable" taking care of a noncircumsized boy baby.

To be "sent away" refers to the nonofficial but widely acknowledged practice of out-of-country adoptions for non-Jewish children, particularly by prospective Scandinavian parents. These are carefully screened, and prospective adopters must actually come to Israel to complete the arrangements. Another solution is sending babies to child-care settings in the occupied areas, and one such agency will be described at a later point.

Foster care is not a relevant service for Arab families, since children born in-wedlock are not given up. As the Bedouin student said, "A Bedouin never gives up a child. Never, not even a girl." There is the extended-family system available for child care if the parents cannot function. Arab children do have problems, however, and special services are limited or nonexistent.

In East Jerusalem an American psychiatrist developed a child guidance clinic, serving Arab children from ages two to fifteen. Since 1974, when it was established, about six hundred children were seen, and there is an active load of about twenty. The program includes treatment for these children and work with their families, as well as diagnosis, testing, and follow-up with another forty-five children. Cases are referred from the welfare department, which is in the same building as the center, and from schools or health settings.

Ethnic factors manifest themselves in this service in many ways. In the first place, there are very few programs for Arab children, and the needs are substantial. Second, language, custom, religion, and other cultural factors in the life of the Arab family need to be understood before diagnosis can be made and treatment undertaken. Arab families reportedly resist psychotherapy, which is seen as a Western concept. There is a myth that a disturbed person is "crazy" because a curse has been put upon him.

Ethnic differences arise in relation to staffing the treatment service. An American Jewish psychiatrist had recently left, and was considered by staff to be ineffective. He knew neither Arabic nor Hebrew, nor was he acquainted with Arabic culture. At the time of the visit the center was staffed with a full-time Arab social worker, a part-time Jewish social worker, a half-time Jewish psychologist, and a full-time Arab secretary. The Arab social worker complained that the Jewish psychologist insisted that all records be kept in Hebrew. He knew Hebrew, Arabic, and English, she knew Arabic and English, and the other social worker knew Hebrew and English. If the records were in English, all could read them.

In response to the question of whether there should be separate institutions for Arab and Jewish children, the Arab social worker answered in the affirmative. She said the Arab child would not feel at home in the Jewish institution—there would be differences in language, religion, and custom. It could only add to the problems of children who already have difficulties. She reported that they have tried to send Arab children to Jewish vocational schools for training and there have been many quarrels and difficulties.

On the continuum of ideology suggested in the ethnic research—melting pot to cultural pluralism to promotion of ethnic identity—both Arab and Jewish workers in this setting opted for an ideology favoring cultural pluralism. Melting pot was out of the question when it came to services for Arabs and Jews. Ethnic identity was not considered to be a relevant issue. The Jewish psychologist suggested that promotion of identity only arises when ethnic groups are separated from their origins and not sure where they belong, as the Blacks in America. In Israel the Arabs have their own pride, background, and identity. The Jews also have their identity, language, and customs. Both Arabs and Jews are in their own societies and do not have to build an identity concept. The problem is for each group to live according to its own culture—a pluralistic approach.

When this child-guidance clinic in East Jerusalem opened and referrals were sought, the staff was inundated with cases of retardation. This reflects several factors—there were few services for Arab children, and the most pressing problems were presented first. Emotional difficulties and therapy for problems of adjustment was a sophisticated Western concept—severe retardation was more apparent and aroused more concern. Retardation was regarded as both a shame and a curse, and handicapped children were often hidden away from view.

To meet the special needs of these children, a day-care center was established to serve the severely retarded in East Jerusalem, those with IQ scores of lower than 65. This center, housed on the ground floor of a school building, is supported by government funds but is jointly sponsored by a voluntary agency. It serves thirty Arab children, ages three to ten, and the director and staff are all Arab except for the nurse, who is foreign. Children are trained to perform activities of daily living, to feed and toilet themselves, and to write, count, and get along in a group.

According to the director of this day-care center, these children are socially as well as educationally retarded, and they come from homes where they have been hidden from view. They are responding well to the acceptance and training. The major problem is lack of trained staff. Not one person working with the children is trained in special education, so all programs are trial and error.

Cultural needs are recognized in this center for the retarded. For example, the food is prepared in the accustomed way, but the diet is strengthened by adding vegetables and cutting down on bread. The dining pattern at home for these families is to have one big dish, and everyone sits on the floor and eats out of the big dish with his or her hands. In the center children each have their own dish and are taught to eat with a spoon. One child who learned this insisted on her own dish at home. Some of the problems of diet are that the men come home and eat first and then the women eat, and then the children. If the dish is a meat stew, little meat remains for the children. Another example of center training is in the bathroom at the center, where there are both Arab (hole in ground) and Western toilets. Children use Arab toilets when they first come, then learn to use Western.

The Arab director of this center strongly believes there should be separate institutions for Arab and Jewish children, maintaining that they have different religions, languages, and cultures. Arab children in a Jewish institution are in the minority and do not feel comfortable. She says the question is related to both political and geographical factors. For example, one institution for both might be possible in Haifa, where there is more of a mixed population, but not in Nazareth.

A similar position in favor of separate institutions was taken by an Arab social worker who directs recreational activities. His programs serve about five thousand non-Jewish youth (primarily Arab but also Armenian, African, and Greek Orthodox). Separate programs are organized near their living quarters, since the participants have strong roots in their neighborhoods. The only sport shared with Jewish youth is swimming, since the only available pool is in the YMCA building. Otherwise this worker supports separate programs on ethnic lines, feeling that all people need their own reference groups, even in sports, and that they feel more secure with others like themselves. In addition certain ethnic cultural patterns need to be respected. For example, Arab families insist on separate services for boys and girls. Another example of differences is that there are certain religious restrictions on drawing the human form, and this arose in a painting class for Arab youth.

In developing recreational programs ethnic factors must be recognized. For example, according to this youth leader sports contests between Arab and Jewish youth do not go well. The social worker reported that all the latent hatred between the groups comes out on the playing field, and he said, "They play the game as if it were the Middle Eastern wars." He has tried mixed teams, each team including Jews and Arabs, but this also has difficulties since the boys tend to pass the ball only to others like themselves on their own teams. On the whole the preferred ideology was that of cultural pluralism, recognizing that Arab youth have strong pride in belonging to their own group.

Ethnic issues in the administration of welfare to families and children in occupied areas were discussed with a senior Arab social worker who had been directly involved. Here the key issue was not cultural content or mixing–matching, but decision-making and power. The assistant director and all workers in the welfare office were Arab, the director was Jewish. It was reported that efforts on the part of Arab workers to improve services were regarded as hostile political acts. Clearly even issues of income support and personal social services for Arabs could not be discussed outside the political context. The need for separate services is accepted on both sides; the key issue is who makes the decisions.

Within Israel, in an area with a large Arab population, a major university has a special program for Arab-Jewish studies, and an Arab-Jewish Center to meet special problems. The Arab students make up 12 percent of the enrollment at the university and they come to school at a younger age than the Jewish students because they do not serve in the army. It was reported that they live apart from the Jewish students. The program at the center seeks to establish a dialogue between Jewish and Arab students, hoping to develop understanding and trust. The ideology is that of an ethnically pluralistic society. Arab faculty from the university have been sent abroad for training so that they can return and serve as role models for the Arab youth.

The final group of services for Arab children visited were two institutions in Bethlehem, both under foreign auspices. One was for about a hundred deaf children, a residential center run by an Italian Catholic order. Children with severe hearing disabilities, from the age of three through the grades, live in the institution during the week and receive intensive training. They have up-to-date machines and teaching methods, the sisters are fluent in Arabic, and the classes visited appeared to show a high level of learning. No signing was used; children are taught to lip-read and to talk, and appropriate hearing aids are fitted. Classes go through sixth grade, and children then go on for vocational training.

There are political, ethnic, and religious factors involved in this institution's service plan. They accept Arab children from the West Bank and Gaza primarily, since there are no services in those areas for the deaf child. Although a Catholic institution, the large majority of the children are Moslem. There are religious services for Christian children, and a teacher of the Moslem religion is being sought. The religious observance of each group is respected.

The second institution visited with foreign support was a children's village, designed to give homes and families to motherless children. Cottage houses headed by "mothers," who are child-caring women, hold eight to ten homeless children from the West Bank. Children of ages from six months to fourteen years are grouped together to stimulate a family constellation. Commitment is made to sustain the child until the age of fourteen, and for most residents this institution is the only home he or she will know until maturity.

Ethnic factors have strong priority in planning this child-care program. The philosophy of the international agency is that each child should be brought up in the accustomed ways of the country. Since this setting primarily serves West Bank Arab foundlings, the cottage mothers are matched to the religion and nationality of the child. All must be Moslems and most have come from the West Bank. Although the agency recognizes the value of family adoption, since this is not in the Moslem tradition, the cottage setting becomes the family substitute. House mothers are encouraged to run the cottage like their own households, and each has her own budget and does her own marketing. "Mothers" come from refugee camps, most had not slept in a bed before, nor used a fork or knife. They are trained in child care and household management. No foreign volunteers are accepted in the cottages; experience has shown it destroys the sense of family. An Arab doctor who visits serves as father figure to the children.

The foreign director of this institution took a strong position on both cultural content and matching of children and caretakers. She supported separate institutions for Arabs, saying they are needed to help people know their own "mentality" and background. Both this institution and the one for deaf children in Bethlehem gave support to two of the three factors from the ethnic agency study—cultural content and the principle of matching rather than mixing. The third factor, decision-making and power, however, was a different matter. In both institutions decision-making and power were in the hands of foreigners, both Europeans. Neither these institutions nor the ones in Israel run by Jewish executives were allowing Arab leadership in seeking solutions to the problems of Arab children. It should be noted that a fourth set of services for Arab children where such leadership might be found was not visited. These would be institutions in the towns with Arab mayors where separate Arab services were maintained.

The Ethnic Continuum in the Israeli Context

The Israeli study confirmed the usefulness of the approach developed in the earlier work in the United States. It was relevant to seek to identify programs on an ideological continuum of melting pot to cultural pluralism to ethnic identity. And the three factors that emerged in the earlier study as characteristics of ethnic agencies—cultural content, mixing–matching, and decision-making and power—all surfaced in one or another way in the programs visited.

Traditional Israeli child-welfare services dealing with Sephardim followed the melting-pot ideology, including a minimum of cultural content, stressing mixing rather than matching, and leaving decision-making to the Ashkenazi executives. For the programs visited, this was the case for adoption, foster care, shelters, day care, and compensatory education for the very young. Matching occurred primarily in employment of paraprofessionals and local workers, who were mainly Sephardic and worked under the supervision of Ashkenazis with professional training. In special programs for older children, mixing was also the goal, but there was growing interest in introducing cultural content relevant to Sephardim in the schools. Ideological differences were mainly seen in community services, where customs and cultures varied and people still related to the country of origin as reference groups. In those settings workers saw a culturally pluralistic approach to services as being a more viable route to integrated community development. The strength of the common religion, language, and aspirations for the national state were often mentioned as the basis for future Sephardic-Ashkenazi relations. The dissident voice was the raising of class issues as being more basic than ethnic ones. The relationship between Ashkenazi and Sephardim in Israel is very complicated, with strong positive as well as negative valences. On the negative side are economic as well as cultural differences. Uniting Sephardim and Ashkenazi, however, are two powerful factors: a common religion and a common enemy.

For the Arab sector, political issues were overriding, and social service policy cannot be analyzed outside the political context. In all programs visited separate institutions were favored by both Arabs and Jews. Where Arabs attended large Jewish institutions, such as a university, separate support systems were needed for Arab students. On the ideological continuum of the ethnic agency study cultural pluralism was the preferred position. Issues of developing ethnic identity were not considered to be a problem, since the Arab people have a strong sense of group affiliation and pride in their own culture. The relevant problem is political identity, however, and in this matter Arabs interviewed rejected allegiance to existing national Arab states, preferring instead their own political entity. One said, "An Israeli Arab is a contradiction in terms."

This review is not based on a systematic sampling of all child welfare services in Israel, but rather reflects visits to twenty-five carefully selected sites and programs offering a wide range of services. The goal was not a national survey but rather the testing of a method of looking at ethnicity in service delivery.

It was found that ethnic factors were incorporated in service delivery in both positive and negative directions. They were considered when a policy of mixing was followed with an ethnically diverse population, and when separate institutions were supported for political reasons. Thus the incorporation of the ethnic component was part of social and national policy. Whether ethnic differences within Israel will persist in spite of the priority for a single national state, whether a culturally pluralistic policy might better achieve the basic goals, and whether the social needs of Arab and Jewish children will ever be discussed outside a hostile political context are questions for the future.

Notes

1. Abraham Shumsky, *The Clash of Cultures in Israel* (New York: Columbia University Press, 1955), p. 18.
2. Judith T. Shuval, *Immigrants on the Threshold* (New York: Atherton Press, 1963), p. 29.
3. Ibid., p. 30.
4. Dorothy Willner, *Nation-Building and Community in Israel* (Princeton, N.J.: Princeton University Press, 1969), p. 3.
5. Judith T. Shuval, "Emerging Patterns of Ethnic Strain in Israel," *Social Forces* 40:4 (May 1962):330.
6. Judith T. Shuval, "Ethnic Stereotyping in Israeli Medical Bureaucracies," *Sociology and Social Research* 46:4 (July 1962):455-65.
7. J. M. Rosenfeld and E. Morris, "Socially Deprived Jewish Families in Israel," in A. Jarus, J. Marcus, J. Oren, and C. Rapaport (eds.), *Children and Families in Israel: Some Mental Health Perspectives* (New York: Gordon and Breach, 1970), p. 432.
8. Ibid., p. 433.
9. Eliezer D. Jaffe, "Child Welfare in Israel," in Jarus et al., *Children and Families*, p. 342.
10. Ibid., p. 334.
11. Rachel Peleg and Chaim Adler, "Compensatory Education in Israel," *American Psychologist* 32:11 (November 1977):945-58.
12. Michael Inbar and Chaim Adler, *A Comparative Study of Educational and Socio-Economic Achievement of North African Immigrants in France and Israel* (Biannual Report, 1975-76, National Council of Jewish Women, Research Institute for Innovation in Education, School of Education, The Hebrew University of Jerusalem, Israel), pp. 48-50.
13. Peleg and Adler, "Compensatory Education," p. 848.
14. *Home Activities for Toddlers and Their Families (HATAF)* (Interim Report, National Council of Jewish Women, Research Institute for Innovation in Education, School of Education, The Hebrew University of Jerusalem, Israel, April 1976), p. 9.
15. *Home Instruction Program for Pre-School Youngsters (HIPPY)*. Final Report, 1973. Aviva D. Lombard, Project Director; and Dan Davis and Judith Kugelmass, *Home Environment: The Impact of the Home Instruction Program for Pre-School Youngsters (HIPPY) on the Mother's Role as Educator*. Interim Evaluation. Both reports published by the National Council of Jewish Women,

Center for Research in the Education of the Disadvantaged, School of Education, The Hebrew University of Jerusalem, Israel, May 1974.

16. M. Smilansky and D. Nevo, *Secondary Boarding Schools for Gifted Students from Culturally Disadvantaged Strata.* A Follow-up Study (Tel Aviv, Israel: Tel Aviv University and the H. Szold Institute, 1971), pp. 2–6.

17. Ibid., pp. 6–54.

7

Ethnicity in Britain: The Heritage of Empire

The British social services were developed to serve a relatively homogenous population and to compensate persons suffering disadvantages as a result of economic inequities in the system. Discussion of social policy issues in Britain in the 1960s focused on categorical versus universal services, centralization versus decentralization, and generic versus specialized services, and there was little reference in the British social work literature to ethnic groups, cultural content, mixing–matching, or decision-making and power by minority clients. By the mid-1970s, however, there was substantial domestic controversy around the issue of immigration of "coloured persons" to Britain. Social service workers began to explore ways to cope with problems of immigrant clients. The concerns were not only with personal social services, but also with policy issues such as eligibility of immigrants for child benefits and tax relief.

To study ethnic factors in service delivery in Great Britain we reviewed the British social welfare literature, and then visited fifteen programs serving West African, West Indian and Asian families and children. Included were public, voluntary, and self-help settings. The comparison of this material with the Israeli and United States studies supported the hypothesis that ethnic factors in service delivery were related to the role of ethnic minorities in the larger political context.

The Ideological Plateau

Cultural pluralism is not a popular concept in England, but neither is the melting pot. In fact, there may be more approval for separate programs in a relatively homogeneous country with small new minority groups, such as England, than in a heterogeneous country with a broader ethnic mix, such as Israel. In Great Britain, relationships with ethnic people in the past occurred primarily in the context of the colonies. A major heritage of the dissolution of the empire was the complicated immigration regulations, which held out certain advantages to the holders of the British passport. Ethnic issues became controversial in that they were also immigration issues, and whereas people in formerly colonial areas might assume their right to "return" to the home country, there was no "law of return" in official British policy comparable to that in Israel. On the contrary, Britain, a small heavily populated country with limited resources and a highly organized labor force, sought population restriction rather than expansion. Since the would-be immigrants were Asian, African, or West Indian, ethnic issues inevitably arose in the policy debate.

Problems of West Indian families in England were noted by Glass, a sociologist, and FitzHerbert, an anthropologist, about ten years before they received major attention from the social work field. In *Newcomers: The West Indians in London*, Glass dealt with increased migration, adjustment problems, and the protests and expectations of this particular group.[1] In *West Indian Children in London* FitzHerbert discussed the West Indian family system, and reviewed case records of 150 families receiving child-welfare services.[2] She worked in a London borough social service office for six months testing certain hypotheses about appropriate service delivery to West Indian families. Her findings were that the social service workers gave an exaggerated picture of deprivation, reflecting "the reluctance of Children's Departments to treat West Indians as a separate cultural group with distinct family patterns and attitudes to child-rearing."[3]

FitzHerbert did not follow traditional social work in that she

strongly pushed families to arrange for substitute child care themselves rather than having social workers move children into
agency placement as a first resort. She admits that some risks were
taken in the nature of the alternate care, but she felt they were
inevitable in order to avoid excessive placement and the resultant
alienation from home and family that agency care involved. Fitz-
Herbert concluded:

> The general principle behind these recommendations is that West
> Indian children should be treated differently from non-West Indian.
>   This is a discriminatory proposal, apparently contradicting the
> Government's immigration policy that, once in the country, every
> subject must be treated alike regardless of race or creed. Unless the
> Government wanted to invite genuine racial discrimination in every
> walk of life, this is the only possible overall policy toward immigrants.
> However, it is in fact more of a slogan than a practical policy, and it
> becomes very ambiguous when it needs to be applied. It implies that
> "equal" treatment will produce social equality and opportunities for
> all. This is not necessarily true.[4]

By the early 1970s the problems of the new arrivals in England
began to burden the welfare system, and social workers were increasingly concerned about meeting special needs. In *Social Work
with Immigrants,* Cheetham discusses social work treatment
methods and social policy in relation to the new client groups. She
states, "Social workers sometimes find that their contact with immigrants raises fundamental questions of social work policy and
technique; by throwing into relief assumptions underlying approaches to the solving of problems, immigrants act as a catalyst in
more general thinking about the functions and methods of social
work."[5] Among the policy issues that arise are questions of boundaries, short-term versus long-term help, universal versus selective services, and communication in authority-dependence relationships, preacceptance of "colour," and recognition of client
pain and suffering. In this seminal work Cheetham makes the
case for an ideological approach in social work closer to cultural
pluralism, and she stresses incorporation of cultural content as
well as improved intergroup empathy.

In the same year that Cheetham's work appeared, Triseliotis
gathered several articles and published them under a similar title,
Social Work with Coloured Immigrants and their Families.[6] His particular concern was with the practitioner's need to understand some
of the tensions arising from immigration, and the way in which

sociocultural factors affect social work process. "This knowledge," Triseliotis said, "should help social workers to recognize in what ways coloured immigrant clients are the same as or different from their customary white British clients, and whether specific behaviour is cultural or symptomatic of pathology."[7]

Ethnic factors in social welfare began to receive attention in Great Britain in relation to broader policy issues. The Community Relations Commission, for example, was established under the Race Relations Act of 1968, and its major concerns were breaking down intolerance and prejudice and helping people of different races and cultures to live and work together in harmony. It encouraged the formation of community relations councils, supported full-time community relations officers, and undertook a substantial program of education and publication. Recognizing the involvement of the minority groups with social welfare services, it issued a series of pamphlets and training documents dealing with various aspects of child welfare. The publications show a commingling of racial concerns and issues of service delivery that did not occur on the American scene. Among the titles are the following: *Fostering Black Children: A Policy Document on the Needs of Ethnic Minority Group Children* (1975); *A Home from Home? Some Policy Considerations on Black Children in Residential Care* (1977); *Caring for Under-fives in a Multi-racial Society* (1977); and *Seen but Not Served: Black Youth and the Youth Service* (1977).

Whereas the earlier work of the British social scientists tended to emphasize the cultural knowledge needed in working with minority groups, the Community Relations Commission did not hesitate to discuss mixing–matching issues, and in some cases even matters of decision-making and power for ethnic minorities. The pamphlet on foster care, for example, states:

> The long-term fostering of Black children in an exclusively white setting can also lead to more disturbing psychological problems for the children themselves, deriving out of stresses having to do with race, colour and identity. . . . In white homes, cut off from the Black community, Black children are exposed in their formative years to a process of anglicisation in which they internalize the essentially white values of their English foster-parents. Over time such children may develop a negative image of themselves and after discharge from the fostering situation may find it difficult to relate to their own parents and the Black community without ambivalence and embarrassment— and this happening at the same time as they are being rejected by

the wider society on grounds of race. There have been cases of children....trying to wash themselves white and denying they are Black.... Recruitment of more Black foster parents, as well as placing Black children in Black homes for ethnic identification, are urged.[8]

In the publication on residential care, the development of self-help projects for Black adolescents is discussed. The pamphlet states:

> To some people the idea of self-help raises the difficult question of the desirability of the all-Black children's home. Although there are those who may find the concept varying there is no doubt that some children are at a stage in their lives when such a setting is appropriate.... Not only young West Indians, but Asian girls, for instance, who need care away from home could well benefit from a hostel with an Asian orientation and with Asian staff who would have a thorough understanding of the girl's culture and situation. It may also provide a better framework for group work with parents.... Such specialized homes should preferably not be seen as a last resort when all else has failed, but as part of a long-term treatment plan.[9]

Finally, in relation to mental health services, the commission finds there is limited use of psychiatric services by minority clients, in particular, in the early phases of illness. It states:

> Our interviews with people working in areas where many of the general practitioners belong to the same minority group as their patients revealed that in such areas more routine use is made of the National Health Service and delayed referral is less common. While it is not essential that patient and doctor should belong to the same ethnic or cultural group, it is important that a doctor should be able to appreciate the kind of life that Black people lead in this country. Black doctors and social workers can help their white colleagues to relate better to Black clients."[10]

The illustrations show the emphasis placed in this literature on mixing–matching issues and the implications raised for separate ethnic institutions. This shift from the earlier focus on culture occurred under two conditions. The first change was the involvement of minority persons themselves in the conceptualization of the issues. Second, there was a changed political context for the presentation of these ideas. Both changes were related to the establishment of the Community Relations Commission. The changes noted may have been more in the literature than in the delivery of services, but nonetheless they opened up new areas for discussion, and challenged old stereotypes.

The new British Race Relations Act of 1976 also affected the focus, personnel, and structure of work on ethnicity.[11] The Commission for Racial Equality was established and a strengthened legislative base gave legal power for pressing court action in cases of reported discrimination. The authorization of power of formal investigation was considered to be a major opportunity for the commission to affect change,[12] but the new directions undertaken by the body were not without controversy. One major issue was whether the legislative and court route would not be more effective than educational work in the community. Other questions were raised about whether either would be meaningful without basic changes in the social system.

One provision in the Race Relations Act of 1976 paid particular attention to the mixing-matching component of services to ethnic groups. Although discrimination in employment on the basis of race was prohibited, certain exceptions were noted. The act states that "being of a particular group is a genuine occupational qualification for a job . . . in four circumstances. The first three involve drama, art, and food. The fourth case is when . . . the holder of the job provides persons of that racial group with personal services promoting their welfare, and those services can most effectively be provided by a person of that racial group."[13] It was on the basis of this section that a social service officer in a local borough was able to request a West Indian worker for a teenage group, even though this meant dipping into the list of eligibles rather than taking the top of the list.

The increasing numbers of minority clients posed problems that were new to the traditional British social services. One response was that the British Association of Social Work set up a Special Interest Group on Intercultural Social Work. From their meetings over a five-year period, 1972–77, a series of papers was published that drew attention to differences in cultural patterns as well as to the special problems of specific ethnic groups, particularly West Indians, Pakistanis, and Indians.[14] Among their concerns was the use of interpreters in social work who cannot communicate the meaning of concepts, so that diagnosis and treatment of non-English-speaking clients becomes a process of questionable validity.

Ethnic factors in British child welfare also arise in relation to social policy issues. The government decision implemented in April 1977 to replace family allowance and tax relief for children with a system of tax free child benefits was generally regarded as a forward step to help low-income families. The ethnic catch, however, was that the tax relief had been available for all minor children of the taxpayer, whether in Great Britain or not, and the new child benefit plan only applied to children domiciled in Great Britain. For the thousands of new immigrants who were supporting children in the West Indies and the Indian subcontinent, the new plan would further depress their wage level, since they would not receive the child benefits and they would lose the tax relief. It was an economic issue with ethnic implications because of the populations concerned. The impact was considered to be racially discriminatory, and both the Joint Council for the Welfare of Immigrants and the Child Poverty Action Group in London proposed various options for remediation.[15] This issue was also raised by the Commission for Racial Equality, which stated, "Clearly the Government recognizes that its policy on this question is inherently unjust to ethnic minority parents with dependent children overseas."[16]

Field Visits to Service Programs

The British literature suggested various ways in which ethnicity was relevant to service delivery. Field visits were made to fifteen selected programs in the boroughs of London and elsewhere among concentrations of ethnic people to study the way in which these suggestions were implemented. The results, in British terms, were "patchy." The interviews and field visits were both to traditional and innovative child-welfare programs, adoption, foster care, day care, residential care, and psychiatric services. The programs served West Indian, West African, and Pakistani children and families, and all had particular concerns about the ethnic factor in service delivery.

In the field of adoption, the key study concept of mixing-matching was a major issue. In the sixties increasing numbers of Black children came into care and were available for adoption. The first response was placement in white homes, but increasingly Black mothers giving up babies asked that they be placed in Black adoptive homes. In the area of fostering, Black social workers were concerned with identity issues for young Blacks going into care. Beginning in August 1974 a group of concerned Black and white social workers began to meet regularly to discuss the problems of Black foster children. From these informal sessions there developed a major educational and recruitment campaign for Black foster and adoptive parents, an enterprise called Soul Kids. Activity took place for one year in nine London boroughs, with moderate success and some unanticipated consequences. For example, there was resentment on the part of some community members that the white social service system was expecting the Black community to take on its own service problems—a perception of the campaign never envisaged by the leadership. The portrayal of sad and neglected West Indian children in publicity posters seeking to attract foster parents was considered by some West Indian leaders to be a criticism of the entire community. The steering group reported that it learned two significant lessons. The first was "that it had been naïve to ask the leaders of the Black population to look at the needs of Black children in care in isolation from the wider social problems faced by Black people." The second lesson was that "there is a place for community work alongside casework, even in the comparatively narrow fields of fostering and adoption."[17]

The restriction of this pilot effort to a one-year campaign was an obvious limitation to the number of successful placements. The organizers reported that another outcome was learning about the need to involve ethnic organizations and leaders if a real impact is to be made in the minority communities. These findings relate to the hypotheses of this study. The Soul Kids campaign supported the mixing-matching concept; where it foundered was in relation to questions of decision-making and power. The "matching" slogan "Black homes for Black kids" was not acceptable because it did not deal with the political questions of who decides that this is appropriate and who controls the program. It seems evident that segregation and separatism are defined by whether or not choice is involved, and what options are open to the concerned minority. Even the matching concept will not be acceptable unless the decision-making rests with the ethnic group.

Although the Soul Kids project did not continue, there were repercussions in new programs initiated in both public and voluntary agencies. In one of the London boroughs a special fostering section, manned by a Black social worker, was directed to make special efforts both to find Black homes and to give special services relating to ethnic factors to white foster parents if no Black homes were available. A special group of foster parents with Black children was meeting regularly to discuss both general child-care problems and special needs of Black children. These included identity issues as well as concrete matters such as hair and skin care and preferred foods.

In recruiting and working with West Indian foster parents, cultural factors were taken into account. Recognizing the prevalence of consensual union, marriage certificates were neither required nor requested. Living patterns, such as the West Indian custom of having two living rooms, one for parents and one for children, were interpreted to British social workers who had been concerned when told that foster children were not allowed to use the living room.

An active program of recruitment of Black adoptive parents, called Parents for Children, was being undertaken by the borough social service officers. Separate programs to meet special needs were considered appropriate under public auspices, and in developing these both cultural content and issues of mixing–matching were taken into account. Social work staff, including Black staff, however, expressed opposition to the establishment of entirely separate agencies for Black children since it was felt that each group can learn from the other, and each needs to understand the other's point of view.

An African social worker in this public agency warned of oversimplification on the basis of color in the matter of Black children and families. She said they did not place African children with West Indian parents because of cultural differences and because of antagonisms between the two groups. African parents would object to a West Indian fostering their child, she said, in part because the Africans identify with middle-class British culture and see the West Indians as a lower class. As for the West Indians, she said they often feel unfriendly to the Africans, and she quoted a West Indian saying about Africans, "If your great-grandparent hadn't sold my great-grandparent, I wouldn't be in this fix." This exchange supports the hypothesis that ethnic factors in service delivery can only be understood in terms of the relevant social and political background.

In addition to the work of the public agency, there are voluntary groups in Britain interested in promoting more appropriate services for minority children. One of these is an independent adoption agency with a history of nontraditional support from agnostic and humanist groups. This agency had experience with interracial placements and with the Soul Kids campaign. It was in the process of negotiating an agreement with a public agency to develop a special program for placement of Black children in Black homes.

In discussing cultural content, the director was concerned about stereotyping the ethnic minorities. She pointed out that the West Indian community itself did not have a homogenous identity, and there were differences among the islands as well as between immigrants to Britain from rural and urban areas. Furthermore, some of the biggest problems in child care are those that are intergenerational. The pattern of leaving young children behind in the islands for years to be cared for by relatives creates misunderstanding and conflict. Those children are not sure where they belong or who their parents are. Then if they experience foster care, there is further confusion. In the islands it is not uncommon for people to care for the children of others on an informal basis, and the biological parents are not cut off. Here the system is legal and structured, and parents cannot understand why they cannot have casual contact with and access to their own children just because they are in placement.

In discussing the desirability of separate agencies on ethnic grounds, this agency director had "an open mind." She said many Blacks were not in favor of separate agencies because they would institutionalize differences. Separate programs, however, could help Black youngsters establish their own identity. The plan to involve an independent voluntary agency in a separate program for Blacks in association with the public sector was seen as less threatening to the Black community than a program run by the government. This model had been suggested in several other settings, and it can be hypothesized that separate programs on an ethnic basis are more likely to occur under voluntary than under public auspices.

Warnings about oversimplification in discussing issues of ethnicity and social services have been given, and a good case in point is the fostering of children of African students, who are in Britain for extended periods in order to qualify in technical and professional fields. In this situation both practice and policy child-welfare issues arise, and they are played out in a complicated context of cultural differences, historical antagonisms, and modern-day prejudices.

Information on the needs of this group came from interviews with the African director of the organization designated to serve families of African students. In terms of the three agency factors conceptualized in our study, neither cultural content nor mixing–matching in relation to children were critical issues. The important factor was decision-making and power—the right of the African group to state its needs and supervise the kinds of services it feels are appropriate.

The special problems faced by African students were stated by Boateng, speaking at a seminar, "The African Child in Great Britain," held in Ibadan, Nigeria, in 1975. He said:

> The University lecturer was only interested in the student's academic performance and not the social reasons why he failed his examinations: the hospital matron, being unmarried herself, would not accept the new applicant to the nursing school if she knew that she was married and so the new entrant kept this side of her life private and confidential; sponsoring parents at home in Africa had no knowledge of the problems involved in studying with a wife and children and therefore simply counted the years to coincide with the day when their son should have returned home with the expected academic laurels; the attitude of the African High Commissions in London was that of fostering diplomatic and trade relations between their country and the host country and that in any case the students came to study and not to raise a family; the children's legislation in England gave priority to children from broken homes, and until the overburdened wife had run away, leaving father and children to fend for themselves, the local authorities and their social workers insisted they were not empowered to come to the aid of the family in difficulties, and, in any case, they had enough family problems from members of the local community on their plate; the British Council provided social and cultural entertainments as well as accommodations for sponsored students but had no facilities for children; the Christian churches were good at providing cups of tea after Sunday services but this had no bearing on the problem. In short it was a hidden problem with a tacit conspiracy to keep it so, as everyone pretended not to know let alone attempting to solve it. The agonised student parent preferred it so, for fear of letting the cat out of the bag and in many cases losing his grant.[18]

The cultural context is not hard to understand. Africans married young, were expected to have children directly after marriage, needed training outside their country, and used the traditional African system of fostering as a child-care option. Two major problems arose. One was whether Black identity was maintained in the use of white foster homes, and the second was the policy conflict between the British social service opposition to long-term fostering and pressure toward permanency for children in care. This position was meaningful for British white children neglected by parents but had very different implications for the Africans, whose legal rights to their own children were threatened.

African parents were reported to prefer white British foster parents and to reject the idea of West Indians fostering their children. They did not see West Indian culture as African, and they related more to the British way of doing things. When the African program director was asked about identity, his response was that African students have no problem of identity—they know who they are, they know where they came from, and they know they will be going home. It is the West Indian immigrants who have the problems of identity, and the sense of the interview was that the Africans didn't want the West Indians "messing up" their children.

In spite of the preference for the British foster parent, it was admitted that problems of communication did arise. The white foster parent does not understand the African extended family, for example, and is surprised and dismayed when the parental visit includes cousins, aunts, and uncles. Yet if visiting is not carried out, the children lose contact with their native culture. Patterns of relating to children differ. The Africans are not inhibited; they keep their children physically close to them, and in the evening they take them along to parties and social events. Yet the African is not permissive with his children; the African child is to be seen but not heard. The British way is different. Children are seen less but heard more. These differences can be confusing to all parties: to foster and biological parents and also to children.

The student society's program has several aspects, including an education program in African countries to inform prospective students of what to expect. In Britain they offer supervised foster care to children of African students for a maximum of eighteen months, with the criterion that there must be regular parental visiting, preferably weekly or biweekly, but no less than monthly. Africans are also encouraged to care for their own children, and housing, day-care and social services are offered to some families if they do so.

An important service for the African student is housing, and one setting that was visited accommodated fifty families living in flats. In order to obtain their apartments, these families had to agree not to place their children in foster care. But because often the mothers were also studying or working, day care was needed. This was provided in a day-care center in an apartment in the complex. This was in fact a separate service for Black children, who were mainly Nigerian with a few Ghanians. The staff was mixed, two African and one white English teacher and two West Indian aides. The director reported that parents had much confidence in the center, and the staff worked with parents on child-rearing and cultural differences. One mother, for example, gave a cane to a teacher with instructions to hit her child if he didn't eat. The teacher returned the cane to the mother, saying, "We don't hit the children" and explaining the center's discipline procedures. She did not actually tell the mother not to hit her child at home, but she hoped that by explaining why children were not hit in school the lesson would be learned.

The day-care director regretted that her center did not have the space, equipment, or toys that British children in the government-supported schools had. But she doubted if the children feel deprived, because they feel "safe and free," and because of the "caring attitude" of the staff to the children. This was a positive example of a separate service, where all three factors of cultural content, mixing–matching, and decision-making and power were under control of the ethnic group. Yet the director did not support separate institutions for the country as a whole. She felt it was good to mix, if possible, since that was the only way to learn about each other. Perhaps the experience of apartheid was too close to the Africans to allow a positive position on government support for ethnic agencies. This encounter reinforced the hypothesis that the separate institution should only exist by the choice of the ethnic group. In structural terms, this means separate institutions may be an appropriate choice for a voluntary agency but not for a public one.

The policy issue affecting West African children in foster care arose from sections of the newly adopted Children Act of 1975.[19] Like the Child Benefits issue, already discussed in relation to West Indian and Asian children, this issue was the result of an anomaly in that a piece of legislation designed to improve the status of British children had an adverse affect on ethnic minorities. The relevant sections of the Children Act refer to the introduction of custodianship, a status between foster care and adoption. The foster parent may request such status if a child has been living in the home for three years. If granted, the parent cannot remove the child from the foster home without a court order, but unlike adoption, government payments for child support continue. The custodian foster parent can relinquish custody at will, having no enduring legal or financial responsibilities to the child. This was a plan designed to encourage permanency for British children in foster care, where there was no active natural-parent involvement. The African student family, however, who may spend four or five years in England, wants foster child care during that time and has every intention of taking its children back to Africa. The attachment of white British foster parents to African children they have fostered has led to what have been called "tug-of-love" court cases, where African parents had to fight in the courts for the right to resume care of their children. And they have often lost.

This situation is of great concern to the leaders of the student society, who see the problems of loss of identity by African children, loss to Africa of young people who have no contact with their culture, and further suffering by the African children if they elect to remain in the British setting, where their wider acceptance as adults is problematic.

Boateng, speaking at the Nigeria Centre in London, basically advised students against placement of children in foster care in Britain. He said, "If you cannot look after your children yourself it is best to send them to the extended family at home in Africa, otherwise by the end of your studies you might have lost your child to the foster parents."[20] He concludes, "Help us to bring out the African children from the foster home in Britain, because we prefer for ourselves and our children independence with danger to servitude in tranquility."[21]

The matter of custodianship was seen not only as a psychological hardship but as an actual threat to group survival. The issue was raised by the minority group leadership, and it involved the factor of decision-making and power. Where this particular case differed from others, however, was that the identity was not "Black" but "African." This is more evidence of the dangers of stereotyping, and further supports the hypothesis that ethnic issues cannot be dealt with outside the political and social contexts in which they arise.

THE TEENAGE ETHNIC CLIENT

Social work with teenagers is complicated by many factors—normal adolescent changes, generational conflicts, educational difficulties, vocational and job impediments. And there are the additional problems of delinquency, sexual relationships, drugs and alcohol. Where there are also ethnic issues, all of these factors can be exacerbated because of difficulties in communication, problems of identity and scapegoating, and a further sense of alienation from the opportunity structure. These problems were seen in several neighborhoods in London, and also in Bradford, in relation to West Indian and Asian youth. The social services recognize some of the special needs, and in a "patchy" way are trying to develop programs more appropriate to the problems of minority teenagers.

The generational differences that occur in almost all societies are exacerbated in Great Britain because they are part of the broader issue of culture conflict. Thus the Black parent from Jamaica, raised in a strict manner, expects his own child, who may have recently come from the islands as a teenager and is exposed to British youth culture, to accept parental discipline as at home. The Pakistani family, with its strict code of behavior, including arranged marriages and separate schools for girls and boys, also has a new problem with rebellious teenagers. To accommodate problem youth and difficult adolescents, there are group homes run by local authorities, and one of these was visited in an area of London that had been the scene of earlier racial riots. Of the twenty-five youth from seven to seventeen years living in this group home, one-half were West Indian, one-fourth native English, and one-fourth of mixed parentage. Being in an area of ethnic mix, the youth mingle freely with local families. To some extent this is encouraged, although it can lead to problems. The director reported that there was widespread use of marijuana in all-night parties in the community, which included children as well as adults, and this sometimes involved the residents of the group home.

There are important problems of identity for these youngsters. Many were born in Britain and resent being treated as immigrants. One teenage resident of the house was asked if he came from Jamaica and he said, "No, Birmingham." On the other hand there are some Black youth who were born in England and deny British allegiance, seeing their roots in Africa.

When asked what was the best thing he had done, the director of the house, who was white, said, "Get Black staff." When he came to the house two years before, the children were 90 percent Black, and the staff was 100 percent white. There had been serious incidents of racial violence. By recruiting Black staff, now 50 percent, it has been possible to reduce conflicts that have a racial base and work with youngsters to separate out which grievances are because of race and which are because of individual behavior of the residents. The West Indian staff was reported to have more understanding of the children's needs and backgrounds. On the other hand, when asked what didn't work, the director answered, "Indian staff with West Indian kids. They see them as neither Black nor English and they just don't stick it." Problems had also occurred between residents at this mixed house and Black youngsters at another group home in the area run by "Black Power" West Indians. The second house is a residential voluntary setting that is all Black, and they are critical of the integrated home with its white director.

The hostel visited was very concerned with cultural content relevant to the West Indian children. Posters, art, music in the house, and recreational activities all reflected this awareness. The need for skin and hair care for Blacks was understood, and even though no special funds were allocated, the director maneuvered his budget to buy hair pomade, six dollars per jar, for use of the Black teenagers.

Cultural factors were present in foods that were served and in the entry in the neighborhood carnival to be held on Easter Monday. Myths and superstitions also surfaced. For example, the director found the girls moving their beds away from the windows when there was a full moon shining in. They had heard this could make a girl pregnant.

Differences in language can be evident even when the same written form is used. Dialect, idiom, and speech patterns vary greatly between the islands and Great Britain, and the West Indians can vary their speech, depending on circumstances. One teenage youth in the hostel reported speaking "in tongue" when talking to his friends, who understood him. He was asked if his social worker understood him, and what he spoke with her. "She understands the part of me that speaks English," he said, "and my friends understand the part that speaks in tongue. That is when I feel more powerful." The director had never heard this youngster speak "in tongue" in the hostel.

Although the staff supported cultural content and mixing–matching in the group home, separate institutions on ethnic grounds were not favored. The director felt this would harden differences and give no opportunity for youth of different minorities to learn about each other. Cultural pluralism was the ideology supported, although the development of ethnic identity was seen as a needed support base for the teenagers.

The dilemmas of meeting ethnic needs were discussed by British social workers in another London borough, also an area with a history of racial conflict. They pointed out that there were problems in both directions. Sometimes a Black client will make a specific request for a white home helper, saying they give better service. And there have been problems in the street with Black social workers who overidentify with the adolescents with whom they work. In spite of this, the Black worker was highly valued. A new male Black worker was being requested by the Social Service Department under the terms of the Race Relations Act, which allows specification of ethnic group if it is deemed to be in the interest of the clients served.

This borough social welfare office was concerned with a wide spectrum of services, and the community relations office was particularly involved in ethnic issues. A West Indian parents' group met regularly for counseling and help in working with their teenagers. West Indians, however, do not want to be seen as a problem community, so they resist too much emphasis on pathology. This had to be considered in setting up programs with an ethnic focus.

In this same London neighborhood there was another agency, with support from public funds but under voluntary auspices, which was Black run and dedicated to the Black community. The latter group had its origins in a community confrontation, when squatters groups took over empty buildings in opposition to the local authority. In time the dissidents were recognized as a formal group that could meet needs of the Black community, especially the youth. Grants were made available for the development of a rehabilitation program for Black youth who have trouble adjusting to authority, and a residential center was established. Forty youth live in this hostel, others come and go as needed. In addition an alternate school was set up to help the dropout youngsters. When asked about the success rate, the director made the point that this Black agency was a "place of last resort" for the delinquent and problem youth. They get the youngsters no one else can manage, and then are expected to produce substantial success rates. It is hard to get a realistic evaluation of the operations of such an ethnic agency, since it starts out with so many handicaps—the most troubled youth, the least resources, the poorest facilities. That it functions at all and holds on to the youngsters is success in itself.

A major problem noted by the agency director was the culture conflict between the life in the islands and in Great Britain. This showed up particularly in methods of discipline, and affected the educational process. In the islands, discipline was strict, and teachers as well as parents could beat their children. Here it is different; the British teachers are young and inexperienced, the schools are crowded, and corporal punishment is not approved. The children, who come from the schools in the islands, are disruptive and there are no controls. As a result the large majority of Black children, according to the agency director, are not being educated.

The parents are caught in both the generational conflict and the culture conflict. They do not take kindly to the white social workers, who they see as overidentifying with the rebellious teenagers, and interfering in family matters. A Black worker can function in a different way, according to the agency director. As an example, he said if he walked down the street and saw one of "his" boys fooling with a car or doing something else he shouldn't he would "clip him, cuff him, and then talk to him." "If a white did that," he said, "there would be murder."

Black programs can be more responsive to accustomed patterns of group behavior. For example, in the youth hostel they tried the 10:00 P.M. curfew, which was typical in the government-sponsored settings. It didn't work. So they experimented with an 11:00 P.M. curfew during the week, and a 2:00 A.M. curfew on weekends. That worked, and if there were infractions they were dealt with. The important thing was not the hour but the concept of conforming to reasonable regulations. A matching policy is followed in staff recruitment. Of the staff of twenty-two, three are white and nineteen Black. Black staff is preferred because these youngsters need to identify with other Blacks who have "made it."

This neighborhood setting had as strong an ethnic base as any seen in all three factors being studied: culture, mixing–matching, and decision-making and power. Yet even here the director was against the general establishment of separate institutions for minority youth. He said that many West Indians have made it because their parents have worked within the system, and he sees the ethnic agency as needed to try to get the dropout youth back into a multiracial society. Part of this effort is to impress on the children pride in themselves and acceptance of responsibility. He said, "The Africans think they are better because the West Indians are the sons of slaves. We say, forget your forefathers, take responsibility for yourselves."

At this agency, and at the alternative school, which was also visited, there was little support for the official government Commission on Racial Equality. Legislation "to make people love you" was not appreciated. It was considered more important that the minority youth develop skills so that people would accept them for their abilities, not because they felt sorry for them. The director of the alternate school conceptualized a further problem with which the ethnic programs must cope. He said that the youth are both "affected by the culture, as well as rejected by it." Thus they take on the values and contradictions of the very society that excludes them, acting out Groucho Marx's comment that he wouldn't join any club that would admit him. West Indian youth were caught in their own conflicts about wanting to be part of the society that rejected them, and the ethnic agency sought to strengthen their own identity, seeing that as preliminary to full participation.

SPECIALIZED NEEDS OF ASIANS

Ethnic factors associated with delivery of services to the Asian people in Great Britain, primarily Indians and Pakistanis, took on a somewhat different form from those of other groups. Family organization was strong, and extended-family structures still prevailed. Issues of adoption, foster care, and residential care for young children were not top priority. There were serious problems for teenagers, however, arising from both generational and cultural conflicts. Psychiatric problems were increasing, with British medi-

cal and social service personnel having difficulties in distinguish-
ing cultural phenomena and custom from pathological behavior,
and indeed in identifying what is pathology within the separate
cultures of the patient population.

At an Indian Youth Conference at Sheffield University in
1976, Anwar reported on a survey conducted on behalf of the
Community Relations Commission in which over one thousand
Asian youth and almost one thousand parents were interviewed.[22]
The major cultural issues were arranged marriages, religion,
dress, education, the mother tongue, freedom, and leisure activities. Both parents and children favored marrying within the
ethnic group. Parents preferred sending daughters home to the
Indian subcontinent to be married, but girls of sixteen years and
over were opposed to this. Dress also led to disagreements. Many
children at school were excluded from physical education because
traditional dress was worn. Sikhs had trouble with the law because
of the requirement that crash helmets be worn while riding
motorcycles and the helmets could not fit over the traditional
turban. Parents preferred separate recreation and school facilities
for boys and girls, but these were not available in most localities.

The rising number of Asian immigrants brought clients of a
new kind to the psychiatric facilities in Britain. Although the
numbers are small in terms of the general population, they posed
problems for the treatment services because of language barriers.
One hospital in Britain, a psychiatric facility with three hundred
beds, recognized the special problems of the Asian population
and developed a separate service for this group. This facility was
visited to see how ethnic factors were incorporated in psychiatric
services.

Focusing first on cultural needs, the new program quickly became involved in mixing–matching issues. The most obvious problem in traditional service delivery was language—typically the
treatment staff spoke English and the patients spoke a variety of
Indian languages. Mental illness carries a serious stigma in the
Asian community. Even when patients come for help, it is often
difficult to develop appropriate diagnoses because cultural patterns and behavior under stress differ substantially from the white
British experience.

In introducing the new ethnic program to the psychiatric hospital, personnel at all levels were educated about cultural differences among communities. Information on diets, languages,

religions, and customs was given to staff. Interdisciplinary teams worked on ethnic recruitment, and language facility in Urdu, Hindi, Bengali, or Punjabi was an important credential. Rather than use professional interpreters, functioning staff in all categories—including nurses, chaplains, social workers, medical doctors, pharmacologists, and psychiatrists—with knowledge of Asian languages are involved. An occupational therapist is employed to do cookery. The patients tell her what food to buy, and they themselves prepare the Asian dishes.

It is difficult to measure success in an experiment of this kind. Reduced patient intake cannot be anticipated; in fact, the introduction of ethnic services will probably increase intake. The more receptive a service is to special needs, the more likely it is to expand the hospital census. It is therefore possible that a community with a better program in terms of meeting patient demands might show up in the national statistics as having a higher rate of mental illness if the criterion is psychiatric hospitalizations. For this reason, in its early stages this program can only be judged in terms of clinical impressions and case records. A day of observation, patient rounds, and staff discussion indicated a level of practice that was highly sensitive to the ethnic background of patients, and a treatment staff that was keenly aware of the complexities of the problems.

Two case conferences that were observed, including patient interviews, will illustrate how ethnicity was involved in both diagnosis and treatment. The first concerned a Pakistani girl of fifteen who ran away from home and threatened to kill herself if she was returned. She wanted to be sent to a children's hostel. She knew she had brought shame on her family by running away, but she could not help herself. An arranged agreement had been settled when she was eleven with a boy in Pakistan she had never met. Her main fear is that her parents will send her back there to consummate a marriage. She hears voices and sees visions, but says this is not so special, and that all her family talks to spirits. This case of teenage runaway was reported to be typical—the clinic sees two or three a week.

The problems here are both psychiatric and ethnic, and, as the senior psychiatrist said, the difficult decision is to determine what is culture and what is "crazy." Often the clinic sees runaways who are not mentally ill but are rebelling against rigid patterns imposed by parents that are in conflict with British social norms. If cases are dismissed on grounds that there is no illness and the girls are returned home, their parents may put them on the next plane to Pakistan. On the other hand, British social workers, who tend to identify with the youngsters and their complaints, may overestimate the teenagers capacity to make it on their own, and too often the girls who break ties with their families may find prostitution their only option.

The second case involved a young Bengali widow who had suffered a breakdown following her husband's death, when she had to face what was expected of her: marriage to her dead husband's older brother. That he was at least forty years older and already had a wife was not relevant—he would be doing the expected thing in keeping his brother's widow and children in the family. The young widow, however, had a new plan. She has a friend with an unmarried brother in Bengal who wishes to come to England. The widow seeks an arranged marriage—the young man could enter the country, although after a long wait, as her fiancé, and she could leave the house of her elderly brother-in-law with her own young children. The psychiatrist must decide whether this is pathology or sensible planning.

The ethnic programs in the psychiatric setting incorporate both cultural and matching factors in delivering services. They are, in fact, frequently intertwined, since the helping person with language facility will usually be of the same ethnic group. Interpreters are not considered appropriate, since only the trained person of the same culture as the patient can grasp the nuances of patient responses. By utilizing matching at all levels, although with a team rather than on a one-to-one basis, chances of an appropriate diagnosis and treatment plan are enhanced. Decision-making and power remain in the hands of the British Chief of Service, but the team approach, which is both interdisciplinary and intercultural, leads to sharing power at different levels of operations.

There are also situations in which power is held by the ethnic group, and it is necessary for the majority culture to make the accommodation. At the psychiatric facility visited there had been unexplained reactions to psychotropic medications. It was finally realized that some patients were also taking native medicines from the local Hakim, the "medicine man," which interacted badly with Western drugs. A Pakistani pharmacologist became involved in a study of this interaction of native and Western drugs, and hospital staff worked with patients to try to learn what specific medicines they were taking. Attempts were made to relate to the Hakim, to study his products, some of which were entering the country as "health foods." Since no controls could be exerted over the patterns of native medication, it was the Western medication that had to be watched to see that it did not interact negatively with whatever patients were taking.

An important complication, not only in this program but in working with any immigrants with different cultural and ethnic backgrounds, is that there is no clear baseline. Instead there is an interaction between the old and the new, and the life-style that emerges inevitably accomodates both. Thus knowing the culture of the Bengali, the West Indian, or the West African is necessary, but not sufficient, to provide social services appropriate for living in Great Britain. Laws on monogamy and on compulsory school attendance, for example, are likely to be enforced even if they conflict with the immigrant culture because they have special significance to the host country. But habits of food, taste, socializing, and child-rearing will persist as long as they remain primary group functions and avoid the bureaucracy.

The accommodation of the ethnic group to the new culture, however, is more likely to occur than the reverse process. But a British melting pot is an unlikely prospect; the cultures are too fixed and the people too heterogeneous. Furthermore, it hasn't worked well in more likely situations, such as the Irish, as long as there are political differences. Economic issues are also critical to intergroup and racial relations. Many of the West Indian adults whose teenage children are now part of the problem were themselves recruited from the islands for employment in such industries as transport at a time when there was a tight labor supply in Britain. It is when the job market constricts that newcomers are resented.

Legislation may liberalize or restrict the problems of the immigrants in Britain, but it will not remove the need for social services. How these are delivered will reflect both the stance of the minority groups and the attitudes of the larger population. The question is whether British society will try to retain a homogeneous quality while accommodating to pockets of minority people, or whether there will be substantial movement to an ideology of cultural pluralism, with appreciation of the benefits of a pluralistic society. The minority groups also face a dilemma—separate services to meet special needs might be easier to achieve if the former route is taken, full acceptance in the larger society depends on the pluralistic ideology and may carry fewer targeted benefits. The issue may be one of timing. Will separate short-term programs strengthen the groups for eventual acceptance, or will they divert attention from the long-term goals?

Notes

1. Ruth Glass, *Newcomers: The West Indians in London* (London: Allen and Unwin, 1960).
2. Katrin FitzHerbert, *West Indian Children in London.* Occasional Papers on Social Administration No. 19 (London: G. Bell and Sons, 1967).
3. Ibid., p. 107.
4. Ibid., p. 110.
5. Juliet Cheetham, *Social Work with Immigrants* (London: Routledge & Kegan Paul, 1972), p. 172.
6. J. P. Triseliotis, ed., *Social Work with Coloured Immigrants and Their Families* (London: Oxford University Press, 1972).
7. Ibid., p. vii.
8. *Fostering Black Children: A Policy Document on the Needs of Ethnic Minority Group Children* (London: Community Relations Commission, 1975), pp. 23–34.
9. *A Home from Home? Some Policy Considerations on Black Children in Residential Care* (London: Community Relations Commission, 1977), pp. 25–26.
10. *Aspects of Mental Health in a Multi-Cultural Society* (London: Community Relations Commission, 1976), pp. 32–33.
11. *Race Relations Act 1976* (London: HMSO, 1977), chap. 74.
12. *Strategy Statement: A Programme for Action* (London: Commission for Racial Equality, 1977).
13. *Race Relations Act*, pt. II, sec. 5, subsec. 2, para. (d).
14. *Studies in Inter-Cultural Social Work* (Birmingham, England: BASW Publications, 1977).
15. John Plummer, *Divide and Deprive: A Report on the Implications of Government Proposals to Withdraw Child Tax Allowances and Deny Child Benefits to Immigrant Parents whose Dependent Children Live Overseas* (London: Joint Council for the Welfare of Immigrants and Child Poverty Action Group, 1978).
16. *Child Benefit—But Not for All?*, Commission for Racial Equality, London, February 1978.
17. *Report of the Steering Group of The Soul Kids Campaign: London, 1975–76* (London: Association of British Adoption and Fostering Agencies, 1977).
18. Report of a seminar on "The African Child in Great Britain," Ibadan, Nigeria, 1–3 March 1975, mimeographed (London: Commwealth Student's Children Society and the Department of Sociology, University of Ibadan, 1975), p. 5.
19. *Children Act 1975* (London: HMSO, 1977), chap. 72.

20. B. B. Boateng, "Commonwealth Students' Children in the United Kingdom" (Lecture at Nigeria Centre, London, January 29, 1977), p. 9.
21. Ibid., p. 10.
22. Muhammed Anwar, "The Problem of the Generation Gaps in the Asian Community," in *Leadership and Media in the Asian Community* (Report of a conference, National Association of Indian Youth, Sheffield University, 3–5 September 1976).

Part IV

The Typology

8

Toward a Typology for Ethnic Services

The typology for incorporating ethnic factors in social welfare is emerging, and it is relevant to all five groups studied. This is a concept whose time has come. All over the country there is evidence that ethnicity is becoming a more recognized part of service delivery.

For example. In September 1979, the *Los Angeles Times* ran the following story:

Department of Adoptions Forms Chicano Unit

A new "Chicano Unit"—a special staff of bilingual, bicultural Spanish-speaking adoption workers—has been formed at the Los Angeles County Department of Adoptions, director Helen Ramirez announced. "The unit was created because our children and the adoptive applicants, as well as birth parents who are considering placing a child with the agency for adoption, all need to have workers who understand their cultural background and their language," said Dolores Rodriguez, who will direct the new unit.[1]

The attitude survey reported in chapter 4 showed substantial support for bilingual–bicultural programs. What is new in Los Angeles, however, is that a unit designed to give such services was established within a county government office. The implications

187

reach beyond the parents and children involved. To establish such a unit anywhere in the public sector means coping with civil service rules, seniority, special qualifications, and possibly union contracts. What was considered to be impossible ten years ago is now only difficult.

For example.   In June 1979, the Puerto Rican Association for Community Affairs (PRACA) held a conference in New York City that focused on poverty and foster care. Judge Gilbert Ramirez, who addressed the group, called for "a little bit less of racism, paternalism and custodianism." New York State Commissioner of Social Services, Barbara Blum, agreed there was need for the kind of "cultural sensitivity the public sector has not always exhibited."[2] Thus two officials publicly endorsed consideration of ethnicity and recognized the deficits of the presumed equity of the public services.

The Puerto Rican Association has moved far beyond just raising ethnic issues as a protest gesture. What is new here is that an ethnic association has taken on the service delivery job. In response to the lack of recognition by traditional agencies of the special needs of Puerto Rican children PRACA has founded its own child-care program, Criemos los Nuestros, ("Let Us Raise Our Own"), which places Hispanic children in Spanish-speaking homes. Also new is that this is a program run by an ethnic group with public funding.

This example speaks to all three factors raised in the agency study reported in chapter 3. The service is concerned with cultural issues, in particular language; with matching of child and foster parent on ethnic lines; and, through its parent organization, with issues of consciousness and ethnic identity. Not only are these issues joined, but the question of separate agencies also arises. In this case the separate effort has voluntary ethnic agency sponsorship, although child support comes from government funds. The conference at which Judge Ramirez and Commissioner Blum spoke gave the ethnic agency movement visibility, and the involvement of public officials gave credibility to their decision to "raise their own" with public funds.

For example.   On May 5, 1979, Public Law 95–608, the Indian Child Welfare Act of 1978, was implemented. This legislation was primarily designed to prevent unwarranted removal of Indian children from their homes, to mandate recognition of the authority of tribal courts, and to establish standards for the placement of Indian children in both foster care and adoption. The act requires that in any involuntary proceeding in a state court regarding an Indian child both the parents and the tribe must be notified of the right to intervene. In addition it holds that where an Indian child is a ward of a tribal court, the Indian tribe shall retain exclusive jurisdiction, regardless of the residence of the child. This is a highly significant provision since it does not limit tribal jurisdiction to children on reservations. In adoption placements of an Indian child preference must be given to a placement with a member of the child's extended family, other members of the child's tribe, or other Indian families. In foster placement the same preferences are stated, with the addition of a fourth alternative, an institution for children approved by an Indian tribe or operated by an Indian organization that has a program suitable to meet the Indian child's needs.

This is legislation where the intent is clear. The usual child-welfare shibboleths of "best interests of the child" and "psychological parent," each based on a case decision, are subordinated to the ethnic issues. Cultural factors, matching rather than mixing, and group identity and survival are all involved. They are to be implemented in separate ethnic agencies, backed by national legislation. The rationale is that the child's best interest cannot be attained without reference to his or her group identity.

There is powerful legitimization here for ethnic services, but how it will work in practice depends on other factors, including availability of funds and effective service systems. One caution is that the concept of ethnic services may be a necessary, but not a sufficient, basis for good care. To say that all Indian teenagers in trouble are under the jurisdiction of tribal groups is not to say that the tribes have either the money or the staff resources to meet the needs of these youngsters. One complication is that the legislation is federal, but social services vary from state to state, and there is great unevenness in the availability and quality of programs for youth. The implementation of the Indian Child Welfare Act will be a test of the national commitment to ethnic services for this group.

For example.   In recent years there has been an influx of thousands of new Chinese immigrants to New York City. To meet the needs, the Chinatown Planning Council established a series of school-age day-care centers to care for children of working mothers. By May 1978 the council was responsible for seven such centers, serving over seven hundred children, and there were eight hundred more applicants on their waiting lists. Although accepting traditional child development concepts, these centers stressed family life, parent participation, and Chinese language and cultural programs. Most of the staff are bilingual. Although the primary thrust was for the Asian immigrant child, these centers are open to all children in the area, regardless of race, color, or creed.

What is new in this program is that it has an ethnic focus and is sponsored by a neighborhood organization mainly representing one group, but it maintains an open door to others in the cachement area. This model is of particular relevance to mixed communities in the inner city where there are families of different ethnic origins. In this case the Chinatown Planning Council represents geographic rather than ethnic boundaries. The program and policy reflect the ethnicity of the neighborhood residents, but since the residents are not entirely homogeneous, place must be made for members of other groups.

Where there is a mix of groups, even if one is dominant, new issues arise. These relate to how to incorporate all the factors of culture, matching, and identity within the framework of the multiethnic agency. Some mechanisms for shared power need to be worked out so that the "minority within the minority" does not experience the same isolation and alienation felt by the "minority within the majority."

For example.   In 1976 Barbara Solomon, professor of social work at the University of Southern California, published *Black Empowerment*.[3] This is a work that tries in a systematic way to translate the "power" concept to a practice base. She suggests that the social work role with Black clients is to facilitate and "empower" the recipients of services to function in their own behalf. Enabling people to fulfill needs is not a new idea for practitioners,—what is new here is the explicit use of the Black experience, the awareness by the worker of ethnic issues, and the joining of practice theory and ethnic factors to facilitate service delivery.

The field has moved since this study began in 1974, when we were widely advised not to undertake it, since "ethnicity was too sensitive and controversial" and "no one would respond" to our questions either by mail or in person. Since the meager pickings of the 1963 literature search, the faces of the professional journals have changed, and it is the rare issue that does not have an article on one or another aspect of ethnic needs or concerns. Ethnic factors in service delivery are also discussed, but usually only for one ethnic group and not in terms of a typology for generalized services.

The exception to this is in the substantial efforts of social workers supporting the "new pluralism," a phenomenon primarily associated with concerns of white ethnic and religious groups. Leadership in this work has been given by the Institute on Pluralism and Group Identity of the American Jewish Committee, which has a substantial publication list on ethnicity in relation to mental health, education, and occupations. In a paper presented at the Council of Social Work Education Annual Meeting in 1976, Friedman discussed the controversy which has arisen around the validity of the "new ethnics." He stated that many of the social scientists who "label rising group identity and group pride as healthy and appropriate behavior for Blacks, Indians and Chicanos" suggest that it has "unhealthy connotations when it is expressed by Italians, Poles, Jews, and other white ethnics. Their rationale is that the nonwhite groups are disadvantaged and the others advantaged."[4] Friedman suggests that this is a simplistic approach to the issue of ethnicity and that "the new pluralism should not be discussed as bigotry in the service of class exploitation."[5]

Another disservice to the "white ethnic" cause is to consider it only as an attempt to join the bandwagon of affirmative action, and secure a piece of the pie. There are political opportunists in all groups, but it is no more a disgrace to change your name from Cohen to Conant than to change it from Ort to Ortiz. Both are responses to social pressures. The preference for the familiar, the sense of consciousness of kind and generational continuity is pervasive among all groups. What is familiar, of course, may vary. In Jerusalem I heard the wife of a prominent Soviet emigré to Israel, when asked to what she attributed the excellent adjustment of her family to the move they made, reply "We get along well because here, as in all countries, the intelligentsia relate to other intelligentsia." Within the broader political framework that was what was familiar, that was where she found her kind.

This need for belonging for the white ethnic is particularly keen for the elderly, and with good reason. We have discussed Litwak and Dono's suggestion that ethnicity can be an intervening variable between primary groups and bureaucracies, and the nursing home and other facilities for the elderly are substituting for what in the past was mainly a primary-group function. The need continues in the bureaucratic structure of the modern hospital. A ninety-year-old member of my family was recently admitted by ambulance to emergency care in a Catholic, primarily Italian-run hospital. In the corridors of the intensive-care unit I found a young intern with a yarmulke on his head, in the Orthodox Jewish tradition. I asked him to watch for when the elderly patient regains consciousness and to say a few words in Yiddish to him. The problem, I explained, is that he doesn't know where he is, and if he opens his eyes and sees the crucifix on the wall above, he may think he has died and gone to the wrong heaven.

If ethnicity is a valid concern for white ethnics, then what is the justification for claiming that their concerns are different from those of the other groups in this study: Blacks, Asian Americans, American Indians, Puerto Ricans, Chicanos? There are two answers to this question, one related to social indicators, the other to social institutions. The five groups studied have been particularly disadvantaged in all sectors of our economy, and each has faced a kind of institutional racism not now experienced in the United States by Caucasians of European background. The minority groups are disproportionately high among those in poverty, and among clients for social services. Development of a delivery system that allows for their access to entitlements is a high priority for the social welfare community.

Another way to respond was expressed by Leon Chestang, who was a discussant on a report of this study at a session of the National Conference on Social Welfare.[6] Asked the very same question, Why is it different?, he responded with reference to the two worlds in which Black and other minority people live. He described the two worlds experienced by all people—the nurturing world of home and family, and the sustaining world of school, job, and the larger society, a dichotomy with some elements of the primary group–bureaucratic organization already defined. Chestang suggested that there is a qualitative difference in the way in which the white and Black ethnic moves back and forth between these two worlds. For the white, his ethnicity may be easily expressed in the nurturing world and forgotten in the sustaining one. But the Black, he said, takes his Blackness with him. Solomon, in *Black Empowerment*, writes, "In a racist society, race tends not only to transcend ethnicity in the responses elicited from others in the social system, it tends even to shape the cultural content that defines the group's ethnicity."[7]

If this analysis is valid, then the racial ethnics have a problem different in kind as well as degree from the white ethnics since the institutions in their sustaining environment are not so likely to allow their ethnicity to pass unnoticed. Their race will not be ignored, even if their cultural distinctiveness is suppressed.

Having discussed these differences, however, let me add that what has been learned in this study about a typology of ethnic services is relevant for white ethnics as well as racial minorities. But assimilation is not a viable option for the latter groups, and "symbolic ethnicity" is not likely to encapsulate their racial identities.

Study Findings and Typology of Services

- Ethnic factors are relevant for services, and there is widespread interest nationally and by all groups in how such factors should be incorporated in the delivery system.
- There are important differences among social workers on how ethnicity is viewed, as shown by the fact that significant differences were found between traditional workers and those in innovative, ethnically oriented settings on twenty-eight of the thirty items on the attitude scale.
- There were also significant differences in attitudes according to ethnicity of worker, regardless of setting.
- Agencies serving ethnic clients differed among themselves in degree of ethnic commitment when measured on three indexes of culture, consciousness, and matching–mixing on ethnic lines.
- Parents tend to commingle attitudes on poverty, welfare, and ethnic discrimination in their responses to the quality of service delivery and their dissatisfactions with it.
- Parents may perceive service needs differently than social workers and may be more concerned with upward mobility and individual opportunity than with group goals.

The extensive agency visits, program observations, individual and group visits, and responses to the study instruments provided a multifaceted view of ethnicity and service delivery. It led to the conceptualization of ethnicity as a variable that does not have a fixed dimension, like age or sex. Ethnic group may be fixed—but ethnicity is a variable with accordionlike properties which can expand or contract, depending on a series of other factors. The factors that determine the extension of the instrument make up the typology we have been seeking.

There are three levels to be considered in describing the conditions under which ethnicity is activated—they can be described in the traditional way as micro, mezzo, and macro.

At the micro level, we look at two elements: the situation and the alternatives. For example, the alternative of a caretaker who loves children is preferred over the option of unknown commitment to children from a member of the same group. But the alternative of "same-group membership" for someone to tell one's problems to is preferred over a credentialed professional of another group. At the same time the ethnicity of a dentist has a lower priority than that of a social worker. Here the situation calls for training and skill which encompasses ethnic diversity of patients. These two factors, situation and alternatives, are relevant on a case basis in every situation where ethnic issues arise.

When issues of ethnicity and service delivery are examined at the mezzo, or intermediate, level, characteristics of the groups involved are relevant. At least four variables are important in determining the strength of ethnic commitment.

Recency of migration or immigration affects the kinds of services needed and their ethnic content. The third-generation college-bound Chinese teenagers we visited in an established settlement house in San Francisco's Chinatown had little in common with new immigrant youth from Hong Kong. Tribal affiliation and tribal law had less relevance in service delivery for the Indian family in Phoenix than for their relatives who lived on the reservation.

Geographical locale is a second important variable. It is related to migration, but has political implications as well. We asked a Chicano consultant what to call United States residents who come from Mexico, and he asked us, "Where did you interview them?" When told it was in the south of Texas, he said, "Call them Mexican Americans. If you had said Los Angeles, I would say call them

Chicanos." This response reflects not only rural–urban differences but political differences in identity.

A third factor affecting this accordion process of ethnic relevance is class and caste. Black social workers in the attitude study gave significantly more credence to credentials than did workers of any other group. They also had a higher percentage of credentialed workers among themselves. Thus in choosing a "worker with credentials" over a "member of one's own group" they started from the base of knowing that there was a pool of credentialed workers in their own group. Such a choice was not made so easily by social workers of ethnic groups where there were very few credentialed workers.

Although upper-class membership does not erase ethnic differences, it is associated with wealth and power so that deprivations are eased, and discrimination, if it exists, takes more benign and subtle forms. Here Schermerhorn's designation of the dominant elite is relevant, and class must be considered in any typology of ethnicity.[8] Service delivery is not likely to involve upper-class ethnics, but social attitudes toward them on the part of helpers and aides, as well as their positions on policy issues, are important considerations.

The homogeneity of the ethnic group is the fourth factor to be considered in determining the strength of the ethnic variable. We have used the term *Indian* in this study to refer to Native Americans who belong to hundreds of different tribes. These tribes speak different languages, have different customs and histories, and may be friendly or hostile to each other. Under conditions of threatened annihilation, they come closer to cooperation on matters of mutual interest. But they are not a homogeneous group by any means.

Another broad generalization has been the labeling of persons from Asia as Asian Americans. These include people of very different backgrounds and cultures. Most of the data reported here on Asian families and children refer to Chinese, but Filipino and Japanese clients were also included. The commonalities were in relation to opposing prevailing myths and stereotypes and seeking improved service delivery.

Homogeneity is a variable that is relative. Just as there is a danger of overgeneralizing, there is also danger in stressing differences to the point where no unity or coalitions can be achieved for the groups involved. To say that German Jews differ from

Russian Jews, southern Blacks from West Indian Blacks, Cherokees from Navajos, and Puerto Ricans from Chicanos is not to say there are no Jewish, Black, Indian or Hispanic ethnic issues.

The four factors relevant at the mezzo level—recency of migration, geographic locale, class and caste, and homogeneity—all refer to characteristics of the groups in any national setting. Beyond that, at the macro level, are the factors that affect consideration of ethnicity across national bounderies. The work in Israel and England provides data for observing how national interests and policies affect the incorporation of ethnicity in service delivery.

The comparative material can be broadly generalized by saying that in the United States almost everyone was an immigrant, in Israel almost everyone is an immigrant, and in England "once an immigrant always an immigrant." This is no accident, but reflects the national interests, history, and current state of politics in each country. National governments choose when and where to recognize ethnicity as befits their perceptions of their national interests and priorities. Cultural pluralism in the United States is essentially documented by demography, but its social acceptance was contingent on the political movements of ethnic groups, resulting in concessions from the sources of national power. Ethnicity in service delivery received more support from the "maximum feasible participation of the poor" in community programs than from any ideological concern with "role" or "identity."

In Israel ethnicity has been selectively attended to, with the overriding national concern for wartime unity dominating all other issues. Thus the highest value in Israel is on religious identity for Jews, and languages and national origins of immigrants were devalued. Services are designed to develop homogeneity, which supports the national purpose. The major model has been "absorption–modernization," with more recent modifications which recognize the value of Sephardic culture, some need to promote national redistribution of wealth, and some goals of affirmative action. Concern about the viability of the new public policy to accelerate integration has been expressed by Jaffe, who states, "If integration means loss of identity, status and pride for only one segment of the population, and increased power and continued ethno-centrism for another segment (which happens to be a numerical minority), then we are surely headed for years of turmoil."[9] Whatever issues are raised on ethnic Jewish subcultures in Israel, the decisions are bound to be taken on political rather than social grounds.

A third pattern of political process on ethnic issues occurs in Great Britain, where the image of national cultural homogeneity is maintained, and those who do not fit the pattern are declassified as "immigrants," including the youngster interviewed in Notting Hill who insisted that he wasn't from Jamaica but from Birmingham. The British situation is complicated in two additional ways. The heritage of empire creates legal issues about status and rights of those who hold or held British passports. Second, ethnicity has become an issue for partisan party campaigns and election decisions may turn on ethnic politics.

To sum up—at least eight factors would enter the typology to determine the extent to which ethnicity is involved in service delivery. At the case, or micro, level, consideration must be given to the situation and the alternatives. At the group, or mezzo, level, attention should be paid to the recency of migration, the locale, class or caste, and the homogeneity of the group. Finally, these decisions are made in a social context, the macro level, which includes issues of national purpose and national politics. The ethnic variable is present for almost all people in almost all cases; it will expand or recede in significance in relation to the case, the group, and the social context.

In 1944 Myrdal suggested that there was an "American dilemma,"[10] a lack of congruence between our professed commitment to equality in the United States and our actual practices of discrimination and deprivation, particularly for Black people. In the thirty-six years since this issue was stated, some of the problems have been faced, if not solved. The emergency of ethnic pride, ethnic identity, and ethnic power have been part of that process.

Now we face a new set of choices, which we call the ethnic dilemma. In what ways, and to what extent, should ethnicity become a major variable in service delivery? Would separate institutions meet ethnic needs, or would they further fragment the delivery system? Would matching rather than mixing provide superior services, or would it lead to a differential level of help? If public services support distinct ethnic programming, are they accountable to the public at large or to their own ethnic communities? These are valid questions for the field. The data on agency services reported here help answer some of them. Further descriptive, demonstration, and experimental work is needed to inform us about differential outcomes resulting from incorporation of ethnicity in service delivery. The ethnic dilemma, finally, can only be resolved in terms of the ethnic purpose and the extent to which that purpose is facilitated by the incorporation of ethnic factors in service delivery.

Notes

1. *Los Angeles Times*, September 10, 1979.
2. *New York Times*, June 2, 1979.
3. Barbara Solomon, *Black Empowerment: Social Work in Oppressed Communities* (New York: Columbia University Press, 1976).
4. Murray Friedman, "The New Pluralism and Social Work Education" (Paper presented at the Council on Social Work Education Annual Meeting, Philadelphia, Pennsylvania, March 3, 1976, published by the National Conference of Jewish Communal Service, New York, October 1976), p. 2.
5. Ibid.
6. NCSW Annual Meeting, Cleveland, Ohio, May 20, 1980.
7. Solomon, *Black Empowerment*, p. 53.
8. R. A. Schermerhorn, *Comparative Ethnic Relations: A Framework for Theory and Research* (New York: Random House, 1970), pp. 12–14.
9. Eliezer D. Jaffe, "Ethnic Preferences of Israelis" (Unpublished document, Jerusalem, 1979).
10. Gunner Myrdal, *An American Dilemma* (New York: Harper & Row, 1944).

Appendixes

A

Statistical Tables
Supporting Findings

1. Agencies Visited, by State and Ethnic Group Served
2. Factor Loadings for Agency Items, by Factors
3. Reliability of Agency Indexes
4. Analysis of Variance, Culture Factor of Agency Index
5. Recipients and Respondents in National Sample, by Region
6. Comparative Data on Major Demographic Characteristics of the National Sample vs. the Ethnic Agency Sample: Percentage Distribution
7. Mean Alienation Scores of Workers, by Ethnicity and Sample
8. Worker and Agency Commitment Scores, by Ethnic Match
9. Correlations Among Parts I, II, and III of the Ethnic Agency Scores, and with Worker Attitude Scores, by Matched Groups

Table 1.   **Agencies Visited, by State and Ethnic Group Served (N = 54)**

STATE	Asian American	Black	American Indian	Mexican American	Puerto Rican
			ETHNIC GROUP		
Arizona	—	—	6	—	—
California	7	—	—	—	—
New York	5	—	—	—	9
North Carolina	—	—	8	—	—
Pennsylvania	—	11	—	—	—
Texas	—	—	—	8	—
Total	12	11	14	8	9

Table 2.   **Factor Loadings for Agency Items, by Factors**

ITEM		LOADING
	CULTURE	
2	Ethnicity of director	.46
3	Ethnic composition of staff	.55
9	Ethnicity of board	.42
16	Use of ethnic curriculum	.62
18	Ethnic staff in programming	.76
21	Use of ethnic food	.80
22	Ethnic art	.79
23	Ethnic music	.86
24	Ethnic history	.57
25	Ethnic holidays	.59
	CONSCIOUSNESS	
11	Support ethnic institutions	.51
12	Leadership on ethnic issues	.69
13	Relate to ethnic power structure	.52
14	Relate to ethnic community	.53
15	Train for ethnic awareness	.46
20	Develop pride in ethnic institutions	.62
26	Support group identity	.56
29	Support ethnic ideology in programming	.56
30	Support separate ethnic agencies	.55
	MATCHING	
1	Percent of nonethnic clients	(−) .49
4	Preference for ethnic staff	(−) .68
5	Support matching policy	(−) .45
6	Prefer workers of same ethnicity as client	(−) .82
28	Success with ethnic staff	(−) .54

Table 3. **Reliability of Agency Indexes**

Index	Cronbach Alpha
1	.847
2	.735
3	.543

Table 4. **Analysis of Variance, Culture Factor of Agency Index**

Groups	Mean	SD	N	Variance
Index	1.76	0.89	54	0.80
Asian	2.11	0.78	12	0.62
Black	1.31	0.94	11	0.88
Mexican	2.41	0.51	8	0.26
Indian	1.08	0.69	14	0.48
Puerto Rican	2.31	0.37	9	0.14

Analysis of Variance Table

	Mean Square	DF	F-Test	Significance
Among Groups	4.06	4	7.38	$p < .001$
Within Groups	0.55	49		

Table 5. **Recipients and Respondents in National Sample, by Region**

Region	Recipients (N = 2733) Percent	Respondents (N = 1606) Percent
Northeast	6	7
Mid-Atlantic	27	27
Central	27	29
South	18	14
Southwest	5	6
Pacific	17	17
Total	(100)	(100)

Table 6. **Comparative Data on Major Demographic Characteristics of the National Sample vs. the Ethnic Agency Sample: Percentage Distribution**

CHARACTERISTIC	NATIONAL SAMPLE	ETHNIC AGENCY SAMPLE
Age	(N = 1603)	(N = 578)
Under 29 years	19	48
30–39 years	29	24
40–49 years	20	15
50–59 years	20	10
60 years or older	12	3
Total	(100)	(100)
Median Age	41 years	30 years
Ethnicity	(N = 1599)	(N = 574)
Asian American	1.5	11.0
Black	6.1	26.0
Indian	.2	12.0
Mexican American	.4	11.0
Puerto Rican	.4	11.0
White	90.8	27.0
Other	.6	2.0
Total	(100.0)	(100.0)
Religion	(N = 1597)	(N = 563)
Catholic	22	32
Jewish	14	4
Protestant	48	45
Other	3	4
No affiliation	13	15
Total	(100)	(100)
Marital status	(N = 1594)	(N = 577)
Single, never married	30	32
Married	57	52
Separated	1	6
Divorced	8	7
Widowed	4	3
Total	(100)	(100)
Annual family income	(N = 1591)	(N = 565)
Under $5,000	2	9
$5,000–9,999	4	38
$10,000–14,999	23	24
$15,000–19,999	30	14
$20,000–24,999	17	9
$25,000 and over	24	6
Total	(100)	(100)
Median Family Income	$18,377	$10,545

Characteristic	National Sample	Ethnic Agency Sample
Highest educational level attained	(N = 1603)	(N = 574)
Below B.A.	—	43
B.A. Degree	2	18
Some Masters work	9	13
M.S.W. Degree	81	17
Other Masters Degree	1	6
Some Doctoral Work	5	2
D.S.W. Degree	1	—
Other Doctoral Degree	1	1
Total	(100)	(100)
Years in practice	(N = 1598)	(N = 527)
Under 1 year	3	13
1–5 years	21	50
6–10 years	22	17
Over 10 years	54	20
Total	(100)	(100)
Professional status	(N = 1601)	(N = 569)
Administrator	26	7
Supervisor	30	12
Caseworker	30	25
Teacher	—	14
Child Care Staff	—	25
Teacher Aide	—	9
Student Status	6	5
Other	8	3
Total	(100)	(100)
Professional area	(N = 1598)	(N = 563)
Practice	76	42
Policy/Admin.	16	6
C.O.	2	2
Teaching	2	19
Research	1	1
Other/Generic	3	2
Paraprofessional	—	28
Total	(100)	(100)
Experience with minority children	(N = 1562)	(N = 558)
Only worked with	1	19
More than with white	17	62
Equal with white	33	17
Less than with white	48	2
Never worked with	1	—
Total	(100)	(100)

CHARACTERISTIC	NATIONAL SAMPLE	ETHNIC AGENCY SAMPLE
Type of agency setting	(N = 1502)	(N = 583)
Protective Services	30	8
Adoption/Foster Care	25	6
Inst. Residence	10	22
Multi-Service	12	11
Child Mental Health	5	8
Youth Services	4	8
Day Care	1	34
Service in own home	—	3
Other*	13	—
Total	(100)	(100)
Agency auspices	(N = 1502)	(N = 583)
Public	54	52
Private, nonsect.	29	33
Private, sectarian	17	15
Total	(100)	(100)

*Other category includes non–child welfare settings such as corrections; hospitals; teaching in school of social work.

Table 7.   **Mean Alienation Scores* of Workers, by Ethnicity and Sample**

SAMPLE	ETHNICITY		TOTAL SAMPLE
	White	*Ethnic*	
National	0.96	1.16	1.1
Ethnic Agency	1.09	1.68	1.5

*For discussion of scale used see Leo Srole, "Social Integration and Certain Corollaries: An Exploratory Study," *American Sociological Review* 21 (1956): 706–716.

Table 8. **Worker and Agency Commitment Scores, by Ethnic Match**

SCORE	MATCH (N = 375) MEAN	NONMATCH (N = 208) MEAN
Agency		
Culture	18.30	14.55
Consciousness	12.32	7.89
Matching	14.28	13.04
Worker: Attitude	.96	.78

Table 9. **Correlations among Parts I, II, and III of the Ethnic Agency Scores, and with Worker Attitude Scores, by Matched Groups**

AGENCY SCORE	I. CULTURE	II. CONSCIOUSNESS	III. MATCHING
Matched group (N = 375)			
I. Culture			
II. Consciousness	.343*		
III. Matching	.253*	.252*	
Worker attitude score	.195*	.325*	.177*
Nonmatched group (N = 208)			
I. Culture			
II. Consciousness	.105		
III. Matching	−.180†	.388*	
Worker attitude score	.017	.322*	.180†

*p < .001
†p < .01

B

Ethnic Agency Worker Attitude Instrument

STATEMENT OF PURPOSE

As part of the study "Ethnic Factors in Child Welfare," an attitude questionnaire has been designed to measure the reactions of child welfare workers to ethnicity in the delivery of services. The instrument incorporates a series of forced choice items. Its content and focus are based on issues identified in the literature as being of major concern to ethnic minority groups. There are no "right" or "wrong" answers, - the purpose is to make the issues explicit and secure a national measure of attitudes.

We ask that all respondents remain anonymous. Give the first response that occurs to you or seems closest to your own reactions. Don't worry over any one item - the overall scale score will provide the needed data. Please answer all items.

Thank you for your cooperation. We hope this research will contribute to improved service delivery for all children.

Shirley Jenkins, Ph.D.
Professor and Study Director

January 1975

208

PART I

Instructions

Below are 10 areas dealing with services to children. Each has
two statements. These are neither "right" nor "wrong," but express an attitude or opinion. You may agree or disagree with
either statement or with both statements, but to different
degrees.

Please read both statements first, then circle either "a" or "b"
indicating which statement appeals to you most or comes closest
to the way you feel.

1) a. When a qualified homemaker comes to the house, the most
      important thing is that she loves children.

   b. It is most important that a qualified homemaker who is
      sent to a house be of the same race and ethnic group
      as the children.

2) a. The young child who knows and speaks two languages has
      an advantage in life.

   b. It is confusing for a young child to have to cope with
      two languages.

3) a. In a day care center, lunch should be an appetizing
      balanced nutritional meal.

   b. Lunch in a day care center should include the kinds of
      foods the children are used to at home, as well as being
      nutritional.

4) a. If you need help from a social worker, you are more
      likely to get it if the worker is of the same race or
      ethnic group as you are.

   b. A trained worker with a social work degree is more
      likely to help you with problems than one without a
      degree.

5) a. Different cultures and groups have their own values and
      ideas of what are the most important things in life.

   b. When you get down to it, most people, from all groups,
      have pretty much the same values and ideas about what
      is important.

6) a. When public agencies give services, they are accountable,
      first, to the families they serve, and second, to the
      public at large.

   b. Representatives of the community and of minority groups
      should see that the people of their own group get the
      services to which they are entitled from public agencies.

7) a. Unless the majority of an agency Board serving minority
        children is of the same race or group as those children,
        we cannot be sure the clients' interests will be well
        served.

    b. If the majority of an agency staff working with minority
        children is of the same race or group as those children,
        then the ethnic composition of the Board does not matter.

8) a. Sometimes ethnic issues in social work are raised which
        serve the interests of the total minority community, but
        not necessarily the clients being served.

    b. There is no difference between the interests of minority
        clients and the community to which they belong.

9) a. One good thing about institutions where there are children
        from different races and backgrounds is that a child can
        learn to make friends and get along with different kinds
        of people.

    b. If a child is in an institution where there are children
        from different races and backgrounds, he will feel more
        secure if he makes friends primarily with children who
        are like himself.

10) a. A minority child can rarely experience a real sense of
        belonging with parents of another race or ethnic group.

    b. A child gets more sense of belonging in adoption than in
        foster care or an institution, even with parents of another
        group.

PART II

Instructions

In delivering services to children several appropriate options
are available. Ten situations are noted below with three possible options for each. Circle either "a," "b," or "c" according to which option you consider most desirable.

1) In placing a child in foster care, after studying the child
    and evaluating the foster parents, the worker should:

    a. give importance to ethnicity and race in placement, but
        not as the determining factor.

    b. take note of race and ethnic background, then place the
        child with the best rated parents.

    c. only place the child with foster parents of the same race
        or ethnic background, even if it means extensive recruit-
        ment.

2) In an after-school day care center with children from different
    backgrounds, some of whom can speak different languages, the
    program should:

    a. be sure there is some time when children speak their own
        language.

    b. encourage all children to speak English.

    c. let children speak whatever language they wish.

3) In assigning adolescent boys to cottages in a residential
    treatment center, you would:

    a. allow the boys to group themselves together by race and
        ethnic background, if they wished.

    b. place boys together in what you consider will be the best
        therapeutic milieu.

    c. assign boys recognizing race and ethnic background, but not
        as the main consideration.

4) If a white couple wants to adopt a black child, you would
    explore motives and evaluate the home, and if both are
    acceptable:

    a. approve the adoption.

    b. allow the adoption only if no black homes are available.

    c. not approve the adoption as not in the best interests
        of the child.

5) Different ethnic groups have many different holidays. In an
    institution where there are children from different backgrounds
    and cultures:

    a. to avoid friction, celebrate only the traditional holidays
        like Thanksgiving and Independence Day.

    b. help each cultural group to celebrate its own holidays
        for its own members.

    c. have children from all ethnic groups participate in the
        celebration of all holidays.

6) If a boy in an institution confronts his woman social worker
    with the idea that, in his own culture, men are regarded as
    superior to women, she should:

    a. work to change attitudes in the direction of equality of
        the sexes.

    b. discuss cultural differences among people.

    c. accept the fact that this is a cultural attitude and not
        challenge it.

7) If you are a mother seeking services for your child you would

    a. look for a good agency run by members of your own group, since then your needs would be met and you would be understood.

    b. look for the agency with the best reputation for high quality services.

    c. look for a good agency where members of your group have been served.

8) Members of minority groups who wish to run separate programs for their own children should:

    a. be encouraged to do so and given public funds.

    b. be discouraged from setting up separate programs.

    c. be allowed to do so but not given public funds.

9) Decisions in a day care center should be primarily made by:

    a. teachers and social workers.

    b. parents, with input from teachers and social workers.

    c. representatives of community groups, with input from teachers, social workers, and parents.

10. The trained social worker from a racial or minority group can

    a. work well with children from all groups.

    b. be most effective with children from his or her own group

    c. work with all children but have a special understanding of children from his or her own group.

PART III

Below are 10 statements relating to issues of concern to ethnic
minority groups. Please check the extent of your agreement or
disagreement with each statement.

	AGREE		DISAGREE	
	Strongly	Slightly	Slightly	Strongly

1) To achieve in American
   society, the Indian child
   must learn to compete and
   strive, even if this is
   in conflict with traditional tribal values.

2) A permissive day care center can undermine the traditional discipline that
   the Mexican American child
   has at home.

3) Asian Americans do not
   frequently come to agencies
   for services, indicating
   they have fewer problems
   than other minority groups.

4) Spanish should be a compulsory course in schools
   of social work, since
   students may be working
   with Puerto Rican clients.

5) The important thing in a
   child welfare agency is to
   have good practice; there
   is no such thing as a
   "white practice" or "black
   practice."

6) Bussing Asian children
   to academically better
   schools outside the
   Asian community could
   do more harm than good
   to the children.

7) The Mexican American
   child can be helped to
   adjust to Anglo society
   if he is in a day care
   center where English is
   spoken and he experiences
   a cultural pattern other
   than his own.

	AGREE		DISAGREE	
	Strongly	Slightly	Slightly	Strongl
8) The isolation of life on the reservation does not mean inevitable cultural deprivation for the Indian child.	___	___	___	___
9) The belief that there is no social stigma attached to illegitimacy in the black community has served to rationalize the lack of child welfare services for black children.	___	___	___	___
10) The Puerto Rican child is better off in a good foster home with agency supervision than with relatives who have many problems of their own.	___	___	___	___

PART IV

Instructions

Below are five items reflecting general social attitudes. Please check the extent of your agreement or disagreement with each statement.

	AGREE		DISAGREE	
	Strongly	Slightly	Slightly	St
1) These days a person doesn't really know who he can count on.	___	___	___	__
2) In spite of what people say, the lot of the average man is getting worse, not better.	___	___	___	__
3) Most public officials are not really interested in the problems of the average man.	___	___	___	__
4) Nowadays, a person has to live pretty much for today and let tomorrow take care of itself.	___	___	___	__
5) It's hardly fair to bring a child into the world the way things look for the future.	___	___	___	__

PART V

Demographic Information

Please answer the following items. No names please.

(1) Age

___Under 20 years
___20-29
___30-39
___40-49
___50-59
___60 or over

(2) Ethnicity

___Asian American
___Black
___Mexican American
___Native American
___Puerto Rican
___White
___Other (please specify)
_____

(3) Sex

___Male
___Female

(4) Religion

___Catholic
___Jewish
___Protestant
___None
___Other (please specify)
_____

(5) Marital Status

___Single, never married
___Married
___Separated
___Divorced
___Widowed

(6) Do you have children
     of your own?

___Yes
___No

(7) Annual Family Income

___Under $5,000
___$5,000-$9,999
___10,000-14,999
___15,000-19,999
___20,000-24,999
___25,000 or above

(8) Highest Educational Level
               Attained

___Some high school
___High school graduate
___Some college
___B.A. or B.S. degree
___Some masters coursework
___M.S.W.
___Masters in another area
    (please specify)_____
___Some doctoral coursework
___D.S.W
___Doctorate in another area
    (please specify)_____

(9) Last date in school Month and Year
    _____

(10) Professional Status

___Child Care Worker
___Case Worker
___Teacher
___Supervisor
___Agency Administrator
___Social Work Faculty
___Research
___Student (Undergraduate)
___Student (Graduate)

(11) Professional Area

___Practice (Casework/Groupwork)
___Community Organizing
___Policy and Planning
___Research
___Teaching
___Other (please specify)
_____

(12) Years in Practice
___Student Status
___Under 1 year
___1-5 years
___6-10 years
___Over 10 years

(13) Agency Auspices

___Private, sectarian
___Private, non-sectarian
___Public

(14) Type of Agency Setting
(Check all which apply)
___Adoption
___Foster Care
___Day Care
___After School Care
___Institutional Residence
___Child Mental Health Clinic
___Youth Services
___Other (please specify)
_____

(15) In your working experience in child welfare, have you worked:

____ only with minority group children
____ with more minority group children than white children
____ with about equal numbers of white and minority children
____ less with minority group children than white children
____ never worked with minority group children

(16) Is the clientele your agency deals with composed of:

_____ only minority group children
_____ more minority group children than white children
_____ about equal numbers of white and minority children
_____ fewer minority group children than white children
_____ no minority group children

(17) If your agency works with minority group children, which groups are represented:

_____Asian American
_____Black
_____Mexican American
_____Native American
_____Puerto Rican
_____Other (please specify)
_____

(18) In which geographic area is your agency located:
_____New England
_____Middle Atlantic
_____Central
_____South
_____South West
_____Pacific

(19) In which type of area is your agency located:
_____Rural(under 2,500)
_____Small Town(under 10,000)
_____Small City(under 50,000)
_____Medium City
_____Large City-Central City
_____Large City-Suburbs

Comments:

_____

_____

_____

_____

C

Validity of the Attitude Scale

Not all the items of the thirty on the attitude instrument were equally useful in determining ethnic commitment. To reduce the number and improve the validity, the first step was to secure an item-criterion correlation analysis. This developed indexes based on groupings of items with the highest intercorrelations.* Where one item was part of the index, the index was adjusted to exclude the item to avoid autocorrelation. By examination, the index with the best grouping or highest level of intercorrelations was selected as a base for further analysis. This enabled a selection of items to be made from the total number on the instrument, based on criterion-related validity, the criterion being the total score.

In analyzing these results, correlations were found to be positive but relatively low. These must be evaluated, however, in terms of the nature of the subject and the exploratory character of the survey. Attitudes sought ranged over several dimensions, as well as several content areas, thus high correlations were not anticipated in this initial trial.

*The procedure followed is based on the method proposed by George W. Bohrnstedt, "A Quick Method for Determining the Reliability and Validity of Multiple-Item Scales," *American Sociological Review* 34(August 1969): 542–48.

For the ethnic agency sample, the first index developed included fifteen of the thirty items, and showed item-criterion correlations ranging from .221 to .476. The majority were .30 or higher. This scale was therefore selected as having acceptable validity for the ethnic agency sample.

Responses from the national sample showed lower validity as well as lower ethnic commitment. One of the indexes developed from the item-criterion correlation analysis, based on national agency responses, did show a cluster of three items with appropriate correlations, from .311 to .324. This index was selected as representing the best grouping of correlated items for the national sample.

The validity of the scale as administered is considered to be low but appropriate for the content when applied in the ethnic agency population. There is less confidence in the validity when applied to the national sample, which may be attributed to disparate and heterogeneous responses, and some items where actual reversals occurred in hypothesized attitudes. An example of this was the reversal on the school lunch response, in which ethnic workers chose the "balanced lunch." The data analysis proceeded, therefore, to examine all items with a view to reducing the scale to those items with highest validity, which were also appropriate for use in the widest population.

Inspection of items was done according to several criteria. In addition to validity, relevance for use in both an ethnic agency and a traditional sample was examined. In addition the content was studied for ambiguousness in wording, repetition of other items, or reference to only one subgroup. As a result two subsets were selected, one with nine items and one with five items (five of the nine). It was decided to explore further the distribution of scores for both subsets, as well as to undertake multiple-regression analysis on both before selecting either as the recommended short form. Validity and reliability measures, previously taken on the original thirty-item instrument, were recomputed for both the five-item and the nine-item scales. As a result it was found that the nine-item scale had substantially higher reliability than the five-item scale, as measured by the Cronbach Alpha scores, and little difference in validity, as measured by the item-criterion intercorrelations. Therefore, the nine-item scale is recommended as the instrument of choice to measure ethnic commitment. It is simpler and more valid than the original thirty-item instrument used to obtain the study responses.

Selected Bibliography

General and Theoretical References

"Color and Race." *Daedalus*, spring 1967.

FRANCIS, E. K. *Interethnic Relations: An Essay in Sociological Theory.* New York: Elsevier, 1976.

GLAZER, NATHAN, and DANIEL PATRICK MOYNIHAN, eds. *Beyond the Melting Pot.* Cambridge, Mass.: M.I.T. Press, 1963.

———. *Ethnicity: Theory and Experience.* Cambridge, Mass.: Harvard University Press, 1975.

GOODMAN, JAMES A. *Dynamics of Racism in Social Work Practice.* Washington, D.C.: National Association of Social Workers, 1973.

GREELEY, ANDREW M. *Ethnicity in the United States: a Preliminary Reconnaissance.* New York: Wiley, 1974.

JONES, TERRY. "Institutional Racism in the General United States." *Social Work* 19:2 (March 1974): 218–25.

MILNER, DAVID. *Children and Race.* London: Penguin, 1975.

MINDEL, CHARLES H., and ROBERT W. HABENSTEIN, eds. *Ethnic Families in America, Patterns and Variations.* New York: Elsevier, 1976.

MYRDAL, GUNNAR. *An American Dilemma: The Negro Problem and Modern Democracy.* New York: Harper & Row, 1944.

National Conference of Jewish Communal Service. *The New Pluralism and Social Work Education: A Challenge to the Profession of Social Work.* New York: The Conference, 1976.

ROTHMAN, JACK, ed. *Issues in Race and Ethnic Relations: Theory, Research and Action.* Itasea, Ill.: F. E. Peacock, 1977.

SCHERMERHORN, R. A. *Comparative Ethnic Relations: A Framework for Theory and Research.* New York: Random House, 1970.

SOTOMAYOR, MARTA. "Language, Culture, and Ethnicity in Developing Self-concept." *Social Casework* 58:4 (April 1977): 195–203.

TURNER, JOHN B. "Education for Practice with Minorities." *Social Work* 17:3 (May 1972): 112–118.

Bibliographies

BRAVO, ENRIQUE R., comp. *An Annotated Selected Puerto Rican Bibliography.* New York: The Urban Center, Columbia University, 1972.

National Institute of Mental Health, Center for Minority Group Mental Health Programs. *Bibliography on Racism.* Department of Health Education and Welfare Publication No. (HSM) 73-9012. Washington, D.C.: Government Printing Office, 1972.

DAVIS, LENWOOD G. *The Black Family in the United States: A Selected Bibliography of Annotated Books, Articles and Dissertations on Black Families in America,* Westport, Conn. Greenwood Press, 1978.

Institute of Puerto Rican Studies at Brooklyn College. *The Puerto Rican People: A Selected Bibliography for Use in Social Work Education.* New York: Council on Social Work Education, 1973.

Project Thrive, National Urban League. *A Selected Annotated Bibliography on Black Families.* Department of Health Education and Welfare Publication No. (OHDS) 78-30140. Washington, D.C.: Government Printing Office, 1978.

Social Work Education and Practice (General)

COHEN, LUCY M., and CARMEN FERNANDEZ. "Ethnic Identity and Psychocultural Adaptation of Spanish-speaking Families." *Child Welfare* 52:7 (July 1974): 413-21.

DAVIS, LARRY E. "Racial Composition of Groups." *Social Work* 24:3 (May 1979): 208-213.

KAUTZ, ELEANOR. "Can Agencies Train for Racial Awareness?" *Child Welfare* 55:8 (Sept.-Oct. 1976): 547-51.

MIZIO, EMELICIA. "White Worker-Minority Client." *Social Work* 17:3 (May 1972): 82-86.

PINDERHUGHES, ELAINE B. "Teaching Empathy in Cross-Cultural Social Work." *Social Work* 24:4 (July 1979): 312-16.

STROBER, SUSAN B., and MILTON GRADY. "Effects of Race Relations Training on Racial Awareness." *Social Work Research and Abstracts* 14:2 (Summer 1978): 12-20.

TRADER, HARRIET P. "Survival Strategies for Oppressed Minorities." *Social Work* 22:1 (January 1977): 10-13.

WILLETS, RUTH J. "Cross-cultural Training in Operating Community Care Homes." *Social Work* 23:1 (January 1978): 31-35.

Comparative Ethnic References

COLE, JOAN, and MARC PILISUK. "Differences in the Provision of Mental Health Services by Race." *American Journal of Orthopsychiatry* 46:3 (July 1976): 510-25.

GOEBES, DIANE D., and MILTON F. SHORE. "Some Effects of Bicultural and Monocultural School Environments on Personality Development." *American Journal of Orthopsychiatry* 48:3 (July 1978): 398–407.

JENKINS, SHIRLEY. "The Ethnic Agency Defined." *Social Service Review* 54:2 (June 1980): 249–61.

_____ and BARBARA MORRISON. "Ethnicity and Service Delivery." *American Journal of Orthopsychiatry* 48:1 (January 1978): 160–65.

SILVERMAN, ARNOLD, and WILLIAM FEIGELMAN. "Some Factors Affecting the Adoption of Minority Children." *Social Casework* 58:9 (November 1977): 554–61.

TEPLIN, LINDA A. "A Comparison of Racial/Ethnic Preferences among Anglo, Black and Latino Children." *American Journal of Orthopsychiatry* 46:4 (October 1976): 702–709.

Cross-cultural and International References

CHEETHAM, JULIET. *Social Work with Immigrants.* London: Routledge & Kegan Paul, 1972.

EVERSLEY, DAVID, and FRED SUKDEO. *The Dependents of the Coloured Commonwealth Population of England and Wales.* London: Institute of Race Relations, 1969.

FITZHERBERT, KATRIN. *West Indian Children in London.* London: G. Bell and Sons, 1967.

GLASS, RUTH. *Newcomers: The West Indians in London.* London: Allen and Unwin, 1960.

JAFFE, ELIEZER D. *Ethnic Preferences of Israelis.* Jerusalem, Israel, 1979. Unpublished manuscript.

ROSE, E. J. B., and associates. *Colour and Citizenship: A Report on British Race Relations.* London: Oxford University Press, 1969.

TRISELIOTIS, J. P., ed. *Social Work with Coloured Immigrants and Their Families.* London: Institute of Race Relations, Oxford University Press, 1972.

References on Separate Ethnic Groups

AMERICAN INDIANS (NATIVE AMERICANS)

BOYER, BRYCE L. "Psychoanalytic Insights in Working with Ethnic Minorities." *Social Casework* 45 (November 1964): 519–26.

BROWN, EDDIE F., and TIMOTHY F. SHAUGHNESSY. *Education for Social Work Practice with American Indian Families.* Tempe: Arizona State University, School of Social Work, n.d.

CINGOLANI, WILLIAM. "Acculturating the Indian: Federal Policies 1834–1973." *Social Work* 18:6 (November 1973): 24–28.

CLARK, ERMA. "A Nursery School on the Ute Indian Reservation." *Childhood Education* 42:7 (April 1965): 409–413.

COOLEY, RICHARD C., and others. "Outreach Services for Elderly Native Americans." *Social Work* 24:2 (March 1979): 151–53.

DAVIES, MARY J. "Adoptive Placement of American Indian Children with Non-Indian Families." *Child Welfare* 40 (June 1961): 12–16.

DIZMANG, LARRY H., et al. "Adolescent Suicide at an Indian Reservation." *American Journal of Orthopsychiatry* 44:1 (January 1974): 43–49.

FANSHEL, DAVID. *Far From the Reservation: Transracial Adoption of American Indian Children: Follow-up Study.* New York: Child Welfare League of America Press, 1972.

FARRIS, CHARLES E. "American Indian Social Worker Advocates." *Social Casework* 57:8 (October 1976): 494–503.

———. "A White House Conference on the American Indian." *Social Work* 18:1 (January 1973): 80–86.

———, and LORENE S. FARRIS. "Indian Children: The Struggle for Survival." *Social Work* 21:5 (September 1976): 386–89.

FREEMAN, DANIEL. "Adolescent Crisis of the Kiowa-Apache Indian Male." In *Minority Group Adolescents in the United States*, edited by E. B. Brody. Baltimore: Williams and Wilkins, 1968, pp. 17–47.

GOOD TRACKS, JIMM G. "Native American Noninterference." *Social Work* 18:6 (November 1973): 30–34.

GUNDLACH, JAMES H., et al. "Migration, Labor Mobility, and Relocation Assistance: The Case of the American Indian." *Social Service Review* 51:3 (September 1977): 464–73.

ISHISAKA, HIDEKI. "American Indians and Foster Care: Cultural Factors and Separation." *Child Welfare* 57:5 (May 1978): 299–308.

JERDONE, CLARE G. "Day Care for Indian Children." *Young Children* 20:3 (January 1965): 143–51.

KELLER, GORDON. "Bicultural Social Work and Anthropology." *Social Casework* 53:8 (October 1972): 455–65.

LEON, ROBERT L. "Maladaptive Interaction Between the Bureau of Indian Affairs Staff and Indian Clients." *American Journal of Orthopsychiatry* 35:4 (July 1965): 273–80.

LEWIS, RONALD G., and MAN KEUNG HO. "Social Work with Native Americans." *Social Work* 20:5 (September 1975): 379–82.

LOCKLEAR, HERBERT. "American Indian Myths." *Social Work* 17:3 (May 1972): 72–80.

LYSLO, ARNOLD. "Adoptive Placement of American Indian Children with Non-Indian Families, Part I." *Child Welfare* 10:5 (May 1961): 4–6.

MACKEY, JOHN, ed. *American Indian Task Force Report.* New York: Council on Social Work Education, 1973.

McNICKLE, D'ARCY. "The Sociocultural Setting of Indian Life." *American Journal of Psychiatry* 125:2 (August 1968): 115–19.

RED HORSE, JOHN G., et al. "Family Behavior of Urban American Indians." *Social Casework* 59:2 (February 1978): 67–72.

STUART, PAUL. "United States Indian Policy: From the Dawes Act to the American Indian Policy Review Commission." *Social Service Review* 51:3 (September 1977): 451–63.

ASIAN AMERICANS

"Asian and Pacific Islander Americans: Heritage, Characteristics, Self-Image, Conflicts, Service Needs, Organization." *Social Casework* 57:3 (March 1976).

CATTELL, STUART. *Health, Welfare and Social Organization in Chinatown, New York City*. New York: Community Service Society, 1962.

CHEN, PEI-NGOR. "The Chinese Community in Los Angeles." *Social Casework* 51:10 (December 1970): 591–98.

———. "Samoans in California." *Social Work* 18:2 (March 1973): 41–48.

———. "A Study of Chinese-American Elderly Residing in Hotel Rooms." *Social Casework* 60:2 (February 1979): 89–95.

FONG, STANLEY L. M. "Assimilation of Chinese in America: Changes in Orientation and Social Perception." *American Journal of Sociology* 71 (November 1965): 265–73.

———. "Identity Conflicts of Chinese Adolescents in San Francisco." In *Minority Group Adolescents in the United States*, edited by E. B. Brody. Baltimore: Williams and Wilkins, 1968, pp. 111–32.

HUANG, KEN, and MARC PILISUK. "At the Threshold of the Golden Gate: Special Problems of a Neglected Minority." *American Journal of Orthopsychiatry* 47:4 (October 1977): 701–713.

KIM, BOK-LIM C. "An Appraisal of Korean Immigrant Service Needs." *Social Casework* 57 (March 1976): 139–48.

———. "Asian-Americans: No Model Minority." *Social Work* 18:3 (May 1973): 44–53.

———. "Casework with Japanese and Korean Wives of Americans." *Social Casework* 53:5 (May 1972): 273–79.

KIM, S. PETER, et al. "Adoption of Korean Children by New York Area Couples: A Preliminary Study." *Child Welfare* 58:7 (July/August 1979): 419–27.

KURAMOTO, FORD H. "What Do Asians Want? An Examination of Issues in Social Work Education." *Journal of Education in Social Work* 7 (fall 1971): 7–17.

McDERMOTT, ROBERT E. "Oriental Adoptive Placements." *Catholic Charities Review* 49:4 (April 1965): 24–25.

MURASE, KENJI, ed. *Asian American Task Force Report*. New York: Council on Social Work Education, 1973.

NICOL, MARJORIE SLOAN. "Characteristics of Chinese-American Children with Problems." *Smith College Studies in Social Work* 36:3 (June 1966): 234–56.

OWAN, TOM C. "Improving Productivity in the Public Sector through Bilingual-Bicultural Staff." *Social Work Research and Abstracts*, NASW, 14:1 (Spring 1978): 10–18.

PETERSEN, WILLIAM. *Japanese Americans*. New York: Random House, 1971.

PONCE, DANILO E., and VINCENT LEE. "Intraethnic Violence in a Hawaii School: A Mental Health Consultation Experience." *American Journal of Orthopsychiatry* 47:3 (July 1977): 451–55.

RATLIFF, BASCOM W., and others. "Intercultural Marriage: The Korean-American Experience." *Social Casework* 59:4 (April 1978): 221–26.

SOLLENBERGER, RICHARD T. "Chinese-American Child Rearing Practices and Juvenile Delinquency." *Journal of Social Psychology* 74 (February 1968): 13–23.

SUE, STANLEY, and HARRY H. L. KITANO. *Asian-Americans: A Success Story.* Special publication of *Journal of Social Issues* 29:2 (1973).

———, and HERMAN MCKINNEY. "Asian Americans in the Community Mental Health Care System." *American Journal of Orthopsychiatry* 45:1 (January 1975): 111–18.

YAMAMOTO, JOE. "Japanese American Identity Crisis." In *Minority Group Adolescents in the United States*, edited by E. B. Brody. Baltimore: Williams and Wilkins, 1968, pp. 133–56.

BLACKS

ANDREWS, ROBERTA G. "Permanent Placement of Negro Children through Quasi-Adoption." *Child Welfare* 47:10 (December 1968): 583–86.

BILLINGSLEY, ANDREW. *Black Families in White America.* Englewood Cliffs, N.J.: Prentice-Hall, 1968.

———, and JEANNE M. GIOVANNONI. *Children of the Storm: Black Children and American Child Welfare.* New York: Harcourt Brace Jovanovich, 1972.

BROOKS, CAROL M. "New Mental Health Perspectives in the Black Community." *Social Casework* 55:8 (October 1974): 489–96.

CHESTANG, LEON W. "The Dilemma of Biracial Adoption." *Social Work* 17:3 (May 1972): 100–10.

CHIMEZIE, AMUZIE. "Transracial Adoption of Black Children." *Social Work* 20:4 (July 1975): 296–301.

CROSS, ANDRA, "The Black Experience: Its Importance in the Treatment of Black Clients." *Child Welfare* 53:3 (March 1974): 158–66.

DAVIS, MACK I., et al. "Separate and Together: All-Black Therapy Group in the White Hospital." *American Journal of Orthopsychiatry* 44:1 (January 1974): 19–25.

DUBOIS, W. E. B. *The Negro American Family.* Cambridge, Mass.: M.I.T. Press, 1970 (original edition Atlanta University, 1909).

EARL, LOVELENE, and NANCY LOHMANN. "Absent Fathers and Black Male Children." *Social Work* 23:5 (September 1978): 413–15.

FAULKNER, AUDREY OLSEN, et al. "Life Strengths and Life Stresses: Explorations in the Measurement of the Mental Health of the Black Aged." *American Journal of Orthopsychiatry* 45:1 (January 1975): 102–110.

FISCHER, CLARENCE B. "Homes for Black Children." *Child Welfare* 50:2 (February 1971): 108–11.

FRANCIS, ARACELIS, ed. *Black Task Force Report: Suggested Guide for the Integration of Black Content into the Social Work Curriculum.* New York: Council on Social Work Education, 1973.

FRAZIER, E. FRANKLIN. *The Negro Family in the United States.* Chicago: University of Chicago Press, 1966 (original edition 1939).

GALLAGHER, URSULA. "Adoption Resources for Black Children." *Children* 18:2 (March–April 1971): 49–53.

GILBERT, GWENDOLYN, "Counseling Black Adolescent Parents." *Social Work* 19:1 (January 1974): 88–95.

GLASGOW, DOUGLASS. "Black Power through Community Control." *Social Work* 17:3 (May 1972): 59–64.

GROW, LUCILLE J., and DEBORAH SHAPIRO. *Black Children—White Parents: A Study of Transracial Adoption.* New York: Child Welfare League of America, 1975. See also Amuzie Chimezie, "Bold but Irrelevant," Grow and Shapiro on "Transracial Adoption," and Deborah Shapiro and Lucille J. Grow, "Not so Bold and Not so Irrelevant: A Reply to Chimezie," *Child Welfare* 56:2 (February 1977): 75–91.

HALLOWITZ, DAVID. "Counseling and Treatment of the Poor Black Family." *Social Casework* 56:8 (October 1975): 451–59.

HERZOG, ELIZABETH, et al. *Families for Black Children: The Search for Adoptive Parents: An Experience Survey.* Washington, D.C.: Government Printing Office, 1971.

———. "Some Opinions on Finding Families for Black Children." *Children* 18:4 (July–August, 1971): 143–48.

HILL, ROBERT. *Strengths of Black Families: A National Urban League Research Study.* New York: Emerson Hall, 1971.

HOWARD, ALICIA, et al. "Transracial Adoption: The Black Community Perspective." *Social Work* 22:3 (May 1977): 184–89.

HUSBANDS, ANN. "The Developmental Tasks of the Black Foster Child." *Social Casework* 51:7 (July 1970): 406–409.

JOHNSON, C. LINCOLN. "Transracial Adoption: Victim of Ideology." *Social Work* 21:3 (May 1976): 241–43.

JONES, DARIELLE, "African-American Clients. Clinical Practice Issues." *Social Work* 24:2 (March 1979): 112–18.

JONES, EDMOND D. "On Transracial Adoption of Black Children." *Child Welfare* 51:3 (March 1972): 156–64.

KATZ, LINDA. "Transracial Adoption: Some Guidelines." *Child Welfare* 53:3 (March 1974): 180–88.

MADISON, BERNICE Q., and MICHAEL SCHAPIRO. "Black Adoption-Issues and Policies: Review of the Literature." *Social Service Review* 47:4 (December 1973): 531–55.

MANNING, SETON W. "The Changing Negro Family: Implications for the Adoption of Children." *Child Welfare* 43:9 (November 1964): 480–85.

McADOO, HARRIETTE. "Family Therapy in the Black Community." *American Journal of Orthopsychiatry* 47:1 (January 1977): 75–79.

NEILSON, JACQUELINE. "Tayari: Black Homes for Black Children." *Child Welfare* 55:1 (January 1976): 41–50.

"The Negro American." *Daedalus*, Fall 1965, and "The Negro American," 2, *Daedalus*, Winter 1966 (complete special issues).

PERRY, LORRAINE R. "Strategies of Black Community Groups." *Social Work* 21:3 (May 1976): 210–15.

PIERCE, CHESTER M. "Problems of the Negro Adolescent in the Next Decade." In *Minority Group Adolescents in the United States,* edited by E. B. Brody. Baltimore: Williams and Wilkins, 1968, pp. 17–47.

SAUNDERS, MARIE SIMMONS. "The Ghetto: Some Perceptions of a Black Social Worker." *Social Work* 14:4 (October 1969): 84–88.

SCANZONI, JOHN H. *The Black Family in Modern Society*. Boston: Allyn & Bacon, 1971.

SHANNON, BARBARA. "The Impact of Racism on Personality Development." *Social Casework* 54:9 (November 1973): 519–25.

SHARRAR, MARY LOU. "Attitude of Black Natural Parents Regarding Adoption." *Child Welfare* 50:5 (May 1971): 286–89.

SMITH, OSCAR S., and RALPH H. GUNDLACH. "Group Therapy for Blacks in a Therapeutic Community." *American Journal of Orthopsychiatry* 44:1 (January 1974): 26–36.

SOLOMON, BARBARA BRYANT. *Black Empowerment, Social Work in Oppressed Communities*. New York: Columbia University Press, 1976.

TAYLOR, RONALD L. "Psychosocial Development among Black Children and Youth: A Re-examination." *American Journal of Orthopsychiatry* 46:1 (January 1976): 4–19.

WILLIE, CHARLES V. "The Black Family and Social Class." *American Journal of Orthopsychiatry* 44:1 (January 1974): 50–60.

MEXICAN AMERICANS (CHICANOS)

AQUILAR, IGNACIO. "Initial Contacts with Mexican-American Families." *Social Work* 17:3 (May 1972): 66–70.

ATENCIO, THOMAS C. "The Survival of La Raza Despite Social Services." *Social Casework* 52:5 (May 1971): 262–268.

CURREN, D. J., ed. *The Chicano Faculty Development Program: A Report*. New York: Council on Social Work Education, 1973.

DERBYSHIRE, ROBERT L. "Adolescent Identity Crisis in Urban Mexican Americans in East Los Angeles." In *Minority Group Adolescents in the United States*, edited by E. B. Brody. Baltimore: Williams and Wilkins, 1968, pp. 73–110.

GIBSON, GUADALUPE. "An Approach to Identification and Prevention of Developmental Disabilities Among Mexican-American Children." *American Journal of Orthopsychiatry* 48:1 (January 1978): 96–113.

Interstate Research Associates. *Approaches for the Institutionalization of Bilingual-Bicultural Head Start Programs Serving the Chicano Child*. Washington, D. C.: The Associates, 1972.

JOHNSON, DALE L., and others. "The Houston Parent-Child Development Center: A Parent Education Program for Mexican American Families." *American Journal of Orthopsychiatry* 44:1 (January 1974): 121–28.

KNOLL, FAUSTINA RAMIREZ. "Casework Services for Mexican-Americans." *Social Casework* 52:5 (May 1971): 279–84.

MALDONADO JR., DAVID. "The Chicano Aged." *Social Work* 120:3 (May 1975): 213–16.

MALDONADO, LIONAL A. "Internal Colonialism and Triangulation, a Research Example." *Social Service Review* 53:3 (September 1979): 464–73.

MANGOLD, MARGARET M., ed. *La Causa Chicana: The Movement for Justice*. New York: Family Service Association of America, 1972.

MIRANDA, MANUEL R., ed. *Psychotherapy with the Spanish-Speaking: Issues in Research and Service Delivery*. Los Angeles: Spanish Speaking Mental Health Research Center, University of California, 1976.

MONTIEL, MIGUEL. "The Chicano Family: A Review of Research." *Social Work* 18:3 (March 1973): 22–31.

_____. "Recent Changes among Chicanos." *Sociology and Social Research* 55:1 (October 1970): 47–51.

PENALOSA, FERNANDO. "Mexican Family Roles." *Journal of Marriage and the Family* 30 (November 1968): 680–89.

RUIZ, JULIETTE, ed. *Chicano Task Force Report*. New York: Council on Social Work Education, 1973.

SALCIDO, RAMON M. "Undocumented Aliens: A Study of Mexican-American Families." *Social Work* 24:4 (July 1979): 306–311.

SOTOMAYOR, MARTA. "Mexican American Interaction with Social Systems." *Social Casework* 52:5 (May 1971): 317–23.

United States Commission on Civil Rights. *Toward Quality Education for Mexican Americans*. Washington, D.C.: Government Printing Office, 1974.

WAGNER, NATHANIEL N., and MARSHA J. HOUGH. *Chicanos: Social and Psychological Perspectives*. St. Louis: C. W. Mosby, 1971.

PUERTO RICANS

ABAD, VINCENTE, et al. "A Model for Delivery of Mental Health Services to Spanish-Speaking Minorities." *American Journal of Orthopsychiatry* 44:4 (July 1974): 584–95.

ARAOZ, DANIEL LEON. "Male Puerto Rican Parental Self Image (How Puerto Rican Men in New York Feel About Being Fathers)." Ph.D. dissertation, Columbia University, 1969.

BRESS, IRWIN. "The Incidence of Compadrazgo among Puerto Ricans in Chicago." *Journal of Social and Economic Studies* 12:4 (December 1963): 475–80.

BUDNER, STANLEY, et al. "The Minority Retardate: A Paradox and a Problem in Definition." *Social Service Review* 43:2 (June 1966): 174–83.

CAMPOS, ANGEL P. "Proposed Strategy for the 1970's." *Social Casework* 55:2 (February 1974): 111–16.

CORDASCO, FRANCESCO. "The Puerto Rican Child in the American School." *Journal of Negro Education* 36:2 (September 1967): 181–86.

_____, and EUGENE BUCCHIONI. *The Puerto Rican Community and Its Children on the Mainland: A Source Book for Teachers, Social Workers and other Professionals*. Metuchen, N.J.: Scarecrow Press, 1972.

_____. *The Puerto Rican Experience: A Sociological Sourcebook*. Totowa, N.J.: Littlefield, Adams and Co., 1973.

DELGADO, MELVIN. "Puerto Rican Spiritualism and the Social Work Profession." *Social Casework* 58:8 (October 1977): 451–58.

_____. "Social Work and the Puerto Rican Community." *Social Casework* 55:2 (February 1974): 117–23.

_____. "A Hispanic Foster Parents Program." *Child Welfare* 57:7 (July/August 1978): 427–31.

FITZPATRICK, JOSEPH P. *Puerto Rican Americans: The Meaning of Migration to the Mainland*. Englewood Cliffs, N.J.: Prentice Hall, 1971, pp. 92–100.

GARBER, MICHAEL, et al. "The Ghetto as a Source of Foster Homes." *Child Welfare* 49:5 (May 1970): 246–51.

GHALI, SONIA BADILLO. "Culture Sensitivity and the Puerto Rican Client." *Social Casework* 58:8 (October 1977): 459–68; Commentary, Emelicia Mizio, pp. 469–74.

GONZALES, AUGUSTIN. "The Struggle to Develop Self-Help Institutions." *Social Casework* 55:2 (February 1974): 90–93.

LONGRES, JOHN. *Perspectives from the Puerto Rican Faculty Training Program.* New York: Council on Social Work Education, 1973, pp. 8–18.

MIRANDA, MAGDALENA, ed. *Puerto Rican Task Force Report.* New York: Council on Social Work Education, Inc. 1973.

MIZIO, EMILICIA. "Impact of External Systems on the Puerto Rican Family." *Social Casework* 55:2 (February 1974): 76–83.

———. "Puerto Rican Social Workers and Racism." *Social Casework* 53:5 (May 1972): 267–72.

MONTALVO, BRAULIO. "Home-School Conflict and the Puerto Rican Child." *Social Casework* 55:2 (February 1974): 100–10.

NORMAND, WILLIAM C., et al. "Brief Group Therapy to Facilitate Utilization of Mental Health Services by Spanish-Speaking Patients." *American Journal of Orthopsychiatry* 44:1 (January 1974): 37–42.

PREBLE, EDWARD M.A. "The Puerto Rican American Teenager in New York City." In *Minority Group Adolescents in the United States*, edited by E. B. Brody. Baltimore: Williams and Wilkins, 1968, pp. 48–72.

RIVERA, J. JULIAN. "Growth of Puerto Rican Awareness." *Social Casework* 55:2 (February 1974): 84–89.

RODRIGUEZ, DE, LIGIA VAZQUEZ. "Social Work Practice in Puerto Rico." *Social Work* 18:3 (March 1973): 32–40.

ROGLER, LLOYD H. *Migrant in the City: The Life of a Puerto Rican Action Group.* New York: Basic Books, 1972.

SCOTT, JOHN F., and MELVIN DELGADO. "Planning Mental Health Programs for Hispanic Communities." *Social Casework* 60:8 (October 1979): 451–56.

SEXTON, PATRICIA C. *Spanish Harlem: An Anatomy of Poverty.* New York: Harper & Row, 1966.

SURACI, ANTHONY B. "Reactions of Puerto Rican and Non-Puerto Rican Parents to Their Mentally Retarded Boys." Ph.D. dissertation, New York University, 1966.

TENDLER, DIANA. "Social Service Needs in a Changing Community: A Study of the Use of Voluntary Social Agencies by Puerto Rican Clients." Ph.D. dissertation, New York University, 1965.

TORRES-MATRULLO, CHRISTINE. "Acculturation and Psychopathology among Puerto Rican Women in Mainland United States." *American Journal of Orthopsychiatry* 46:4 (October 1976): 710–19.

Index

A

Abortion, 52, 60, 130, 149, 150
Acculturation, 6, 62
Adler, Chaim, 136
Adoption, 30, 32–36, 50, 54, 81,
    89, 90, 92
  American Indians, 34–36, 63,
    189
  Blacks, 32–34
  in Israel, 128, 129–130, 149–151
Affirmative action, 7
Afro-Americans: *see* Blacks
Alienation, 79
American Indians, 4, 6, 7, 195,
    196; *see also* Ethnic agency;
    Parents' perceptions of ethnic
    issues; Worker attitudes, sur-
    vey of
  adoption, 34–36, 63, 189
  assimilation, forced, 23–24
  cultural patterns, 12–13, 15–18
  education, 23–24, 56–57
  family, 12–13, 50, 53–54
  foster care, 63, 189
  intergroup relations, 65
  language, 19, 56–57
  separate institutions issue, 59
  social structure, 60
  stereotypes, 23–24, 49–51
Anomie, 79
Anwar, Muhammed, 179
Aquilar, Ignacio, 25–26
Arab children, 149–156
Ashkenazi Jews, 127, 128, 134,
    138–140, 143, 145, 146
Asian Americans, 6, 7, 195; *see also*
    Chinese Americans; Ethnic
    agency; Japanese Americans;
    Parents' perceptions of ethnic
    issues; Worker attitudes, sur-
    vey of
  busing, 60, 84
  family, 51, 53
  language, 55–56
  separate institutions issue, 57–58
  stereotypes, 51
Asians, in Britain: *see* Great Brit-
    ain
Assimilation, 6, 23–24